American Language Hub

LEVEL 2
Student's Book

DANIEL BRAYSHAW
JON HIRD

macmillan education

Contents

Welcome

USEFUL PHRASES

Classroom

0.1 **A** Write the words in the correct order to make useful questions for the classroom. Listen and check.

1. repeat / please / that, / Can / you / ?
2. say / do / How / you / English / *trabajar* / in / ?
3. slowly, / Could / speak / more / please / you / ?
4. do / pronounce / How / you / that / ?
5. spell / do / that / you / How / ?
6. *excellent* / What / mean / does / ?

Dates

B SPEAK Work in pairs. Answer the questions.

1. Which months have exactly 30 days?
2. What are the days of the week?
3. How do you say the ordinal numbers 1–20?
4. What date is it today?

PRONUNCIATION

Word stress

0.2 **A** Listen and underline the stressed syllables. Then listen again and repeat the words.

happy polite amazing beautiful

The /ə/ sound

0.3 **B** Listen and underline the schwa /ə/ sound. Then listen again and repeat the words.

television magazine support campus

Third person -*s* endings and simple past regular endings

0.4 **C** How do you pronounce the underlined sounds? Listen and repeat. Choose the correct option.

1. works /s/ /z/ /ɪz/
2. has /s/ /z/ /ɪz/
3. finishes /s/ /z/ /ɪz/
4. played /d/ /t/ /ɪd/
5. watched /d/ /t/ /ɪd/
6. wanted /d/ /t/ /ɪd/

GRAMMAR

Tenses, structures and auxiliary verbs

A Choose the correct words to complete the questions.

1. What *do* / *does* / *are* you do?
2. *Are* / *Is* / *Can* you cook?
3. *Were* / *Will* / *Are* you reading a good book right now?
4. What *is* / *am* / *are* your parents' names?
5. Where *do* / *does* / *is* your best friend live?
6. Can you *swimming* / *swim* / *to swim*?

B SPEAK Work in pairs. Ask and answer the questions in Exercise A.

VOCABULARY

Word sets

A Look at the word sets. Cross out the odd one out. Check your answers with a partner and explain your choices.

1. serious ~~old~~ friendly happy
2. at five o'clock next to me in the afternoon on Tuesday
3. across from the bank four years ago near the school behind the library
4. egg bottle bag can
5. two years ago in a month last Friday yesterday evening
6. banana apple bread orange

Parts of speech

B Match the parts of speech in the box with the words in **bold**.

~~adjective~~ adverb article auxiliary noun preposition verb

1. My **favorite** subject is English. *adjective*
2. I **read** emails in English at work. ______
3. There are 12 students **in** our class. ______
4. **Do** you speak any other languages? ______
5. We have **a** test today. ______
6. This is my new English **book**. ______
7. Please listen **carefully**. ______

Question words

C Complete the questions with the words in the box.

How many How much ~~What~~ When Where Who Why

1. *What* 's your name?
2. ______ are you from?
3. ______ is your birthday?
4. ______ brothers and sisters do you have?
5. ______ do you know in this class?
6. ______ are you studying English? Do you need it for work?
7. ______ time do you spend studying English each week?

D SPEAK Work in pairs. Ask and answer the questions in Exercise C.

1 RELATIONSHIPS

> My best friend is the one who brings out the best in me.
>
> Henry Ford

Iñupiat friends play in the first of the winter snow, Nome, Alaska.

OBJECTIVES

- find out about someone new
- talk about different types of people
- describe someone's personality
- greet people and give personal information, make introductions
- write information about yourself

Work with a partner. Discuss the questions.

1 Who's your best friend?
2 Look at the picture. Who was your best friend when you were a child?
3 What qualities do you look for in a friend?

1.1 Breaking the ice

Find out about someone new

G question forms V people P the alphabet

LISTENING

A Complete the definitions with the words in the box.

conversation relationship successful tip topic

1 A private and informal talk between two people is a ________________.
2 A useful suggestion is a ________________.
3 When you achieve the result you want, you are ________________.
4 A subject that you write or speak about is a ________________.
5 When two or more people or things are connected in some way, they have a ________________.

B SPEAK Work in groups. Discuss the questions.

1 What is happening in the photo at the top of the page?
2 Where do people usually meet for the first time?
3 How do you usually start a conversation with someone you have just met?

1.1 **C LISTEN FOR KEY WORDS** Listen to an interview with psychologist Isabelle Ackerman.

1 What topic does she talk about?
2 What should you start a conversation with?
3 What are two safe topics of conversation to 'break the ice'?

Glossary

break the ice (phrase) to do or say something that makes people feel less shy or nervous in a social situation
politics (n) the activities of governments which control a country or area
psychology (n) the study of the mind and how it affects behavior
religion (n) the belief in the existence of a god or gods
social life (n) the time you spend enjoying yourself with friends

1.1 **D LISTEN FOR DETAIL** Listen again and complete each tip with the correct verb.

ask discuss feel give know say

1 ________________ something positive about the place or situation you are in, and then ask a question.
2 ________________ about other people.
3 Don't be negative about other people because you don't know who they ________________.
4 Ask lots of questions and ________________ lots of answers.
5 When you ________________ more relaxed, ask some personal questions.
6 Don't ________________ topics like religion or politics with someone you don't know.

E SPEAK Work in groups. Discuss the questions.

1 What did you think of the tips in the podcast?
2 What other topics are easy to talk about with new people?

GRAMMAR

Question forms

1.2 **A WORK IT OUT** Complete the questions with the words in the box. Listen and check your answers.

are did (x2) do (x2) have is (x2) were

1 What *do* you say to a stranger at a party or a new colleague at the office?
2 ________ it OK to talk about some topics, but not others?
3 ________ you ever met someone new and had no idea what to talk about?
4 ________ you having fun?
5 What ________ your favorite band?
6 ________ you enjoy the ceremony?
7 ________ you at school together?
8 Where ________ you study?
9 ________ you have children?

B Look at the questions in Exercise A. What tense are they? Write *simple present*, *simple past*, *present progressive* or *present perfect* next to each one.

C Choose the correct words to complete the rules. Use Exercise B to help you.

Question forms

1 We use the auxiliary verb (*do, does, did*) ***before*** / ***after*** the subject.
2 We use *be* (*am, is, are, was, were*) ***before*** / ***after*** the subject.
3 We use present perfect *have* ***before*** / ***after*** the subject.

D Go to the **Grammar Hub** on **page 122**.

E Rewrite the questions with the verb in parentheses in the correct place.

1 why you studying English? (*are*)
______
2 you have any brothers or sisters? (*do*)
______
3 you ever met a famous person? (*have*)
______
4 you do anything nice last weekend? (*did*)
______
5 you like tea or coffee? (*do*)
______
6 you a late-night or early-morning person? (*are*)
______
7 who your funniest friend? (*is*)
______
8 who the first person you talked to this morning? (*was*)
______
9 you ever been to a wedding? (*have*)
______
10 what the last good movie you saw? (*was*)
______

F **SPEAK** Work in pairs. Ask and answer the questions in Exercise E.

VOCABULARY
People

A Go to the **Vocabulary Hub** on **page 146**.

B **SPEAK** Work in pairs. Answer the questions.

1 How many relatives do you have? How often do you see them all?
2 How many of your colleagues or other students in your class are also your friends?
3 Do you find it easy to talk to strangers? Why/Why not?

PRONUNCIATION
The alphabet

1.3 **A** Listen and repeat.

a b c d e f g h i j k l m n o p q r s t u v w x y z
A B C D E F G H I J K L M N O P Q R S T U V W X Y Z

1.4 **B** Work in pairs. Write the letters of the alphabet in the correct place. Listen and check.

/e/	/uː/	/ɑː/	/iː/	/aɪ/	/oʊ/	/eɪ/
f	*u*	*r*	*e*	*i*	*o*	*a*

C **SPEAK** Work in pairs. Look again at Vocabulary Exercise A on **page 146**. Take turns spelling the words.

SPEAKING

A Find out some information about your classmates. Write six questions using the ideas below to help you. Then write two more questions using your own ideas.

- ice breakers
  Hi, my name's ______. It's nice to meet you. So, …
- personal questions
- family and friends
  Do you come from a large family?
- interests and hobbies
- childhood and school
- work and study
- favorite things/places
- last weekend/vacation
  Where did you go for your last vacation?

B Work in pairs. Work with someone you do not know well and follow the instructions.

1 Stand up and meet the other people in the class. Take turns asking and answering the questions you wrote in Exercise A.
2 When you have broken the ice, sit down with your partner and tell him/her about the people you met. Was it easy to break the ice or do you need some more help?

Find out about someone new

1.2 Blogs and bloggers

Talk about different types of people

V types of people P using a dictionary G frequency words and phrases

READING

A Work in groups. Discuss the questions.

1 Which websites do you visit most often and why?
2 Which blogs, vlogs (video blogs) or video channels do you know or follow?
3 What kind of topics do you enjoy reading about online?

B **READ FOR MAIN IDEA** Read *Three of the best* quickly. Which blog sounds most interesting to you and why?

C **READ FOR DETAIL** Read again. Complete each sentence with the name of a blogger, Emma, Maria or Michela.

1 ____________ is interested in visiting people around the world.
2 ____________ has children.
3 ____________ writes about a variety of subjects.
4 ____________ has a high number of readers.
5 ____________ is interested in trying new things.
6 ____________ wants people to understand that everyone is beautiful.

D **SPEAK** Work in pairs. Discuss the questions.

1 Is running a blog a difficult job?
2 Why do these people spend so much time on their blogging activities?
3 What topic would you blog about?

VOCABULARY
Types of people

A Work in pairs. Make a list of different types of people. You have one minute.

father of two, music fan, …

B Go to the **Vocabulary Hub** on **page 146**.

C **SPEAK** Work in pairs. Write down the names of three people you know and describe them to your partner. Say what type of person each one is. Ask questions about the people your partner describes.

PRONUNCIATION
Using a dictionary

Macmillan English Dictionary

www.macmillandictionary.com

The *Macmillan English Dictionary* gives clear, simple explanations and real life examples showing you how and when the word is used.

A Look at this entry from the *Macmillan English Dictionary*. Match the definitions (1–5) with the labels (a–e).

1 definition
2 part of speech
3 stressed syllable and pronunciation
4 different meaning
5 frequency rating

gorgeous – definition and synonyms ★[a]
[b]ADJECTIVE Pronunciation /ˈɡɔː(r)dʒəs/[c]

[d]**1** very beautiful
Mandy was there, looking gorgeous as usual.

[e]**2** very enjoyable or pleasant
The weather was absolutely gorgeous.

B Look up the following words in the *Macmillan English Dictionary*. Underline the stressed syllable and write down the part of speech and one meaning for each word.

cloud expedition positive rare

Three of the best

Blogs by Calvin Norton

With over 150 million blogs online, there is something for every type of person from the **animal lover** to the **gamer** to the **sports fan.** But, if you are looking for something a little different, here are my top three blogs.

1 Brain Pickings

Maria Popova is a **book lover**, **music fan** and writer. Her blog *Brain Pickings* is a collection of articles about history, news, books and culture. Maria is interested in reading and spends hundreds of hours each month doing research for her blog. It's an extremely popular blog and many people enjoy Maria's interesting mix of articles.

2 The Atlas of Beauty

The Atlas of Beauty is a picture blog showing beauty in different cultures. Romanian photographer, **blogger** and **traveler** Michela Noroc takes pictures of women of all ages, races and nationalities living their everyday lives. It's a wonderful collection which shows that beauty can be found everywhere.

For more interesting blogs, listen to Calvin on this week's Emma Fry Show

GRAMMAR

Frequency words and phrases

.5 **A** Listen to an interview with Calvin Norton about another blog, *Humans of New York*, and answer the questions.

1 What is the blog about?

2 What type of people does Brandon Stanton interview?

.6 **B** Listen and complete each sentence from the radio show with one word.

1 ________________ a week, we bring you reviews and recommendations from the wonderful world of the internet.

2 I'm ________________ out in the real world.

3 I'm ________________ at home, online in front of my laptop.

4 But luckily for us, you ________________ escape.

5 Now and ________________, a blog is so good that I just have to mention it again.

6 Stanton focuses on the lives of normal New Yorkers ________________ of the time.

7 He includes someone well known ________________ so often.

8 It's a very simple idea, but it ________________ gets boring.

3 *Emma's Bucket List*

After her father and step-father died, Emma Stewart Rigby decided to live a full and exciting life. Emma, a **mother of three**, made a list of 246 things to do before she dies and in her blog she writes about her experiences. Emma is a **people person** and gives a lot of friendly advice on life. She's also a **foodie**, and her bucket list includes unusual foods or interesting restaurants she plans to try. A great blog for ideas on how to live life to the max!

Glossary

blog (n) a website containing short articles called posts that are changed regularly
blog (v) to write short articles for a website on your opinions, interests and experiences
culture (n) activities which involve music, books and other arts
subscriber (n) someone who joins and follows a blog

C **WORK IT OUT** Write the four frequency words in Exercise B in the correct place.

Frequency words

100%
always
usually
often
1 ________________
sometimes
2 ________________
3 ________________
hardly ever
0%
4 ________________

D Complete the frequency phrases in the table with words from Exercise B.

once twice three times	[1] ________________	day week month year
every [2] ________________ often		
[3] ________________ and then		
most of the [4] ________________		

E Choose the correct words to complete the rules. Use Exercise B to help you.

Frequency words and phrases

1 We usually put frequency words ***before*** / ***after*** the main verb and ***before*** / ***after*** the verb *be*.

2 We use frequency phrases ***at the beginning*** / ***in the middle*** of a sentence.

3 We also use frequency phrases ***in the middle*** / ***at the end*** of a sentence.

F Go to the **Grammar Hub** on **page 122**.

G **SPEAK** Work in pairs. Discuss the questions.

1 Would you enjoy the blog *Humans of New York*?

2 Why do you think it is so popular?

SPEAKING

A Interview each other about websites, blogs or vlogs you like. Write notes about:

- what they are about
- why you like them
- examples of interesting things on them
- what type of people would enjoy them and why

B Work in groups. Interview each other. Which ones sound most interesting?

Talk about different types of people

1.3 Personality

Describe someone's personality

G indefinite pronouns **V** personality adjectives, adjective + preposition
P word stress in multisyllable adjectives **S** previewing a text

READING

A SPEAK Work in pairs. Discuss the questions.

1 Which do you do more often: write by hand or use a keyboard?
2 Which do you find easier? Why?
3 What kind of things do you write by hand (e.g. shopping lists)?

B Preview the text, and then answer the questions. Use the information in the box to help you.

Previewing a text

Before you read a text, look quickly at the title and any headings, pictures or diagrams. Use this information to decide what kind of text it is, what it's about and why someone might want to read it. This will make the text easier to understand.

1 What is the text about?
2 Is it from a science paper or a popular magazine? How do you know?
3 What do you think you will learn from the text?
4 Can you trust the information in the article?

C READ FOR MAIN IDEA Read *What does your handwriting say about you?* Was your preview correct?

D READ FOR SPECIFIC INFORMATION Read again and answer the questions.

1 What is graphology a study of?
2 How do graphologists help in court cases?
3 Do all graphologists agree that there is a link between handwriting and personality?

E SPEAK Work in pairs. Discuss the questions.

1 Do you believe there is a connection between handwriting and personality? Why/Why not?
2 Is it important for children to learn to write by hand these days? Why/Why not?

What does your *handwriting* say about you?

Everybody has their own style of handwriting, but can someone's handwriting tell you what they are like? The study of handwriting is called graphology. Graphologists are usually involved in legal cases. They are responsible for matching criminals to their handwriting or deciding if signatures are real.
Some graphologists think handwriting can show anything: what kind of job you will be good at, how healthy you are and even what kind of partner you might be happy with.
If you are interested in what your handwriting says about you, check out our information.

Letter size

Small: You're probably a **hard-working** person. People with small handwriting are rarely **lazy**.

Medium: The research says you're **sensible**; you think carefully about the decisions you make.

Large: Big writing – big personality! People with large writing are usually interested in parties and social events and are rarely shy.

Letter shape

Q Rounded letters: Rounded letters suggest you are a **creative** person. Are you good at art or music?

A Pointed letters: You are **curious**. Your favorite question is 'Why?'!

Dotting your i

Dot high over the i: The research says you have a good imagination.

Dot low over the i: You are a **well-organized** person. Are your desk and room neat?

Spacing between words

Wide spacing: You're an **independent** type and you are happy on your own.

Narrow spacing: You're very **sociable** and you need other people in your life.

Your signature

Difficult to read: You are a private person. Like your signature, you can be difficult to read.

Easy to read: **Confident** people usually have signatures that are easy to read. You know what you are good at and you don't mind telling other people about it.

Does your handwriting match your personality? Don't be disappointed with the results if not. Not every graphologist believes there is a connection.

Glossary

legal (adj) relating to the law or lawyers
spacing (n) the amount of space between things

GRAMMAR
Indefinite pronouns

A WORK IT OUT Look at the extract from the article and choose the correct words to complete the rules.

Everybody has their own style of handwriting, but can someone's handwriting tell you what they are like?

Indefinite pronouns

1 We use indefinite pronouns to talk about people or things *so we can say / without saying* who or what they are.
2 We use indefinite pronouns with *-body* and *-one* to talk about *people / things*.
3 After indefinite pronouns, we use *singular / plural* verbs.
4 We use *'s* with indefinite pronouns for *possessives / plural nouns*.

B PRACTICE Find and underline another example of an indefinite pronoun in the article.

C Go to the **Grammar Hub** on **page 122**.

VOCABULARY
Personality adjectives, adjective + preposition

A Match the personality adjectives in **bold** in *What does your handwriting say about you?* with the speakers below.

1 'I believe I can do anything if I try. I don't usually worry about things.' *confident*
2 'I love my job. I work a lot, but that's OK.' ______
3 'I can paint pictures, write stories and make music.' ______
4 'I plan my time carefully and I always know where to find my things.' ______
5 'I don't like work. I like doing nothing! My perfect day? Staying in bed with a pizza.' ______
6 'I like to think about things carefully before I do them.' ______
7 'I have a lot of friends and we meet and go out all the time.' ______
8 'I like learning new things and I ask a lot of questions.' ______
9 'I like to do things myself.' ______

B Look at the underlined phrases in the article. Complete the questions with the correct preposition.

1 Are you involved *in* any clubs, groups or teams? Which ones?
2 What are you good ____?
3 Who is responsible ____ doing the cooking in your home?
4 Are you happy ____ your cell phone? Why/Why not?
5 What websites, magazines or TV shows are you interested ____?
6 Are you interested ____ books and reading?

C SPEAK Work in pairs. Ask and answer the questions in Exercise B.

PRONUNCIATION
Word stress in multisyllable adjectives

A Listen and complete the table with the words in the box.
1.7

hard-working independent lazy sensible

1 ●•	2 ●••	3 •●•	4 ••●•
		hard-working	

B Listen again and repeat the words.
1.7

C Look again at the article. Find the other personality adjectives in **bold** and write them in the correct place in Exercise A. Listen and check and repeat.
1.8

D SPEAK Work in pairs. Practice saying the words. Listen and check your partner's pronunciation.

SPEAKING HUB

A Work in pairs. You are going to study your classmates' handwriting. Follow the instructions.

1 Sign your name and write this sentence on a piece of paper.
The quick brown fox jumps over the lazy dog.
2 Swap papers and use the information in *What does your handwriting say about you?* to write five things about your partner's personality.

B DISCUSS Using your notes, tell your partner what their writing says about them.

Describe someone's personality

Café Hub

1.4 Hello again

F – greet people and give personal information, make introductions
P – word stress and intonation

My name is Gaby. I'm originally from [1] ________, but now, London is my home. I'm a [2] ________. I like traveling and I drink a lot of [3] ________. I live in this [4] ________ with Neena and Zac.

My name's Zac. I live with [5] ________ and Neena. I'm originally from [6] ________. I make [7] ________ games.

My name's Sam. This is my café! I'm [8] ________. I like food. I love [9] ________. I live here in [10] ________.

I'm Milly. This is my clothes store. I'm [11] ________. I watch [12] ________, listen to music and I read a lot. [13] ________ a good friend of mine.

Neena here. I live here in London with my two friends, Gaby and [14] ________. I'm a lawyer. I work in [15] ________.

COMPREHENSION

A ▶ 00:00–02:50 Watch the first part of the video. Complete the paragraphs above.

B Write a question about each person in Exercise A.
Where is Gaby from? What does Zac do?

C **SPEAK** Work in pairs. Test your memory! Close your books and ask each other your questions from Exercise B.

D ▶ 02:50–04:27 Watch the second part of the video and underline the correct verb form to complete each sentence.

1 Neena *is* / *isn't* going to an interview.
2 Sam *is* / *isn't* good.
3 Zac *had* / *didn't have* a good holiday.
4 Zac *has* / *hasn't* asked Milly out.
5 Zac *invites* / *doesn't invite* Sam to the flat.
6 Sam *eats* / *doesn't eat* Zac's croissant.

Glossary

flat **(n) (British)** = apartment **(n) (American)**
holiday **(n) (British)** = vacation **(n) (American)**

FUNCTIONAL LANGUAGE

Greet people and give personal information, make introductions

A Complete the phrases with the words in the box.

doing going hello let's long meet (x2) what

Greeting	Reply
Say hello	
[1] ________	Hi there! / Hey!
Greet new people	
Nice/Good to [2] ________ you.	Nice/Good to [3] ________ you, too.
Greet friends	
How are you? How's it [4] ________? How are you [5] ________?	I'm good. How about you?
What's new?	Not much.
It's great to see you! [6] ________ a nice surprise!	[7] ________ time, no see.
Say goodbye	
See you later. See you soon. I've gotta (got to) go.	[8] ________ do something soon.

B ▶ Watch the video again. Check your answers to Exercise A.

MILLY

SAM

NEENA

ZAC

GABY

USEFUL PHRASES

A Match the useful phrases (1–8) with the pictures (a–h).

1 Dream job! ____
2 I love it here! ____
3 Good luck! ____
4 What can I tell you? ____
5 Come with me. ____
6 What else? ____
7 Come over to the flat this weekend. / Will do. ____
8 Here we are. This is home. ____

a

b

c

d

e

f

g

h

B Watch the video again and check your answers to Exercise A.

C How do you say these phrases in your language?

PRONUNCIATION

Word stress and intonation

A 03:02–03:34 Watch part of the video. Read out the conversation at the same time as Sam and Zac. Copy the word stress and intonation.

Sam: Hey Zac. It's great to see you. What a nice surprise.
Zac: I know. Long time, no see.
Sam: Do you want a coffee?
Zac: Sure, and a croissant.
Zac: So, how are you doing?
Sam: I'm good. How about you? Did you have a nice holiday?
Zac: Yeah. Always good to see family. What's new with you?
Sam: Not much. Same, same.

B SPEAK Work in pairs. Practice the conversation. Listen and check your partner's pronunciation.

SPEAKING

A Walk around the class. Introduce yourself to everybody.

A: Hello, my name's Sven. Nice to meet you.
B: Hi, I'm Ahmed. Good to meet you.

B Walk around the class again. Greet the people you know.

A: Hi, Maria. How's it going?
B: Good, thanks. How about you? What's new with you?
A: Not much. I've gotta go. See you later.

C Prepare a 'selfie' presentation. Follow the instructions.

- Write notes about what you want to say. Use the sentence beginnings below to help you.
- Include at least two useful phrases.
- Record your presentation.

Hi! My name's …	I work in …
I'm from … / I'm originally from …	I like …
I'm a …	I watch / listen to …

D SPEAK Work in groups. Compare your presentations. Which is the best one?

Greet people and give personal information, make introductions

➤ Turn to page 158 to learn how to write information about yourself.

Unit 1 Review

VOCABULARY

A Complete the words for types of people.

1 someone who likes animals
a *nimal* l *over*

2 someone who likes spending time with others
p_______ p_______

3 someone who plays video games
g_______

4 someone who is very interested in food
f_______

5 a man who has two children
f_______ o_______ t_______

6 someone who listens to music regularly
m_______ f_______

B Complete the *About me* section of Emma's social media page with the personality adjectives in the box. There is one adjective you do not need.

creative curious ~~hard-working~~ independent sensible sociable well-organized

Hi, I'm Emma and I'm a student nurse. I study and work a lot [1](*hard-working*) and I make lists so I know what I am doing and when [2](__________). I always think carefully before I make decisions [3](__________). I feel it is important to ask a lot of questions [4](__________) in my social life and at work. I have a good imagination and in my free time I like to write songs [5](__________). I also have a great group of friends and I love spending time with them [6](__________).

C Choose the correct prepositions to complete the sentences.

1 In my family, we are all responsible *for* / *on* / *with* doing the housework.

2 I'm not interested *in* / *about* / *to* people who talk about themselves all the time.

3 As a child, I was involved *in* / *with* / *at* a lot of after-school clubs and activities.

4 I'm happy *at* / *with* / *on* my job.

GRAMMAR

A Complete the questions with the correct form of *do*, *be* or *have*.

1 Do you _______ a pet?

2 _______ you from a large family?

3 _______ you have a party for your last birthday?

4 _______ you ever been to your country's capital city?

5 What _______ your favorite book or toy when you were a child?

B Complete the article with the missing words.

Student Life Online
Your college, your site

This week, we asked students what blogs they read. This is what they said.

Erica: Most [1]__________ the time, I read blogs about soccer.

Jake: [2]__________ so often, I read a cooking blog.

Ammar: I [3]__________ ever read blogs. I don't have time.

Mark: Once a [4]__________, on Sunday mornings, I sit down and read my favorite travel blog.

Tina: [5]__________ and then, I read news blogs.

Nazreen: I don't read blogs, but I do use Twitter. I check it at least ten [6]__________ a day.

What are your favorite blogs? Leave your comments below.

C Choose the word which is *not* possible in each sentence.

1 *Everybody* / *Somebody* / *Anybody* can have nice handwriting.

2 I don't agree with *everything* / *anything* / *nothing* that the graphologists say.

3 Everyone *use* / *uses* / *has* a keyboard these days.

4 Do you know *anybody* / *anyone* / *anything* that is sociable?

FUNCTIONAL LANGUAGE

Reorder the words in the boxes to complete the conversations.

name's / Hi, / my / Erwin
myself / me / Let / introduce
meet / Nice / to / you

Erwin: [1] *Hi, my name's Erwin.*

Laura: Oh, hi, Erwin. [2]____________________. I'm Laura, the office manager.

Erwin: [3]____________________. I think you're going to be my boss!

nice / What / surprise / a
days / are / doing / What / you / these

Alan: Dan?

Dan: Alan! [4]____________________! How are you?

Alan: Oh, fine, thanks. [5]____________________?

Dan: I'm still teaching.

2 LIVING

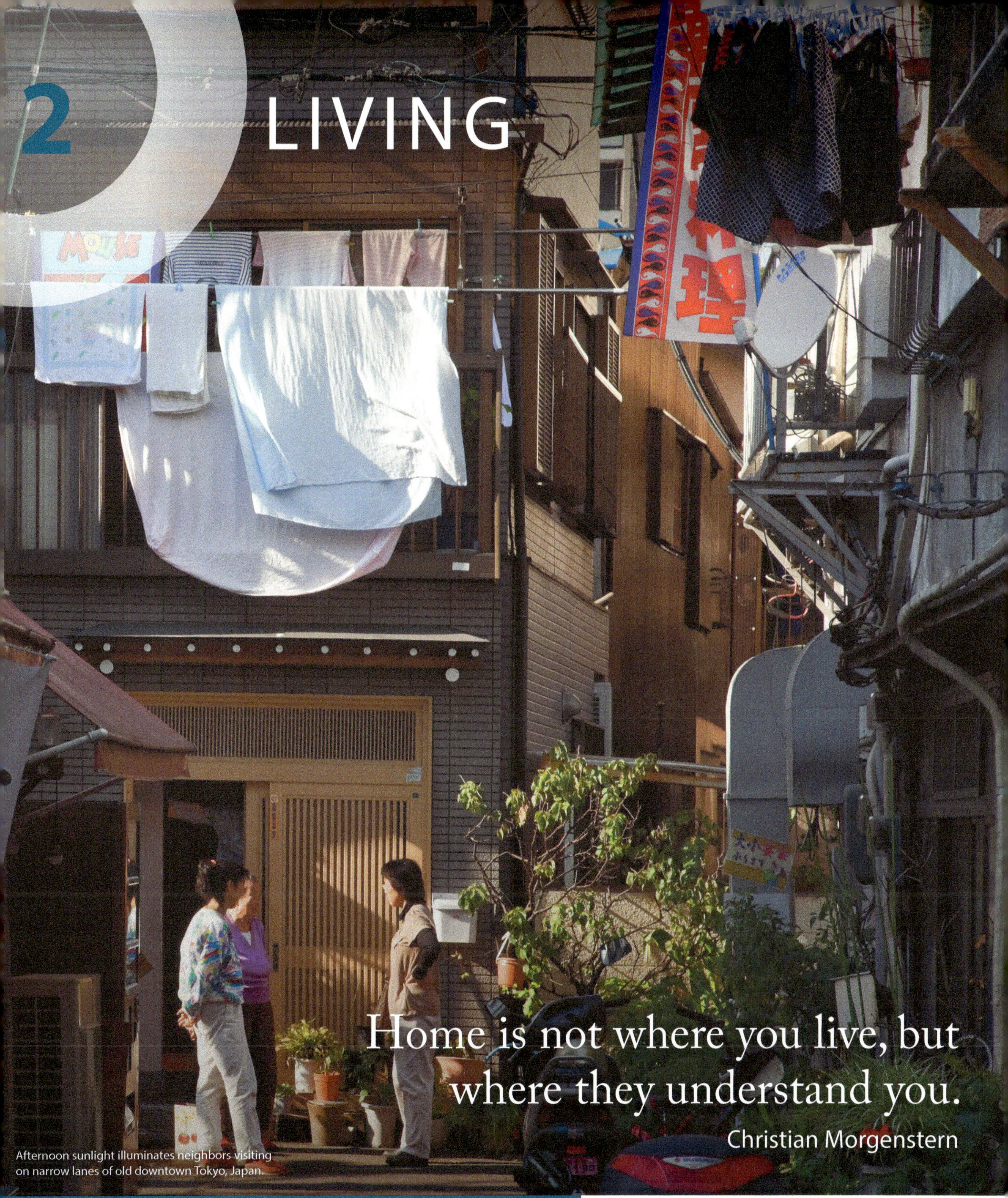

> Home is not where you live, but where they understand you.
>
> Christian Morgenstern

Afternoon sunlight illuminates neighbors visiting on narrow lanes of old downtown Tokyo, Japan.

OBJECTIVES

- talk about your neighborhood
- talk about your life and routine
- talk about life events
- ask for and give advice
- write an email of complaint

Work with a partner. Discuss the questions.

1 Read the quote. Where is 'home' for you?

2 Look at the picture. What do you think the people are talking about?

3 Do you know your neighbors?

2.1 Love where you live

Talk about your neighborhood

G adverbs of degree **V** describing places **P** stress in two-syllable adjectives

READING

A Work in pairs. Discuss the questions.

1. Do you love where you live? Why/Why not?
2. Look at the pictures. What can you see?
3. Look at the glossary. How can a building be environmentally friendly?

B SCAN Read *The forest in the sky* quickly and complete the sentences with the correct word or number from the text.

1. Bosco Verticale is an Italian name that means 'vertical ________________'.
2. The apartment buildings are in the city of ________________ in Italy.
3. There are almost ________________ trees on the balconies of the buildings.
4. The plants help make the noise from the ________________ and people in the street quieter.
5. The apartment buildings are close to the city's services and ________________.
6. The architects plan to build another forest city in ________________ in the future.

C READ FOR DETAIL Read again and answer the questions.

1. What are the four problems of life in central Milan that the writer mentions?
2. How do the Bosco Verticale buildings solve these problems?
3. What is the main problem with buildings like Bosco Verticale?
4. Does the writer think forest cities are a good idea?

D SPEAK Work in pairs. Answer the questions.

1. Do you want to see forest cities in your country? Why/Why not?
   Forest cities are a good idea because …
2. Should we pay more to live in clean cities? Why/Why not?
   I don't think we should pay more to live in clean cities because …

THE FOREST IN THE SKY

Where in the world can you live on the top floor of a 111-meter high-rise building, near the center of a **lively** city, but still have breakfast under a tree on your balcony? Sounds almost impossible! Well, not if you live in the Bosco Verticale (vertical forest) buildings in Milan, Italy. Architect Stefano Boeri has created a completely new approach to designing buildings.

Like many big cities, Milan is **noisy** and **polluted**. It's hot in the summer and in the city center the green spaces are usually fairly **crowded**. But Boeri's team have found a very green answer to these problems.

Almost 900 trees grow high above Milan on the balconies of **modern** buildings. The trees keep the apartments cool in summer and warm in winter. They also produce oxygen, which keeps the air **clean**. The buildings are so **quiet** because the trees and plants stop the noise from the people and traffic in the streets below. Bosco Verticale is really **convenient** for the city's stores, services and transportation, it's **attractive**, and it's environmentally friendly. So, will there be more buildings like this in the future? Well, possibly. The architects want to build a new forest city in China and the Netherlands, but there is one more problem to solve. Buildings like this are extremely expensive. At 65 million euros, Bosco Verticale cost 5 percent more to build than a normal high-rise building. But if we want to live in cool, quiet cities with clean air, it will be worth the cost.

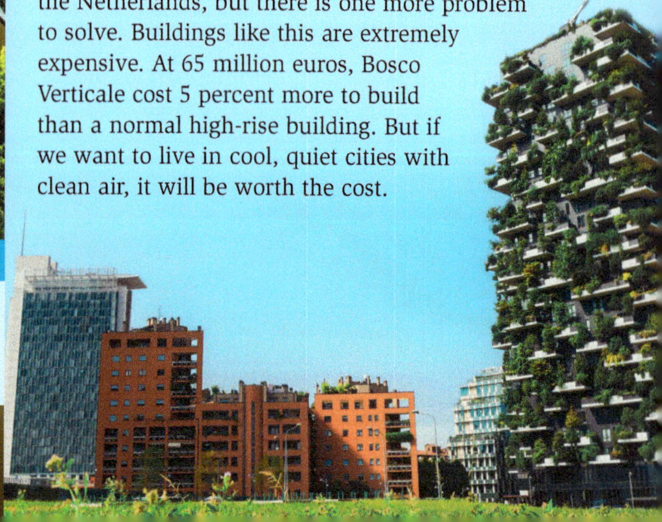

Glossary

architect (n) someone whose job is to design buildings
environmentally friendly (adj) something designed not to harm the natural environment
vertical (adj) standing, pointing or moving straight up

GRAMMAR
Adverbs of degree

A WORK IT OUT Complete the sentences from *The forest in the sky* with the correct adverbs of degree.

1 Sounds ______________ impossible!
2 Stefano Boeri has created a ______________ new approach to designing buildings.
3 Boeri's team have found a ______________ green answer to these problems.

B Underline four more adverbs of degree in the article.

C Choose the correct words to complete the rules.

Adverbs of degree

1 Adverbs of degree are usually used ***before* / *after*** the adjective that they modify.
2 We ***use* / *don't use*** adverbs of degree when we want to make something stronger or weaker.
3 We ***can* / *can't*** use adverbs of degree with adverbs and verbs:
- *She is speaking very fast.*
- *He almost finished the race.*

D Go to the **Grammar Hub** on **page 124**.

E SPEAK Work in pairs. Look at the pictures of unusual buildings and use adverbs of degree to describe them.

A: It's so different from a normal building.
B: It's very strange!

VOCABULARY
Describing places

A Read the sentences and look at the adjectives in **bold**. Then write the opposite adjectives.

1 The air in my city is fairly **clean**. There aren't many factories. *dirty*
2 My neighbors are very **loud**. They usually play music late at night. ______________
3 It's a very **inconvenient** place to live. Our house is far from the stores and public transportation. ______________
4 The shopping center is very **old-fashioned**. It looks like it's from the 1970s. ______________
5 My apartment is in an **ugly** high-rise building. I don't like living there. ______________
6 The main streets are very **dirty**. People regularly drop trash. ______________
7 My neighborhood is very **peaceful**. I rarely hear cars or people in the street. ______________

B Use the adjectives in Exercise A to write five sentences about your neighborhood.

C SPEAK Work in pairs. Say an adjective. Your partner says the opposite. Take turns.

PRONUNCIATION
Stress in two-syllable adjectives

2.1 **A** Listen and underline the stressed syllable in each adjective.

1 dirty
2 quiet
3 modern
4 peaceful
5 noisy

2.1 **B** Listen again and repeat the words.

C Most two-syllable adjectives have the same stress pattern. Read the text below and underline the stressed syllable in all the two-syllable adjectives.

The Chang (Elephant) Building is in Bangkok, Thailand. Some people think it is modern and interesting; some people think it is strange and funny. Other people think it is ugly and totally awful!

SPEAKING

A Tell your partner about your neighborhood. Use these ideas to help you.

- Location – is it convenient? Close to public transportation?
- Appearance – is the area clean, modern?
- People – who lives there? Families or young professionals?
- Environmentally friendly – are there local parks?

B Work in pairs. Take turns to ask and answer your questions.

Talk about your neighborhood

2.2 The boomerang generation

Talk about your life and routine

V verb + preposition G simple present and present progressive P consonant pairs at the beginning of words

LISTENING

A Work in pairs. Discuss the questions.

1 Why do people move out of their parents' home?
2 When do people usually leave home in your country?
3 Why do some adults continue to live at home?
4 What problems could this cause?

2.2 **B LISTEN FOR GIST** Listen to the first part of *The boomerang generation* and answer the questions.

1 What does 'boomerang generation' mean?
2 How old is Richard?
3 Why is Richard living at home with his parents?
4 Does he enjoy living at home?

Glossary

boomerang (n) a curved stick that comes back to you when you throw it
generation (n) a group of people in society who are born and live around the same time
permanent (adj) happening or existing for a long time

2.3 **C** Listen to all of *The boomerang generation* and match two questions with each speaker. Write Richard (R), Gordon (G), Alice (A) or Carla (C).

Who …

1 says their child can live at home for a long time? *C*
2 seems worried about their child? ___
3 isn't working right now? ___
4 plans to do something to thank their parents? ___
5 wants to make a change to their house? ___
6 likes living with their parents? ___
7 is happy they are not alone? ___
8 isn't happy with the house rules? ___

D SPEAK Work in pairs. What are the advantages and disadvantages of living with your parents as an adult?

VOCABULARY

Verb + preposition

2.4 **A** Complete the sentences from the radio show with the correct preposition. Then listen and check your answers.

1 I'm still looking ________ a permanent job.
2 We argue ________ the rules.
3 He can always rely ________ us.
4 I help ________ the housework.
5 I can talk ________ her.

Verb + preposition

Some verbs can be used with different prepositions to mean different things.

argue + about + something

- *We usually argue **about** housework.*

argue + with + someone

- *I usually argue **with** my parents.*

It is possible to join the sentences together:

- *I usually argue **with** my parents **about** housework.*

B Complete the email to Stella with the prepositions from Exercise A.

Re: Help?!
Sent: Friday, November 10, 2017, 2:19 pm
To: stella_28@logbox.com
From: d.smith@screen.nett

Hi Stella,

Thanks for calling this morning. Sorry to hear you're having money problems, but we're happy you decided to talk [1] *to* us about it. You can always rely [2] ________ us. I know you don't like borrowing money, but we'd like to help [3] ________ your rent this month. Let's not argue [4] ________ it this time. You can pay us back when you have a little more money.

You said you'd like to look [5] ________ somewhere cheaper to live. How about coming back to live [6] ________ us for a while? It would only be a temporary solution, but we'd like you to think [7] ________ it. Give us a call and let's talk [8] ________ it.

Lots of love,

Mom and Dad

C SPEAK Work in pairs. What should Stella do? Move home or find somewhere else to live?

A: I think she should definitely …
B: I'm not sure she should …

GRAMMAR

Simple present and present progressive

A WORK IT OUT Read the sentences from *The boomerang generation*. Are they simple present (SP) or present progressive (PP)?

1 I love my parents. ____
2 I'm sleeping in my old room. ____
3 Mom cooks and does all my laundry. ____
4 More and more of my friends are moving back home. ____

B Complete the rules with *simple* or *progressive*.

Simple present and present progressive

1 We use the ____________ present to talk about routines (events that happen every day) and things which are always or generally true.
2 We use the present ____________ to describe what is happening now and to talk about trends.
3 We do not usually use the present ____________ with state verbs like *be, like, want, understand, believe, know, mean, need, cost.*
4 We usually use the present ____________ with time expressions like *now, today, this year.*

C Go to the **Grammar Hub** on **page 124**.

D SPEAK Work in pairs. Complete the sentences with information about your country and discuss with your partner.

1 Recently, more people are living *in apartments in the big cities*.
2 People love ____________, but they don't like ____________.
3 Everyone's talking about ____________ right now.
4 Many young people are studying ____________ right now.
5 Some people are happy because ____________.

PRONUNCIATION

Consonant pairs at the beginning of words

A 2.5 Listen to the words and add them to the correct consonant group.

sl	sm	sn	sp	st	sw
sleep					

B SPEAK Work in pairs. Practice saying these words. Can you add one more example to each group?

SPEAKING

A You are going to ask your partner about his/her life and routine. Use the prompts to make simple present or present progressive questions.

1 think about / moving back home again?
Are you thinking about moving back home again?
2 save money / for anything this year?
____
3 like / cooking for yourself?
____
4 know / your neighbors?
____
5 your own question
____

B Work in pairs. Take turns to ask and answer your questions.

A: Are you thinking of moving back home?
B: I'm not sure. I need to save some money, so maybe!

Talk about your life and routine

2.3 Time flies

Talk about life events

G simple past – regular and irregular verbs P Simple past irregular verbs /ɔː/, /e/ and /eɪ/
V life events S skimming for key words

READING

A Work in pairs. Read the sentence from the article and discuss the questions.

When I was young, … a year was such a long time. Now I'm an adult, time passes so quickly.

1 Do you agree with this sentence? Why/Why not?
2 Can you think of an example when time passed quickly or slowly for you?

B READ FOR MAIN IDEA Read *When did the years get shorter?* quickly and match the headings (a–e) with each theory in the text (1–4). There is one heading you do not need. Use the information in the box to help you.

Skimming for key words

When you read an article for the first time, look for clues to help you understand the main idea of each paragraph.

- Look for key words. These could be numbers or the same words repeated.
- Look for words connected to the main topic.
- Look at the first sentence of each paragraph to help you understand the topic.

a The race against time
b From spring to winter
c New experiences slow down time
d It's all about the numbers
e Counting the days

C READ FOR DETAIL Read again. Are the sentences true (T) or false (F)? Correct the false sentences.

1 Time moved more quickly when the writer was a child. T / F
2 As we grow old, every year becomes a smaller percentage of our life. T / F
3 Many adults feel they have too much free time. T / F
4 Time slows down if we are looking forward to an event. T / F
5 New experiences can help to slow down time. T / F
6 All the theories agree that adults and children experience time differently. T / F

D SPEAK Work in pairs. Which theories in the article best explain why time seems to fly as we get older? Why? Give examples from your own life.

A: I like the one about …
B: I think Theory 3 is best because …

When did the years get shorter?

By Stefan Nyberg

January 10, 2019

Glossary

routine (n) your usual way of doing things
stressful (adj) involving or causing a lot of pressure or worry
theory (n) an idea that explains how or why something happens

When I was young, the school summer vacation was six weeks long – it felt like forever. A year was such a long time! Now I'm an adult, time passes so quickly. Why does time seem to fly as we get older? Psychologists have several theories about this. Here are the most popular ones:

Theory 1: __

The first theory is mathematical. When you were 5 years old, a year was 20 percent of your life, so it seemed like a long time. When you are 50 years old, a year is only 2 percent of your life, so it seems much shorter. Time can feel very different if you are a child or an adult.

Theory 2: __

As children, we didn't have as much to worry about – we started school and studied, then we came home and played with our friends. Adult life is fast, busy and stressful – it's difficult to do everything we want to do. Days can be tiring. Many of us feel that there isn't enough time in the day. Time seems to pass very quickly because as adults we tend to rush to do something and then move on to the next job with no time to stop and think.

Theory 3: __

As children we knew exactly how many days it was until our next birthday or holiday. All that counting and waiting made the days seem to pass much more slowly. Some psychologists suggest adults don't notice time passing because they are focused on 'boring adult stuff', like shopping or housework. The days, weeks and months pass quickly. Suddenly, another year is over and a new one is beginning.

Theory 4: __

The routines of work and family life mean that, for many adults, the days all feel the same. This is different from our early lives, which were full of exciting first-time experiences. Back then, we started school and studied new things. Then we took exams, went on our first dates and learned to drive. When we look back on all these first-time experiences, we feel that the years were much longer because so many new things happened.

All these theories have something in common: there is a clear difference between the way adults and children experience time. Perhaps we need to learn from children and slow down a little more. Stop, look around, notice the blossom on the trees in the spring and the leaves changing color in the fall. The earth will keep spinning, but we are only here for a short time. Let's enjoy it!

GRAMMAR

Simple past – regular and irregular verbs

A WORK IT OUT Complete the sentences (1–4) from *When did the years get shorter?* Then match them with the correct simple past forms in the box below.

1 As children we ________ school and studied.

2 We ______________ exactly how many days it was until our next birthday or holiday.

3 As children, we ______________ have as much to worry about.

4 When ______________ the years get shorter?

negative   regular   question   irregular

B Choose the correct options to complete the rules.

Simple past regular and irregular verbs

Simple past positive

1 To talk about ***finished*** / ***unfinished*** actions in the past.

2 For most regular verbs in the simple past tense, we add ***-ed*** / ***-ing***.

Simple past negative

3 We make the simple past ***negative*** / ***positive*** with subject + *didn't* + base form

Simple past questions

4 We ***make*** / ***don't make*** questions with *Did* + subject + base form + ?

5 Question words (*What, Where, When, Why* and *How*) come ***before*** / ***after*** *did*.

6 After *yes/no* questions, we use *did/didn't* in ***short*** / ***long*** answers.

C Go to the **Grammar Hub** on **page 124**.

PRONUNCIATION

Simple past irregular verbs /ɔː/, /e/ and /eɪ/

2.6 **A** Complete the table with the words in the box. Listen and check.

~~ate~~ ~~bought~~ fought made paid ~~said~~ sent taught

/ɔː/	*bought*
/e/	*said*
/eɪ/	*ate*

B SPEAK Make questions about your childhood using the prompts. Ask and answer them with a partner.

1 Where / meet / your best friend?

2 What / your parents / teach you?

3 You / a happy teenager?

4 Your idea.

VOCABULARY

Life events

A Look at *When did the years get shorter?* again. Find four important life events and match them with the pictures (a–d). How old were you when you did these things?

B Go to **the Vocabulary Hub** on **page 146**.

C SPEAK Work in pairs. At what age do people generally do these things in your country? At what age did your grandparents' generation do these things? Tell your partner.

- learn to swim
- get married
- have a baby
- retire

SPEAKING HUB

A Work in groups. You are going to tell your group about three first-time experiences. Two should be true and one should be false. Use the ideas in the box or your own ideas.

first vacation without your parents
first child   first important exams   first job
first romantic relationship   getting your own place
learning to ride a bike or drive   leaving home
starting school or college

B ORGANIZE Answer the questions. Write notes.

- Where and when did you have this first-time experience?
- Who else was part of the experience?
- What happened? What went well? Were there any problems?
- How did you feel? Did you learn anything from the experience?

C DISCUSS Tell the group about your first-time experiences. Take turns. Can you guess which experiences are true and which are false?

Talk about life events

Café Hub

2.4 Noisy neighbors

F – ask for and give advice P – disagreeing

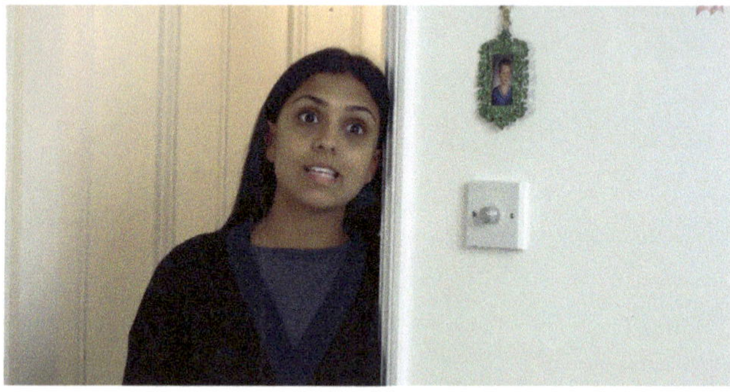

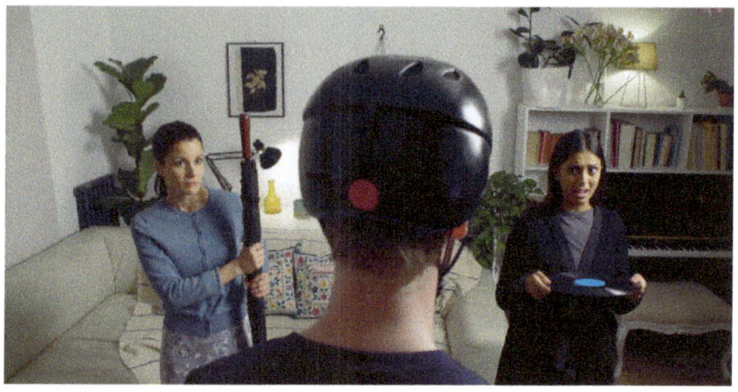

COMPREHENSION

A **SPEAK** Work in pairs. Describe your neighbors to your partner. What are they like? Use words in the box to help you or your own ideas.

friendly noisy old quiet unfriendly young

B Look at the picture. Why do you think Neena, Gaby and Zac are going to see their neighbor like this? Write notes.

Neena's problem	The advice	The decision

C ▶ 00:00–03:40 Watch the first part of the video and check your ideas in Exercise B. What do you think the neighbor is like?

D ▶ 03:40–04:04 Watch the second part of the video. Why does everybody laugh?

FUNCTIONAL LANGUAGE

Ask for and give advice

A Complete the sentences with the correct verb forms. Then decide who said each sentence, Gaby (G), Neena (N) or Zac (Z).

1 What do you think I should ***do / to do***? ____
2 You could ***ask / to ask*** them to turn the volume down. ____
3 How about ***to use / using*** some earplugs? ____
4 Let me ***help / to help*** you out here. Earplugs. ____
5 What ***do / are*** you suggest? ____
6 Why don't you ***go / to go*** upstairs and talk to them? ____
7 I think you should ***go / to go*** and talk to them. ____
8 And why don't we ***come / coming*** with you? ____

B ▶ Watch the video again and check your answers to Exercise A. Write the sentences in the correct place.

Ask for advice

What should I do?

1 ________________
2 ________________

Give advice

You should/shouldn't …

3 ________________
4 ________________
5 ________________
6 ________________
7 ________________
8 ________________

Reply

That's a good idea.
Thanks, I'll try them.
I'm not sure it's a good idea.

MILLY

SAM

NEENA

ZAC

GABY

C Complete the job interview advice for Neena with one word in each blank. Which do you think is the best piece of advice?

1. You ______________ leave plenty of time to get there.
2. I ______________ you should read about the company before the interview.
3. Here's one idea: you ______________ practice a few typical interview questions with a friend.
4. Nervous? ______________ don't you do some breathing exercises to relax?
5. I think you ______________ dress for success.
6. You ______________ have your phone on during the interview.
7. I ______________ think you should ask about salary first.

USEFUL PHRASES

A Match the useful phrases (1–6) with the phrases that come after them in the video (a–f). Then watch the video again and check your answers.

1. Seriously?!
2. What's wrong?
3. Cool!
4. Here you go.
5. What's the problem?
6. You can rely on us.

a. No, it's not cool.
b. All of us.
c. Cool, thanks, Gaby.
d. Someone's playing dance music in the flat above my bedroom.
e. *(very loud dance music playing)*
f. Oh Zac, the people upstairs are playing loud music.

B How do you say these useful phrases in your language?

PRONUNCIATION

Disagreeing

A 00:38–00:49 Watch the scene where Neena disagrees with Gaby again. Read out the conversation at the same time as Gaby and Neena. Copy the word stress and intonation.

Gaby: Really? Cool!
Neena: No, It's not cool. I need to get to sleep.

B **SPEAK** Work in pairs. Make similar conversations. Take turns to comment, disagree and say why. Use the comments in the box or your own ideas.

That's cheap/expensive! That's fair/unfair!
That's funny/serious! That's good/bad!
That's lucky/unlucky!

A: That's cheap!
B: No, it's not cheap. It's really expensive.

SPEAKING

A Work in pairs. Choose one of the problems and write a conversation with one friend giving advice to another one.

1. I usually forget my house keys.
2. My neighbor's dog barks all day.
3. The children in the apartment upstairs are very noisy.
4. My roommate spends too much time in the bathroom.
5. I'm the only person who does the cleaning.
6. My roommate's always hot and I'm always cold.

B Practice your conversation. Take turns giving advice. Then perform it for the rest of the class.

A: I usually forget my house keys.
B: Why don't you leave a key with your neighbor?
A: That's a good idea.

Ask for and give advice

➤ Turn to page 159 to learn how to write an email of complaint.

Unit 2 Review

VOCABULARY

A Complete the ad with the correct prepositions.

Samaritans is a UK charity that helps [1] ___with___ personal problems. Every six seconds, someone calls looking [2] ________ support. Callers can talk [3] ________ volunteers 24 hours a day and can rely [4] ________ them to listen and help. Many callers don't want to talk [5] ________ their problems with people they know well or live [6] ________.
Samaritans volunteers keep all conversations private and are always there to help.

www.samaritans.org

B Complete the profile with the simple past forms of the verbs in the box.

change fall get go to have ~~leave~~

David Attenborough

1926 – born in London
1945 – [1] ___left___ school and [2] ________ Cambridge University
1946 – met and [3] ________ in love with Jane Ebsworth Oriel
1950 – [4] ________ married to Jane; the couple later [5] ________ two children, Robert and Susan
1952 – joined the BBC
1965 – became the head of television channel BBC Two
1973 – [6] ________ jobs and became the writer and presenter we know and love today

GRAMMAR

A Choose the best adverb of degree to complete the sentences. Use the information in parentheses to help you.

1 The idea of a vertical forest building sounds *fairly* / *really* interesting. (*STRONG*)
2 It's ***almost*** / ***totally*** impossible to add trees to every high-rise building. (*WEAK*)
3 The builders worked ***extremely*** / ***a little*** quickly. (*STRONG*)
4 The problem with buildings like this is they can be ***very*** / ***fairly*** expensive. (*WEAK*)
5 The trees are ***almost*** / ***so*** healthy because of rainwater. (*STRONG*)

B Complete the paragraph with the simple past or present progressive form of the verbs in parentheses.

Dreaming of Tokyo

Friends Tatsuo and Daisuki shared a small apartment in Tokyo for three years. Tatsuo [1] ___speaks___ (*speak*) French and recently left for a temporary job in Paris. He [2] ________ (*work*) there as a tour guide for the summer. Apartments [3] ________ (*cost*) a lot in Tokyo and Daisuki can't afford to stay. Right now, he [4] ________ (*live*) with his parents outside the city. They get along well, but Daisuki [5] ________ (*not like*) the two-hour daily train trip into Tokyo.
He is not the only one in this situation. More of his friends [6] ________ (*leave*) the city these days because it's so expensive. Every morning, the train Daisuki [7] ________ (*catch*) is full of young people, making the long trip to work and dreaming of their own place in the city.

C There is one mistake with the simple past in each sentence. Correct the mistake.

1 I ~~falled~~ *fell* in love when I was 18.
2 I weren't good at sports when I was a teenager.
3 I didn't thought money was important when I was a child.
4 When I was young, my parents always knowed when I wasn't telling the truth.
5 I leaved home when I was 19.
6 My father teached me how to drive.
7 I wasn't meet my partner at work.

FUNCTIONAL LANGUAGE

A Complete the missing words in the conversation.

Sophie: Peter, I can't stand the course I'm studying in college. [1]W*hat* d__ you t_ _ _ _ _ I s_ _ _ _ _ _ do?
Peter: [2]M_ _ _ _ you s_ _ _ _ _ _ wait and see if things improve.
Sophie: [3]I s_ _ _ _ _ _ _ _ s__, but I'm pretty sure the course is not for me.
Peter: [4]W_ _ d_ _'_ y_ _ talk to your teacher about it?
Sophie: [5]T_ _ _'_ a good i_ _ _ _.
Peter: [6]D__ you w_ _ _ _ m__ t__ go with you?
Sophie: No, that's OK, but thanks.

3 TRAVEL

Canoeing through the early morning mist near Port Angeles, Washington, US.

OBJECTIVES

- talk about journeys and transportation
- tell a story about a journey
- talk about the kind of vacations you like
- ask for travel information and check understanding
- write an email about a travel experience

Work with a partner. Discuss the questions.

1 What can people learn from traveling?
2 Look at the picture. Do you enjoy doing outdoor activities?
3 Where is the last place you traveled to?

3.1 The four-year journey

Talk about journeys and transportation

G *all / some / most / no / none* **V** types of transportation **P** /p/, /b/, /v/

British man Graham Hughes is the first person to visit all of the countries in the world without flying.

Hughes traveled by sea and over land to complete his record-breaking journey. He traveled on a budget of only US $150 a week and paid for everything himself. Thirty-three-year-old Hughes set off on New Year's Day 2009. His first stop was Argentina, and 1,492 days later, he arrived at his final destination, South Sudan. Hughes crossed the borders of all of the 193 United Nations countries. He traveled long distances by boat, and for shorter trips went by train, rode a bus or occasionally took a taxi. None of his trips were by plane. A lot of people helped him on his journey. Some of them gave him directions and food or let him sleep on their couch for free, and others gave him rides.

Of course, not all his experiences were good. He also had some problems. He crossed the Sahara Desert, but had to go back 2,000 miles because he didn't have the correct visa. The most difficult place to get to was the Seychelles. Graham tried three times from three different countries before he finally made it to the islands.

Glossary

budget (n) the amount of money a person has to spend on something
visa (n) an official document that allows you to enter or leave a country for a specific time period

READING

A Work in groups. Think of a country beginning with each letter of the alphabet. You have two minutes.

B **SCAN** Work in pairs. Read the first line of the article about Graham Hughes. What might the information in the box refer to? Read the article and check your answers.

150 US dollars | 193 countries | 1,426 days | 2,000 miles

C **SPEAK** Work in pairs. Would you like to do a similar journey to Graham? Why/Why not?

D **READ FOR DETAIL** Read again. Are the sentences true (T) or false (F)? Correct the false sentences.

1 The United Nations helped Graham pay for his journey. *T / F*
2 His journey finished in Argentina. *T / F*
3 People were kind to Graham during his journey. *T / F*
4 He didn't always pay for accommodations. *T / F*
5 He visited the Seychelles three times. *T / F*
6 He went on his journey because he wanted to help people from all over the world. *T / F*

E **SPEAK** Work in pairs. Discuss the questions.

1 Would you let a stranger sleep on your couch? Why/Why not?
2 Graham says the world is full of people who want to help each other. Do you agree? Explain your answer.

GRAMMAR

all / some / most / no / none

A **WORK IT OUT** Look at these sentences from the article about Graham Hughes. Then choose the correct words to complete the rules.

Hughes crossed the borders of ***all of*** *the 193 United Nations countries.*
None of *his trips were by plane.*
Some of *them gave him directions and food …*
Of course, not ***all*** *his experiences were good.*
He also had ***some*** *problems.*

all / some / most / no / none

1 We use *all, some, most, no* **before / after** nouns.
2 We **can / can't** use *all, some, most, none* with *of* + pronoun.
3 We **can / can't** use *all, some, most, none* with *of* + *the / this / that / these / those*.
4 We **can / can't** use *no* with *of* + pronoun or *the / this / that / these / those*.
5 With *all* we **have to / don't have to** use *of* before a pronoun or *the / this / that / these / those*.

B Go to the **Grammar Hub** on **page 126**.

C **SPEAK** Work in pairs. Make sentences of your own with *all / some / most / no / none*. Talk about:

- my friends
- my travel experiences
- types of transportation
- Graham Hughes or people like him

VOCABULARY
Types of transportation

A Find five types of transportation in the article about Graham Hughes. Write them in the correct place. Then add the words in the box.

car ferry helicopter minibus trolley

Travel by air	Travel over land	Travel by ocean
plane		

Transportation collocations

With all the transportation nouns in Exercise A, we can use the verbs *go* or *travel* + *by*. We don't use *a* / *an* before the noun. We can also use *take* or *get* + *a* / *an*.

- *He traveled long distances by boat, and for shorter trips went by train, rode a bus or occasionally took a taxi.*

When we talk about plane travel, we usually use the verb *fly*.

- *We flew to Portugal last summer.*

B Add (+) or remove (–) one word to make each sentence correct. Use the Transportation collocations box in Exercise A to help you.

1 I go to work by a bus everyday. (–)
2 My brother occasionally gives a ride on the back of his motorcycle. (+)
3 I took taxi home last Saturday night. (+)
4 I usually get by a trolley to my English classes. (–)

PRONUNCIATION
/p/, /b/, /v/

3.1 **A** Listen and repeat.

1 /p/ plane 2 /b/ boat 3 /v/ visa

3.2 **B** Listen and write the words in the correct place.

/p/	/b/	/v/
	bus	

3.3 **C** Listen, check and repeat the words.

SPEAKING

A Interview your classmates about their travel habits. Find out about:

- daily travel to and from college or work
- trips they regularly make on the weekend
- transportation they use to go on vacation

B Work in pairs. Write questions to find out about:

- the different types of transportation people use in each type of travel in Exercise A
- what they like and dislike about each type of transportation they use
- how much they spend on transportation in a normal week

C Interview another student and make a note of their answers to your questions.

D Work with your original partner again and compare the travel and transportation habits of the people you interviewed.

1 Who uses more types of transportation?
2 Who feels most positive about the transportation they use?
3 Who spends the most on transportation in a normal week?

Talk about journeys and transportation

3.2 Lost at sea

● Tell a story about a journey

G past progressive and simple past **P** *was* and *were* with past progressive **V** prefixes

LISTENING

A What famous stories or movies do you know that involve seas, oceans and islands? What happens?

B **PREDICT** Work in pairs. You are going to listen to a podcast about the Robertson family. Look at the pictures (1–4). What do you think happened?

3.4 **C** Listen and check your answers to Exercise B.

Glossary

brave (adj) a brave decision, action or choice is one that you make even though it involves risk and may cause problems for you

life raft (n) a small rubber boat used for saving people whose boat is sinking

survival expert (n) a person who knows how to stay alive in emergencies if you are far away from help

survive (v) to stay alive, especially in a difficult or dangerous situation, for example injury, illness, war

3.4 **D** **LISTEN FOR DETAIL** Listen again and put the information in the order that you hear it (1–6).

___ The Robertsons got help.

_1_ One of the Robertsons' children asked an unusual question.

___ The Robertsons had no more food.

___ The Robertsons left their old life behind.

___ There was a serious accident.

___ The Robertsons made it back to land.

E **SPEAK** Work in pairs. Discuss the questions.

1 Do you think the Robertsons' decision to sail around the world was a good one? Why/Why not?

2 Why do you think some people do dangerous things?

3 Do you ever do dangerous things, or do you prefer to avoid danger? Give examples.

GRAMMAR

Past progressive and simple past

A **WORK IT OUT** Read the rules and complete the examples with the words in the box.

bought	noticed	sold	started	was passing	were living

Past progressive and simple past

We use the past progressive (*was / were* + verb + *-ing*) for actions or situations that were in progress.

- *In 1970, Dougal and Lyn Robertson and their four children* 1 ________________ *on a farm, in northern England.*

We use the simple past for finished actions or situations, and things that happened one after another.

- *They* 2 ________________ *their business,* 3 ________________ *a boat and on January 27th, 1971,* 4 ________________ *their journey across the Atlantic.*

When used together in the same sentence, the past progressive describes a long action and the simple past describes a shorter action.

- *Their boat* 5 ________________ *the Galapagos Islands when they* 6 ________________ *something large in the water behind them.*

when and *while*

We use ***when*** or ***while*** to link past progressive and simple past verbs.

We can use ***when*** or ***while*** before the past progressive.

- ***When/While*** *they were sailing out into the Pacific Ocean, things started to go very wrong.*

We always use ***when*** before the simple past.

- *They were sailing out into the Pacific Ocean* ***when*** *things started to go wrong.*

AMAZING ADVENTURES

1

2

B Go to the **Grammar Hub** on **page 126**.

C SPEAK Think of an interesting or unusual thing that happened to you on a trip or vacation. Write notes using the questions below. Then work in groups and tell your story.

1 Where and when was the vacation?
2 Who did you go with?
3 What happened that was interesting or unusual?
4 What were you doing when this thing happened?

When I was a teenager, I went camping with my family in Spain. One morning, we were walking to the beach when I found a wallet full of money on the path …

PRONUNCIATION

was and *were* with past progressive

.5 **A** Listen and repeat the sentences. What do you notice about *was* and *were*?

1 We were biking to the beach when I fell off my bike.
2 I was swimming in the ocean when I lost my car keys.

B WORK IT OUT Choose the correct words to complete the rules.

1 We usually use ***weak* / *strong*** pronunciation of *was* and *were* in positive sentences.
2 We do this because we ***stress* / *don't stress*** the main verb.

C SPEAK Work in pairs. Find out what your partner was doing at these times.

1 7 am this morning
2 last New Year's Eve at midnight
3 10 pm last night

VOCABULARY

Prefixes

A Look at the sentences from *Amazing Adventures*. Choose the correct words to complete the rules.

*I mean, they were very **un**lucky, weren't they, Matt?*

*It sounds like an **im**possible situation.*

1 We use prefixes before ***adjectives* / *pronouns*** to change their meanings.
2 Prefixes like *un-*, *im-*, *dis-* and *in-* give the original word a(n) ***opposite* / *stronger*** meaning.

B Complete the words with the correct prefix, *un-*, *im-*, *dis-* or *in-*.

1 I don't believe anything he says. I think he's ____**honest**.
2 Living on rainwater and turtles sounds very ____**healthy** to me.
3 I failed the test; a lot of my answers were ____**correct**.
4 Not many people go to the Galapagos Islands. It's a/an ____**usual** vacation destination.
5 He doesn't like waiting – he's very ____**patient**.

C SPEAK Work in pairs. Think of other examples of things or people that you can describe with the adjectives with prefixes in Exercises A and B.

SPEAKING

A Work in groups and describe a journey. Students A and B – go to the **Communication Hub** on **page 157**. Students C and D – go to the **Communication Hub** on **page 152**.

B Work in pairs. Take turns telling your story to your group.

C Work in groups. Look at all eight pictures as a group and think of a new story that uses them all. Then tell your story to another group.

3

4
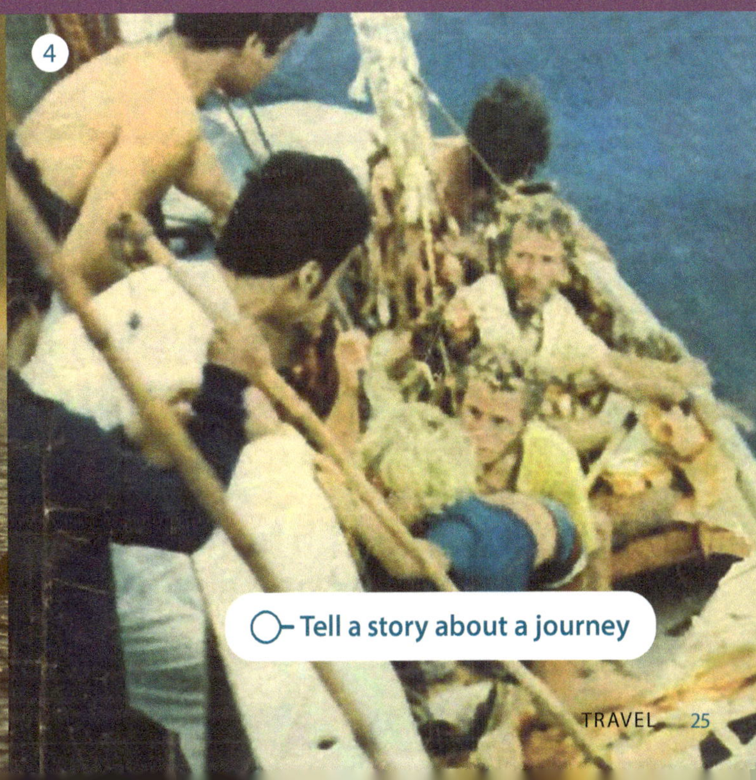

Tell a story about a journey

3.3 Too good to be true

Talk about the kind of vacations you like

G verb + *-ing* and *to* + base form **V** accommodations and amenities **P** /ʃ/, /tʃ/ and /dʒ/ **S** identifying tone

READING

A Work in pairs. Discuss the questions.

1 When you are planning a vacation, how do you choose where to stay?

2 Do you find online reviews helpful or not? Why?

B Read two online reviews for a hotel. Which sounds real and which does not? Why?

★★★★☆

a I love to travel, but I can't afford to stay in five-star hotels or expensive apartments all the time. If you are on a budget like me, the three-star Hotel Jasmine is a great choice. The service is very good and the rooms are small but clean. The location is a little noisy but central. I hope to return to Hotel Jasmine soon.

★★★★★

b This hotel is EXCELLENT!!! The rooms are BEAUTIFUL and the staff are very kind and WONDERFUL!!! I love shopping and the hotel is in the city center!!! I will definitely go on using this hotel – in fact, I refuse to stay anywhere else!!!!!

C **SCAN** Read *Tips for a happy vacation* quickly. Underline any of the ideas you discussed in Exercise B.

D Choose two words which describe the author's tone. Use the information in the box to help you.

1 serious 3 formal
2 informal 4 funny

Identifying tone

The tone of a text can help you understand the author's opinion on the topic. Notice words and phrases the author uses to communicate this.

- Look at the author's choice of adjectives and adverbs.
- Does the punctuation give you any clues? For example, 'quotation marks', exclamation marks, parentheses or capital letters.
- Is the language formal or informal?

TIPS FOR A HAPPY VACATION

You're **planning** to go on vacation and you've **decided** to try somewhere new. You could **consider** using a travel agent, but it's easy to organize your own vacation online these days. All you **need** to do is visit a travel review site, spend time reading travelers' comments and then choose the accommodations with the best reviews. Simple!

Or is it? How do you know that what you are reading is genuine? Research shows that some hotels and restaurants pay people to write fake reviews. Of course, the websites **manage** to find and delete some of these fake reviews, but they aren't always successful. So, before you **choose** to spend your vacation budget on that 'amazing beach resort' or cruise ship that scored ten out of ten, read our tips and learn how to spot a fake review.

TIP ONE: What you see is not always what you get. If the pictures of the apartment, guest house or campsite **seem** to be too good to be true, they probably are. For example, when you see the photograph below, you **expect** to find a nice quiet beach, but in fact, the beach and all the hotels are right next to a building site!

TIP TWO: Nowhere is perfect – fact! Most genuine reviewers **like** to include a mix of positive and negative comments, so a review that's 100 percent positive or negative is more likely to be fake. If you **want** to know what a hostel or chalet is really like, don't read the very best and very worst reviews. Look at the ones in the middle.

TIP THREE: EXCELLENT!!!!!!!! Fake reviewers **like** using capital letters, exclamation marks (!) and lots of extreme adjectives like 'wonderful', 'amazing' and 'excellent'. It can feel like you are being YELLED AT! Genuine reviewers usually **avoid** using so much extreme language. Instead, they usually include helpful details like room size or prices.

Glossary

fake (adj) made to look like something real in order to trick people

genuine (adj) real, rather than pretended or false

E READ FOR DETAIL Read again and answer the questions.

1 Why isn't organizing your own vacation online as simple as it seems?
2 Why might someone want to write a fake review?
3 What does the article aim to teach its readers?
4 What are the characteristics of a genuine review?
5 What are the characteristics of a fake review?

F SPEAK Work in groups. Discuss the questions.

1 What other kinds of online reviews do you read or write, for example, movies, books, games, etc.?
2 Do people rely too much on online reviews? Explain.

GRAMMAR

verb + *-ing* and *to* + base form

A WORK IT OUT Look at the underlined verb patterns from the online reviews. Then complete the rules with the words in the box.

either | *to* + base form | verb + *-ing*

1 I love to travel, but I can't afford to stay in five-star hotels or expensive apartments all the time.
2 I hope to return to Hotel Jasmine soon.
3 I love shopping and the hotel is in the city center!!!
4 I will definitely go on using this hotel – in fact, I refuse to stay anywhere else!!!!!

verb + *-ing* and *to* + base form

1 We use ______________ after these verbs: *agree, can't afford, hope, learn, refuse, would like, would prefer*, ______________, ______________, ______________, ______________, ______________, ______________, ______________, ______________.
2 We use ______________ after these verbs: *(don't) mind, enjoy*, ______________, ______________.
3 We can use ______________ after these verbs (there is little change in meaning): *hate, love, prefer, can't stand*, ______________.

B Look at *Tips for a happy vacation* again. Write the verbs in **bold** in the correct place in Exercise A.

C Go to the **Grammar Hub** on **page 126**.

D SPEAK Work in pairs. Think about the best place you have stayed on vacation. Write a short review. Then swap with a partner and ask questions about your partner's review.

VOCABULARY

Accommodations and amenities

A Look at the words in the box. Which types of accommodations are included in *Tips for a happy vacation?*

apartment | beach resort | campsite | chalet | cruise ship | guest house | hostel | hotel

B Go to the **Vocabulary Hub** on **page 147**.

C SPEAK Work in groups. Take turns describing or drawing items from the **Vocabulary Hub**. The first person in the group to guess each item gets one point.

A: This keeps your room cool when the weather is hot.
B: Air conditioner!

PRONUNCIATION

/ʃ/, /tʃ/ and /dʒ/

A 3.6 Listen to the sounds. Are they the same or different? Then listen and repeat.

1 /ʃ/ chalet 2 /tʃ/ choose 3 /dʒ/ budget

B 3.7 Complete the table with the words in the box. Listen, check and repeat.

~~adjective~~ | ~~beach~~ | genuine | language | manage | picture | ~~ship~~ | shout | show

/ʃ/	/tʃ/	/dʒ/
ship	*beach*	*adjective*

C SPEAK Work in pairs. Practice saying the words. Listen and check your partner's pronunciation.

SPEAKING HUB

A Work in groups. You are going on vacation together to Barcelona for two nights. Together, you have a budget of 600 dollars for accommodations and spending money. Answer the questions:

1 What kind of accommodations would you like to stay in?
2 Which amenities are most important to your group?

B Read about vacation accommodations in Barcelona. Student A – go to the **Communication Hub** on **page 155** and read about Hotel Rambla Park. Student B – go to the **Communication Hub** on **page 156** and read about Gaudí House Hostel. Student C – go to the **Communication Hub** on **page 157** and read about Olympic Apartments.

C PRESENT Describe the accommodations you read about to your group. Decide where you will stay. How much spending money will you have left?

Talk about the kind of vacations you like

Café Hub

3.4 Overslept

F – ask for travel information and check understanding
P – word stress and intonation

COMPREHENSION

A SPEAK Work in pairs. Are you usually early or late for things? Give examples.

B SPEAK Work in pairs. Number the pictures in order (1–6) to describe a morning when Gaby overslept. What do you think happened?

a ☐

b ☐

c ☐

d ☐

e ☐

f ☐

C ▶ Watch the video and compare it with your ideas in Exercise B. What does the ticket officer find? What do you think will happen next?

FUNCTIONAL LANGUAGE

Ask for travel information and check understanding

A Test your memory! Look at the conversation between a customer and a ticket officer. Underline five responses that are different from the video. Try to remember the correct information.

Ask for travel information – trains	
Customer:	[1]Could I have a ticket to St. Albans?
Ticket officer:	[2]Of course. Would you like a single or a return?
Customer:	[3]A single, please.
Ticket officer:	[4]No problem.
Customer:	[5]Do I have to change trains?
Ticket officer:	[6]Yes, you need to change at Watford.
Customer:	[7]What time's the next train?
Ticket officer:	[8]The next train's in about ten minutes. [9]The next train leaves from platform 4B.
Customer:	[10]What time does the train arrive in St. Albans?
Ticket officer:	[11]At 9:13.

B ▶ Watch the video again and check your answers to Exercise A. Write the correct information.

Glossary

single **(adj) (British)** = one-way **(adj) (American)**
return **(adj) (British)** = round-trip **(adj) (American)**

MILLY SAM NEENA ZAC GABY

USEFUL PHRASES

A Watch the video without sound. Yell *Stop!* when you think the ticket officer is about to use one of the useful phrases. Then listen and check.

1 Here, let me help you.
2 Don't worry.
3 Follow me.
4 Don't forget this.
5 You don't want to miss your train.
6 Have a good trip.

B How do you say these useful phrases in your language?

PRONUNCIATION

Word stress and intonation

3.8 **A** Listen and repeat the conversation. Copy the word stress and intonation.

Ticket officer: The next train's in about three minutes from platform two.
Anna: I'm sorry. Did you say three minutes?
Ticket officer: Yes, three minutes!
Anna: OK, thanks. Oh, and where's platform two?
Ticket officer: Go past the coffee shop, then turn right.
Anna: OK. So I need to go past the coffee shop and then … turn left? Is that right?
Ticket officer: No, you need to turn right after the coffee shop.

B SPEAK Work in pairs. Make a similar conversation.

SPEAKING

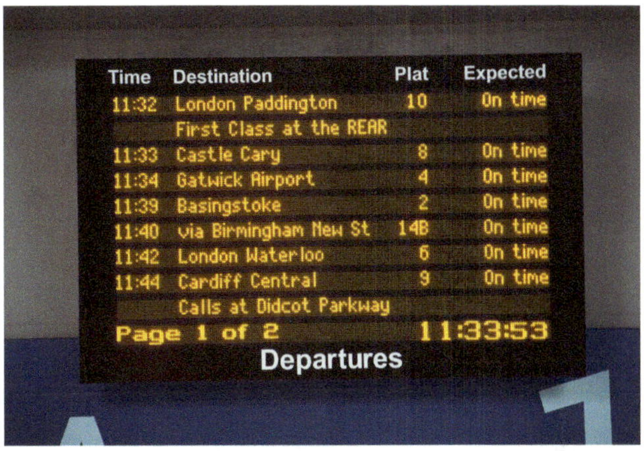

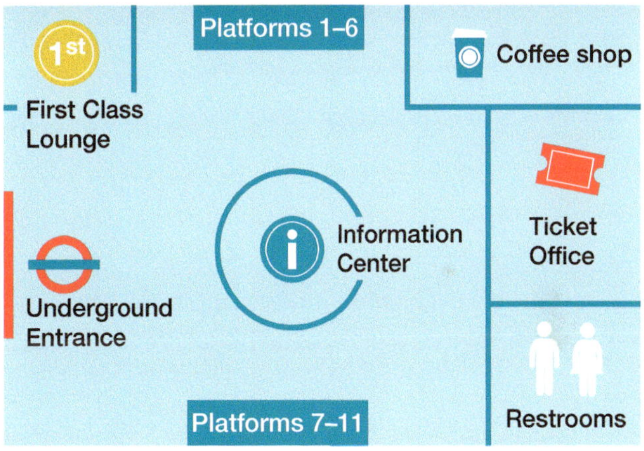

A Work in pairs. Student A is the customer. Student B is the ticket officer. Write a conversation. Use these ideas to help you.

Student A: Ask for information about trains to a place on the departure board.
Student B: Answer Student A's questions.
Student A: Check understanding and then ask for directions to the correct platform.
Student B: Look at the train station plan and give directions.
Student A: Check understanding.

B Practice your conversation. Take turns being the customer and the ticket officer. Then perform it for the rest of the class.

Ask for travel information and check understanding

➤ Turn to page 160 to learn how to write an email about a travel experience.

VOCABULARY

A Label the pictures with the correct forms of transportation.

bus ferry helicopter minibus plane trolley

1 ____________

2 ____________

3 ____________

4 ____________

5 ____________

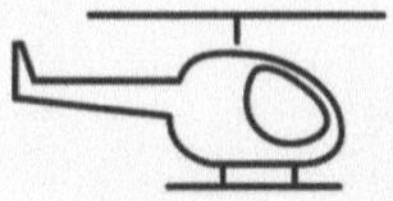

6 ____________

B Write the words in the box in the correct place. Some words can go in more than one place.

accurate happy kind likely organized polite

un-	im-	dis-	in-

C Complete the definitions with the words in the box.

apartment beach resort campsite chalet cruise ship

1 A ____________ is a place where people on vacation can stay in tents.

2 A ____________ is a large, comfortable boat that has similar amenities to a hotel.

3 A ____________ is a place that many people go to for a vacation by the ocean.

4 A ____________ is a wooden house built in a mountain area where people on vacation can stay.

5 An ____________ is a set of rooms, usually on one floor of a large building, where people on vacation can stay and cook their own meals.

GRAMMAR

A Choose the correct words to complete the sentences.

1 *Most* / *Most of* the people I know want to visit other countries.

2 *Some* / *Some of* countries are difficult to get into.

3 *No* / *None* type of transportation is completely safe.

4 *All the* / *All* my money was in my jacket.

B Complete the article with the past progressive or simple past forms of the verbs in parentheses.

Lucky to be alive!

Today, we bring you the story of surfer Mick Fanning.

World champion surfer Mick Fanning is lucky to be alive. In 2015, he [1] ____________ (*surf*) in a competition in South Africa when a shark [2] ____________ (*attack*) him. Thousands of people [3] ____________ (*watch*) on live television when the attack [4] ____________ (*happen*). Mick [5] ____________ (*sit*) on his surf board when he [6] ____________ (*notice*) the shark next to him. The giant fish tried to pull him under the water, but Mick [7] ____________ (*hit*) it on the back, and it [8] ____________ (*swim*) away. A rescue boat [9] ____________ (*wait*) and it brought Mick and another surfer safely back to land.

C Choose the correct form of the verbs to complete the questions. Both forms may be possible.

1 Do you ever refuse ***to leave*** / ***leaving*** a tip in a restaurant? Why?

2 Do you prefer ***to go*** / ***going*** on vacation in the summer or the winter? Why?

3 What do you hope ***to learn*** / ***learning*** when you visit a new country?

4 Would you enjoy ***to visit*** / ***visiting*** a country where no one speaks your language? Why/Why not?

5 Do you like ***to try*** / ***trying*** new foods when you travel? Give an example.

FUNCTIONAL LANGUAGE

A Write the words in the correct order to make questions.

1 have / a / could / I / ticket / to / Central Station / ?

____

2 a / one-way / you / like / would / a / round-trip / or / ?

____

3 does / train / what / the / arrive / in / time / Amsterdam / ?

____

4 next / the / time's / train / what / ?

____

5 do / trains / have / I / to / change / ?

____

6 did / say / platform / sorry, / I'm / 30 / you / ?

____

7 is that right / at the top of the stairs, / so it's left / ?

____

8 do / get / you / to / platform / 9 / how / excuse me, / ?

____

B Work in pairs. Think of different ways to answer the questions in Exercise A.

4 SOCIALIZING

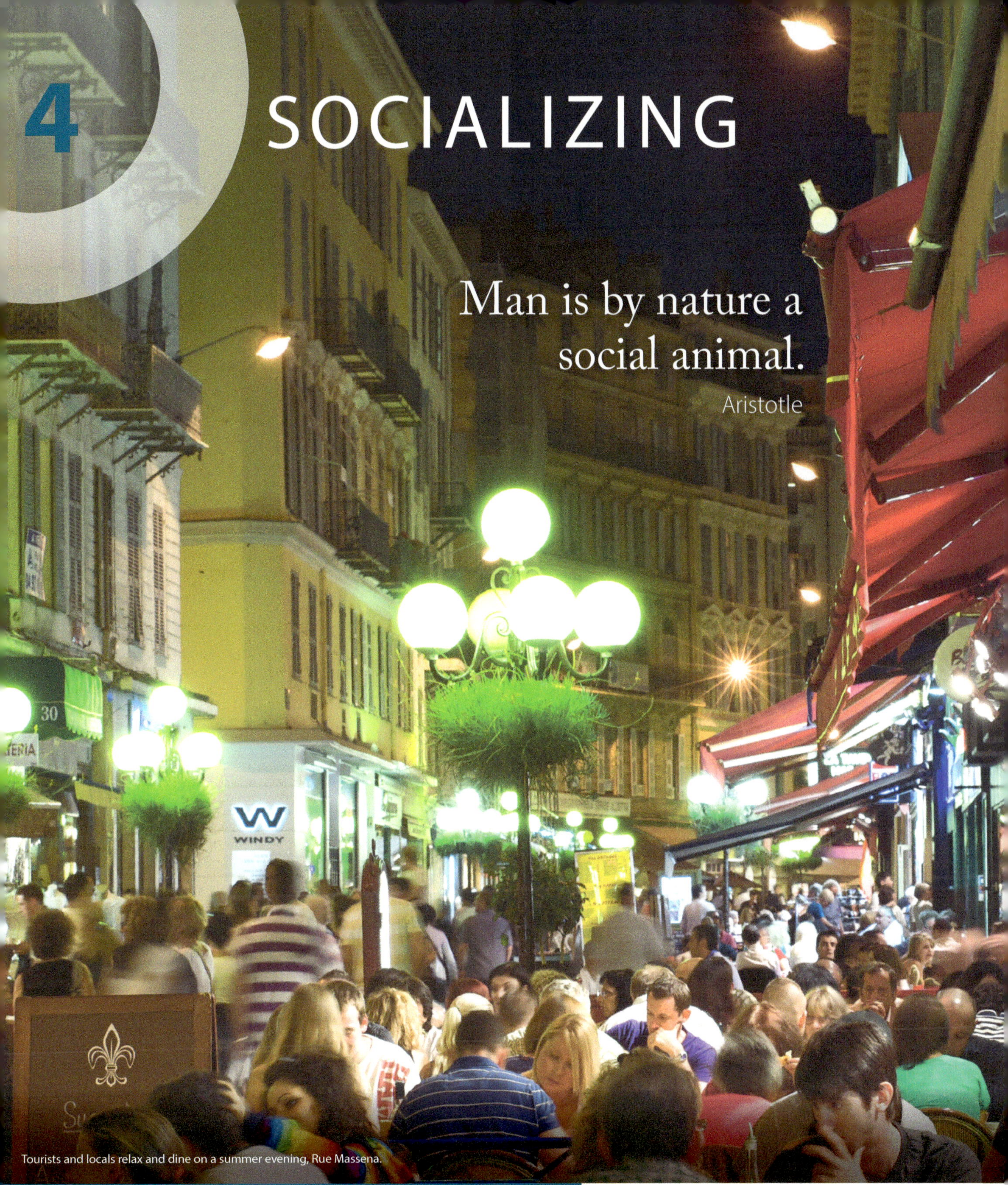

Tourists and locals relax and dine on a summer evening, Rue Massena.

OBJECTIVES

- talk about plans you have made for a weekend with visitors
- present reasons to support or argue against predictions
- ask and answer questions about how you like to spend your free time
- make arrangements to meet up with somebody
- write an invitation and reply

Work with a partner. Discuss the questions.

1 Where do people go out in your country?
2 Look at the picture. Which city do you think it is? Why?
3 What do you enjoy doing with your friends?

4.1 What's the plan?

Talk about plans you have made for a weekend with visit

V free time **G** *be going to* + base form and present progressive for the future **P** *going to*

VOCABULARY

Free time

A SPEAK Work in pairs. Write down as many free time activities as you can in English. You have two minutes. Then compare your list with another pair.

B Complete the diagrams with the verbs in the box.

go for go to hang out play see or go to

1 ______
- the theater / the movies
- a museum / a gallery
- a market
- a friend's place / a party

2 ______
- a meal / a drink
- sushi/pizza/burgers
- a walk / a run / a bike ride
- coffee/lunch/dinner

3 ______
- an exhibit
- a concert / a play / a movie
- a comedy show

4 ______
- cards
- board games
- pool/billiards

5 ______
- in town
- at the mall
- online
- in the park
- with friends

C SPEAK Work in pairs. Which of the free time activities in Exercise B are your favorites, and why?

LISTENING

A Work in pairs. What kind of things do you like to do when you visit a city for the first time?

4.1 **B LISTEN FOR GIST** Listen to a conversation between Sylvia and Greg and circle seven free-time activities in Vocabulary Exercise B that they talk about.

Glossary

arrange (v) to make plans for something to happen, for example by agreeing on a time and place

intelligent (adj) good at understanding difficult ideas and subjects

4.1 **C LISTEN FOR DETAIL** Listen again and choose the correct answer a or b.

1 What is the relationship between Sylvia and Greg?
   a brother and sister
   b boyfriend and girlfriend

2 Who is Claire?
   a Greg's friend
   b Greg's girlfriend

3 Sylvia thinks that Greg will like her friend Duncan because they …
   a are both good cooks.
   b both enjoy eating.

4 After dinner, Sylvia and Greg are going to see …
   a a comedy show.
   b a play by Shakespeare.

5 Greg stops Sylvia explaining the plan for the next day because he …
   a doesn't feel very well.
   b wants to order some food.

D SPEAK Work in pairs. When was the last time you visited friends or family for the weekend? Tell your partner.

GRAMMAR

be going to + base form and present progressive for the future

A WORK IT OUT Read the definitions. Then look at the sentences and decide if they are arrangements (A) or intentions (I).

Arrangements – you have probably booked a ticket or agreed on a time with other people. You usually mention a time, date or place.

Intentions – you have already decided to do something and want to tell someone about it. You don't need to mention a time, date or place.

1 I'm going to introduce you to all my new friends as 'Greggy'. ___
2 Tomorrow evening, she's having dinner with some old friends. ___
3 I think I'm going to bring Mom and Dad here, too. ___
4 We're meeting Duncan and Alicia at three o'clock. ___
5 Alicia says she and Duncan are going to open a restaurant one day. ___

B Choose the correct words to complete the rules. Use Exercise A to help you.

***be going to* + base form and present progressive for the future**

1 We use *be going to* + base form to talk about ***arrangements / intentions***.
2 We use the present progressive (*be* + verb + *-ing*) to talk about ***arrangements / intentions***.

C Go to the **Grammar Hub** on **page 128**.

PRONUNCIATION

going to

4.2 **A** Listen and repeat the pronunciation of *going to* /ˈɡʌnə/ in informal speech.

1 She's going to call later.
2 I'm going to text Angie and Mark.

B SPEAK Work in pairs. Look at the sentences that you marked as intentions (I) in Grammar Exercise A. Practice saying the sentences in an informal way. Pronounce *going to* as /ˈɡʌnə/.

C SPEAK Ask questions about your partner's plans. Talk about your arrangements and intentions.

A: Are you going to have a party in the next few weeks?
B: Yes, I am! It's my birthday next weekend and I'm having a party.

SPEAKING

A Work in groups. Plan a weekend. Choose a group of visitors:

- older family members, for example, an aunt and uncle or grandparents
- younger family members, for example, a brother or sister with their partner and children
- a group of four friends from school or college

B Make plans for next weekend for you and your visitors in and around a city you know well. Write notes on:

- meeting
- sightseeing
- entertainment
- food and drink
- evening activities

C Explain your plan to students from other groups. Which weekend sounds like the most fun?

My old school friends are coming to visit next weekend. I'm meeting them at the train station. Then we're going to have breakfast in town, probably at Vincent Café. The food there is great and it isn't expensive.

Talk about plans you have made for a weekend with visitors

4.2 The future of free time

Present reasons to support or argue against predictions

G making predictions **P** *will* and *won't* **V** suffixes

READING

A Work in pairs. Do you agree with the following sentences? Why/Why not?

In the next ten years …

we will do less work and spend more time socializing.

we will do a lot of our socializing in virtual worlds.

we will socialize with artificial intelligence.

B **READ FOR MAIN IDEA** Work in groups. Student A go to page 156, Student B go to page 153 and Student C go to page 152. Read your article and discuss the questions below.

1 What does the article say about our social lives?

2 What role will technology play?

3 Which expert or business leader is mentioned, and why?

4 What possible benefits of the development does the article mention?

C **SPEAK** Work in groups. Discuss your article and the following questions.

1 Which predictions do you think will happen?

2 Do you think these will be positive or negative developments for our social lives? Why?

GRAMMAR

Making predictions

A **WORK IT OUT** Look at the sentences from the articles about the future of our social lives. Underline the modal verbs used to make predictions.

1 The good news is some people think it might not be long until every weekend is a long weekend.

2 However, experts agree that the way we use social media will change in the future.

3 Some experts even believe that one day it may be possible for robots to feel love.

B Find and underline four more examples of modal verbs in one of the articles you read in Reading Exercise B. Then work in pairs and compare your answers.

C Complete the rules with *will* or *might/may*.

Making predictions

1 We use ______________ (*not*) + the base form of a verb when we are certain about our prediction.

2 We use ______________ (*not*) + the base form of a verb when we are less certain about our prediction.

D Look at the sentences from *Robot relationships*. Then choose the correct words to complete the rules.

… humans will probably develop close relationships with robots.

… it definitely won't be long until robots look, sound and move like humans.

1 We use *probably* to make predictions with *will* and *won't* **less** / **more** certain.

2 We use *definitely* to make predictions with *will* and *won't* **less** / **more** certain.

3 We use *probably* and *definitely* **before** / **after** *will*.

4 We use *probably* and *definitely* **before** / **after** *won't*.

E Go to the **Grammar Hub** on **page 128**.

F Complete the predictions about artificial intelligence with the words in parentheses.

1 Some people ^might not^ want three-day weekends every week. (*might not*)

2 It probably be harder to find a job in the future because of technology. (*will*)

3 I don't think we have robot friends in my lifetime. (*'ll*)

4 We control computers with our minds in the future. (*might*)

5 VR headsets definitely get much cheaper in the next few years. (*will*)

6 Humans won't fall in love with robots in the future. (*probably*)

7 I'm sure we all have robots in our homes 20 years from now. (*'ll*)

8 We stop working completely one day because of technology. (*may*)

G SPEAK Work in pairs. Are there any predictions in Exercise F that you do not agree with?

I think most people will want three-day weekends every week.

PRONUNCIATION

will and *won't*

3 **A** Stressed words are the ones that carry the information. Listen and underline the stressed words.

1 There will be fewer car trips to work in the future.

2 Technology will do more of the work for us.

3 People won't be paid for working fewer days per week.

4 Do you think people will be happier in the future?

5 No, they won't.

6 Yes, they will. They won't have to work so hard.

.3 **B** Listen again and repeat the sentences. Copy the stress.

VOCABULARY

Suffixes

A Go to the **Vocabulary Hub** on **page 147**.

B Add one of the suffixes in the box to the words in parentheses to make nouns. You may need to change the spelling of some of the words. You will need to use some of the suffixes more than once.

-ion -ity -ment -ness

1 I think there is a ______________ (*possible*) that robots will feel love in the future.

2 I agree with the ______________ (*predict*) that virtual reality will be an important part of social media.

3 There is an ______________ (*agree*) between many experts that technology will help our work–life balance.

4 An important ______________ (*develop*) is that robots are now beginning to understand our feelings.

5 I don't believe that robots will be able to experience real ______________ (*happy*) or ______________ (*sad*).

C SPEAK Work in pairs. Look at sentences 1, 2 and 5 in Exercise B. Do you agree with these opinions? Why/Why not?

SPEAKING

A Discuss some predictions about the future. Read three predictions for the future and present reasons to support and argue against each.

Fifty years from now …

1 cash in the form of bills and coins will completely disappear.

2 all cars will be self-driving and there will be very few road accidents.

3 all European children will learn Mandarin at school.

B Work in groups. Discuss the predictions and write down reasons to support and argue against each prediction.

C Work in new groups. Take turns speaking for one to two minutes about one of the predictions.

Present reasons to support or argue against predictions

4.3 Hygge

Ask and answer questions about how you like to spend your free time

G subject and object questions **V** relaxing **P** linking a consonant to a vowel **S** summarizing

READING

A Work in pairs. Which of these things have you done recently? What exactly did you do? Tell your partner.

1 spend the evening at a friend's home
2 relax at home on your own
3 invite people over to your home for the evening
4 get together with your extended family
5 have a night out with friends

B SPEAK Look at the pictures. What are the people doing? How do you think they feel? Use the words in the box to help you.

a cozy blanket a family gathering a fire a hot bath a sleeping pet candles warm socks wool sweaters

C READ FOR MAIN IDEA The pictures all show the Danish idea of *hygge*. What do you think *hygge* means? Read the first paragraph of *Make yourself at home* to check your answer.

Make *yourself* at home

What is *hygge*?

Winters in Denmark are long, dark and cold, but according to the 2016 UN World Happiness Report, Danish people are among the happiest in the world. One reason might be *hygge*, the Danish attitude that focuses on enjoying the simple things in life, such as enjoying a coffee in a relaxed atmosphere with easy-going friends or family.

How do you pronounce *hygge*?

Hygge is easy enough to pronounce – 'hue-gah' – but much more difficult to translate. No single English word describes the idea completely, but being cozy is a big part of it. There may be a connection between the word *hygge* and the English word *hug*, and in Danish *hygge* can be an adjective, verb or noun.

How do I know if it's *hygge*?

Your friends come over on a cold winter evening to sit by the fire, eat homemade food and play board games. That's definitely *hygge*. You have a quiet night in, take a bath, light some candles, then sit down with a good book and a cozy blanket. That's *hygge*, too. You argue about politics, check your phone, play video games and listen to thumping techno music. That's definitely not *hygge*! So how do you know if it's *hygge*? Think warm socks, wool sweaters, sleeping pets and happy family gatherings. Got it now?

Why *hygge*?

Research shows that people who are kind to themselves and take some time out to relax have better mental health and feel happier. *Hygge* encourages us to do this and also to get together with friends and family. Happy groups of people make more caring communities and a happier society. It's no surprise that the Danes are always smiling!

Glossary

cozy (adj) warm and comfortable, and making you feel relaxed
family gathering (phrase) when a family meets and spends time together
translate (v) to change spoken or written words into another language

D READ FOR DETAIL Read the whole article. Then complete the summary with the words in the box. Use the information in the box to help you.

Summarizing

A summary gives the most important points of a text.

Highlight or underline key points and write notes as you read the text. Try to use your own words rather than copy the writer's.

comfortable explain health important technology

Hygge is a Danish custom for people who want to relax and feel [1] ________. It is usually at home and no [2] ________ is involved! *Hygge* can be with other people or by yourself – the [3] ________ thing is to feel happy and cozy. Feeling this way is good for your mental [4] ________. This might [5] ________ why Danish people were described as some of the happiest people in the world by the 2016 UN World Happiness Report.

E SPEAK Work in pairs. Discuss the questions.

1. When did you last do something '*hygge*'? What was it and who were you with?
2. Is there a word in your language that means *hygge* or something similar?

GRAMMAR

Subject and object questions

A WORK IT OUT Read the rules and look at the questions from *Make yourself at home*. Then look at the examples and answer the questions (1–3).

Subject and object questions

We ask subject questions when we don't know *what/who/which/whose* something or someone is.

We ask object questions when we want to know more information about something or someone.

What is hygge?

How do you pronounce 'hygge'?

1. Which is the subject question?
2. Which is the object question?
3. Which question includes an auxiliary verb?

B Look at the questions and possible answers. Then choose the correct words to complete the rules.

What is hygge? It is an attitude that focuses on enjoying the simple things in life.

How do you pronounce 'hygge'? You pronounce it 'hue-gah'.

1. With subject questions, we ***change / don't change*** the word order in the answer.
2. In ***subject / object*** questions, the question word is the object of the sentence.

C Go to the **Grammar Hub** on **page 128**.

D Choose the best question word and decide if an auxiliary verb is needed to complete the questions. Then choose the correct question type: subject (S) or object (O).

1. *Who / Why* is *do / –* your best friend? S / O
2. *When / What do / –* you do with your best friend? S / O
3. *What / Who does smile / smiles* more, you or your best friend? S / O
4. *What / Which do / –* you do to relax? S / O

E SPEAK Work in pairs. Ask and answer the questions in Exercise D.

VOCABULARY

Relaxing

A Work in pairs. Make a list of different ways of relaxing. You have one minute.

B Go to the **Vocabulary Hub** on **page 148**.

PRONUNCIATION

Linking a consonant to a vowel

A SPEAK Work in pairs. Which letters of the alphabet are vowels and which are consonants?

4.4 **B** Listen and repeat the phrases. Which words link together?

1. light a candle
2. take a bath

4.5 **C** Say the phrases and draw an arrow where a consonant sound links to a vowel sound. Then listen and check your answers.

1. have some friends over
2. a relaxed atmosphere
3. the simple things in life
4. friends and family

SPEAKING HUB

A Work in pairs. You are going to write a quiz with the title *Are you a home bird or a party animal?*

B PLAN Ask five questions and give two or three possible answers for each. Use the topics below:

- a favorite way of celebrating
- a typical Saturday night
- your ideal vacation
- going to or having parties
- eating out or cooking at home

C Swap quizzes with another pair and answer their questions. Do you agree with the results?

Ask and answer questions about how you like to spend your free time

Café Hub

4.4 Would you?

Ⓕ– make arrangements to meet up with somebody

Ⓟ– saying *yes* or *no*

COMPREHENSION

A SPEAK Work in pairs. Look at the pictures and discuss where the characters are and what you think happens. Then choose the correct words to complete the sentences.

1 Zac and Milly *have* / *haven't* met before.
2 Zac *knows* / *doesn't know* what to say to Milly.
3 Zac *wants* / *doesn't want* to buy a T-shirt.
4 Milly *likes* / *doesn't like* Zac.
5 Zac *likes* / *doesn't like* Milly.
6 Zac and Milly *arrange* / *don't arrange* to go out together.

B ▶ Watch the video and check your answers to Exercise A.

C ▶ 02:58–04:19 Watch part of the video again. When are Milly and Zac free to meet? Put a check mark (✓) or an ✗ in the correct place.

	Milly	Zac
1 tonight		
2 on Saturday after 1:30		
3 on Sunday at midday		

D SPEAK Work in pairs. Why are they not able to meet tonight or on Saturday?

Glossary

midday **(n) (British)** = noon **(n) (American)**

FUNCTIONAL LANGUAGE

Make arrangements to meet up with somebody

A Complete the questions with the words in the box. There are three words you do not need.

are can could do how maybe what will ~~would~~ would

Make arrangements (invitations)

1 __Would__ you like to hang out tonight?
2 ________ you like to do something, then?
3 We ________ go for a coffee, or eat something?
4 ________ you free on Saturday?
5 ________ about Sunday instead?
6 ________ time?
7 ________ you want to meet at the park?

Say *yes*

Yeah! Sure. / Sounds great. / Awesome!
I'd love to!
Great. Twelve o'clock it is!

Say *no*

I'm so sorry, I can't.
Oh! Wait a minute. I just remembered …

B ▶ Watch the video again and check your answers to Exercise A.

MILLY

SAM

NEENA

ZAC

GABY

USEFUL PHRASES

A Match the useful phrases (1–6) with the phrases which show the correct meaning (a–f).

1 Are you looking for anything in particular?
2 I'm sorry, I need to get that.
3 So, you were saying.
4 Well, it was nice to see you again.
5 Wait, hold on!
6 Sounds great!

a I'm leaving.
b That's a good idea.
c Stay here!
d Do you want to buy something?
e Please continue.
f The phone is ringing.

B How do you say these useful phrases in your language?

PRONUNCIATION

Saying *yes* or *no*

.6 **A** Listen and write the replies in the correct place.

Saying *yes*	Saying *no*

.7 **B** Listen and repeat. Can you hear the difference in intonation between saying *yes* and saying *no*? Copy the word stress and intonation.

C **SPEAK** Work in pairs. Practice saying the replies. Listen and check your partner's pronunciation.

SPEAKING

A Work in pairs. Look at some things you could arrange to do. One item in each word set is not correct. Cross it out and replace it with your own idea.

1 go for … a drink / a walk / a drive / a shop
2 go to … the movie theater / swim / a gig / the beach
3 go … shopping / eating / swimming / dancing / biking

B Work in pairs. Practice making arrangements using the ideas in Exercise A. Take turns inviting each other.

Student A: Invite B to do something.
Student B: Say *no*.
Student A: Suggest another time.
Student B: Say *no*.
Student A: Suggest *another* time.
Student B: Say *yes*.

Make arrangements to meet up with somebody

➤ Turn to page 161 to learn how to write an invitation and reply.

Unit 4 Review

VOCABULARY

A Write the missing words to complete Olivia's email.

To: Natalie
Subject: This weekend

Hi Natalie,

I have a great weekend planned for us. On Friday, I'll meet you at the station – then let's [1] ________ for sushi and go [2] ________ a drink in town.

On Saturday, we can go for a bike [3] ________. I have two bikes, so let's take them and go [4] ________ the market. After we can hang [5] ________ in the park and talk or [6] ________ cards.

On Saturday evening, we're going [7] ________ my friend Alex's place. Then on Sunday, maybe we can [8] ________ a movie before you go.

Can't wait!

Olivia xxx

B Choose the correct words to complete the sentences.

1 This robot can do a lot of different ***active*** / ***activities***.

2 I think we should have a ***discussion*** / ***discuss*** about what will happen in the future.

3 What kind of ***abilities*** / ***able*** do you think machines will have in 50 years?

4 In my opinion, ***happiness*** / ***happy*** is one of the most important things in life.

5 There is the ***possible*** / ***possibility*** that people will stop using social media.

GRAMMAR

A Complete the sentences with *be going to* + infinitive or the present progressive form of the verbs in parentheses. Use contractions.

1 I ____________________ (*not forget*) my friend's birthday again this year.

2 We ____________________ (*meet*) the others tonight on the corner by the coffee shop.

3 Mia ____________________ (*take*) her friend out for dinner tomorrow.

4 I think I ____________________ (*lie down*) for a while before we go out.

5 Go to bed early because we ____________________ (*get up*) at 6 am to drive to the airport.

B Find and correct the mistake in each sentence.

1 It will be easier to meet people in the future probably because of technology.

____

2 People might going on virtual dates online in the future.

____

3 A virtual date probably won't very romantic.

____

4 We might to use technology to help us choose the perfect partner.

____

5 The way people meet and fall in love not may change very much.

____

C Complete the questions and answers with the words in the box. You need to use some of the words more than once.

did do don't it's make
spend went what which

1 '*Which* country is *hygge* from, Denmark or Sweden?' '________ from Denmark.'

2 'Who ________ you spend time with?' 'I ________ a lot of time with my best friend.'

3 '________ is your favorite book?' '________ *The Lord of the Rings*.'

4 'Which board games ________ you play?' 'I ________ play board games.'

5 'How ________ you celebrate your last birthday?' 'I ________ out for dinner.'

FUNCTIONAL LANGUAGE

Look at the beginning and end of the telephone conversation. Put the rest of the conversation in the correct order.

John: Dean, it's your brother. You OK?
Dean: Yep, fine thanks, and you?
__ John: That's great. There's just one thing … Jenny and I are going out.
__ Dean: Not really. No plans. Why?
__ John: Well, yes.
__ John: Well, we have an invitation to a new restaurant and …
__ Dean: And, you need a babysitter!
_1_ John: I'm great, thanks. Listen, are you doing anything this evening?
__ John: Do you want to come over? Jenny has made a curry dish and little Sam says he misses his Uncle Dean.
__ Dean: A curry dish and my favorite nephew? I'd love to!
__ Dean: What?
Dean: Fine, fine. What time?
John: You are the best. How about seven o'clock?

5 WORK

There is no substitute for hard work.
Thomas Edison

Electrical lineman Chen Qi cleans snow from a high-voltage transmission tower, Baima Mountain, Wulong County, China.

OBJECTIVES

- talk about the pros and cons of different jobs and say how they help society
- decide on the rules for a workplace or classroom
- answer questions on topics in which you are an expert
- give information about your work experience in a job interview
- write a cover email

Work with a partner. Discuss the questions.

1 What do you like about your job or the subjects you study?
2 Read the quote. What do you think Edison meant? Do you agree with him?
3 Look at the picture. Would you like to have this man's job? Why/Why not?

5.1 Work

Talk about the pros and cons of different jobs and say how they help society

G – *can, could, be able to* V – work collocations P – /w/ and /v/

READING

A Match the definitions (1–4) with the words in the box.

pay raise salary self-employed well-paid

1 working for yourself ________
2 a fixed amount of money that you earn each month or year from your job ________
3 paid a lot of money ________
4 an increase in the amount of money you are paid to do your job ________

B SPEAK Work in pairs. What are four things, apart from money, that can make people happy at work?

C SCAN Read *What really makes us happy in our jobs?* quickly. Which of your ideas from Exercise B can you find?

D READ FOR DETAIL Read again. Who says these things make them happy in their job, Helen (H), Lena (L), Bret (B) or Ken (K)?

1 they have flexible vacations and working hours ___
2 they learn and use special skills ___
3 their employer gives them clear goals ___
4 they are independent ___
5 they have a relaxed manager ___
6 they have time for the family ___

E SPEAK Work in pairs. Which of the four jobs in the article would you rather have? Why?

What really makes us ***happy in our jobs?***

In a recent survey about jobs and work, 75 percent of children under ten said 'yes' to the question 'Can money buy happiness?' But is being **well-paid** really so important? Can you still be happy at work if you earn a **low hourly wage**? We asked four working adults what, apart from money, they like about their jobs.

Helen Police Officer

I don't work regular office hours – I do shifts. This means I often work in the evenings and sometimes do the night shift. In my last job I could choose when I wanted to work and I found that I liked working in the evenings. I also like that I am able to use all the different skills I learned when I was training to be a police officer.

Bret Waiter

My job is poorly paid, but I only work weekends, so I can study during the week. I work in a big restaurant. When there are no problems, the boss is usually very easygoing.

Lena Sales Manager

I earn an average salary. However, if I make a lot of sales, I get a bonus and I find that motivating. I also enjoy having clear goals, even when I have to work long hours to achieve them. I recently got a promotion which meant a lot of extra work, but I don't mind. I got a small pay raise and as a manager I was able to take an extra afternoon off each week to spend with my kids.

Ken Architect

The best part of my job is being my own boss. Because I'm self-employed, I can choose when I work and can take long vacations when I want to. The only bad part is I don't get a company car!

Glossary

bonus (n) extra money you are paid in addition to your usual salary, usually because you have done well, for example, *a year-end bonus*

promotion (n) a move to a higher level in your job, usually because you have done well

GRAMMAR

can, could, be able to

A WORK IT OUT Look at the sentences from *What really makes us happy in our jobs?* Then complete the rules with *can*, *could* or *be able to*.

I only work weekends, so I can study during the week.

I am able to use all the different skills I learned when I was training.

In my last job I could choose when I wanted to work.

I was able to take an extra afternoon off each week.

can, could and be able to

1. We use *can* and __________ to talk about possibility and ability in the present.
2. We use __________ and *was / were able to* to talk about possibility and ability in the past.
3. We usually use __________ or *was / were able to* for possibilities and abilities at a particular time or for a particular reason.
4. We use __________ immediately before the main verb because *can* has no *-ing* form or *to* + base form.

B Go to the **Grammar Hub** on **page 130**.

C SPEAK Work in pairs. Discuss the questions.

1. What are some of your abilities?
2. What were some of your abilities as a child?

VOCABULARY

Work collocations

A Complete the questions with the correct form of the verbs in the box. Sometimes more than one answer is possible. You need to use some verbs more than once.

be earn get take work

1. Do you or anyone you know __________ shifts? How often do they do a night shift?
2. Do you know anyone who __________ a very high salary? What do they do?
3. Do you think people should __________ an automatic pay raise every year they stay in the same job?
4. Who __________ the longest hours out of all the people you know? What do they do?
5. When was the last time you __________ a day off? What did you do?
6. Would you prefer to __________ a company car or more money?
7. Do people who __________ unemployed get money from the government in your country?
8. Would you be motivated by a job where you earn an average salary, but have the chance to __________ a bonus? Why/Why not?

B SPEAK Work in pairs. Would you like to be your own boss? Why/Why not? Tell your partner.

PRONUNCIATION

/w/ and /v/

5.1 **A** Listen to the sounds. Are they the same or different? Listen and repeat.

1 /w/ work   2 /v/ very

5.2 **B** Listen and write the words in the correct place.

/w/	/v/
wage	*involve*

5.3 **C** Listen and check your answers. Then listen and repeat.

D SPEAK Work in pairs. Can you think of more words with the sounds /w/ and /v/? Make a list.

SPEAKING

A Work in groups. Go to the **Communication Hub** on **page 157** and look at your group's list of jobs. Discuss the questions for each job.

1. Who do you know that does these jobs? How do they feel about them?
   My brother is a social worker. He works with people that have serious problems, but he still enjoys it.
2. Is each job paid a high, medium or low wage or salary?
3. What are the best and worst parts of each job?
4. Give each job a category which describes how it helps society, for example, *important for entertainment, health, education.*

B Work in new groups. Tell the group about the jobs you discussed and the categories you chose in Exercise A. Discuss which categories of jobs are most valuable to society and why.

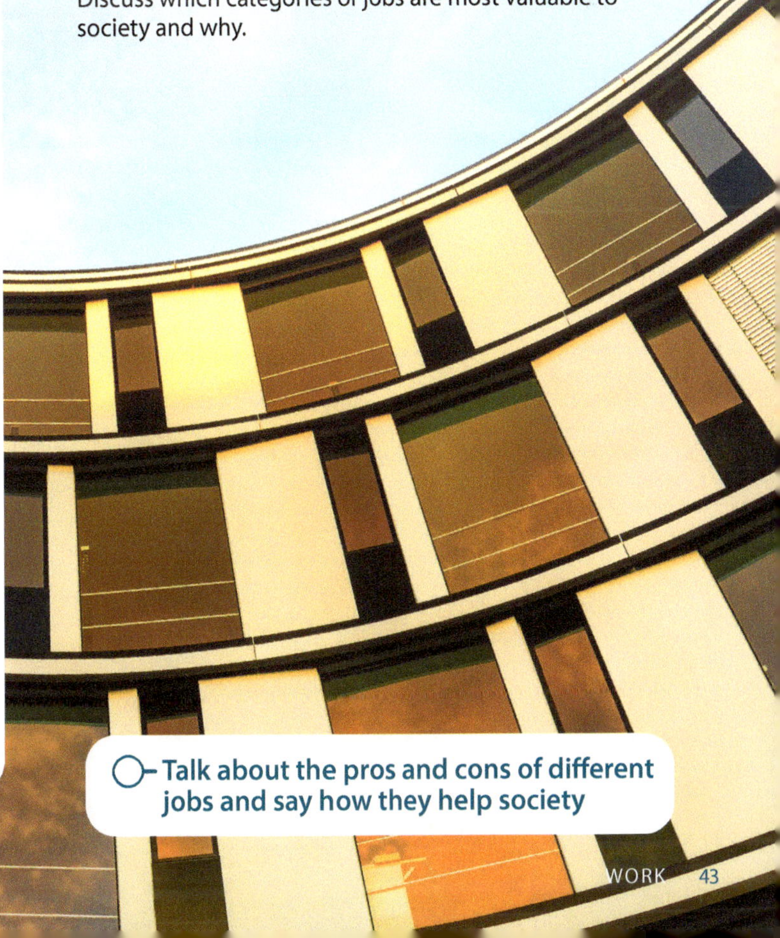

Talk about the pros and cons of different jobs and say how they help society

5.2 Flip-flop entrepreneurs

- Decide on the rules for a workplace or classroom

G obligation, necessity and permission: *must, have to* and *can* **P** *can / can't* and *must / must not* **V** adjectives for appearance

READING

A SPEAK Work in pairs. How important to you are the things on the list when you are buying new clothes? Decide whether they are very important (1), fairly important (2) or less important (3). Compare your ideas.

The product …

a is available in different colors and designs. ___

b is fashionable. ___

c is popular with celebrities. ___

The company …

a pays its staff fair wages. ___

b gives money to charity. ___

c does charity work. ___

B SCAN Read *How do you build a children's home out of flip-flops?* Which things in Exercise A are mentioned?

C READ FOR DETAIL Read again and answer the questions.

1. What was unusual about Rob and Paul's education?
2. How did the brothers become orphans?
3. Why did the brothers start Gandys?
4. Which six adjectives are used to describe the company's flip-flops?
5. What was unusual about the brothers' visit to Buckingham Palace?

D SPEAK Work in groups. Discuss the questions.

1. Who do the biggest charities help in your country? What do they do to help?
2. Do you give money to charity? Why/Why not?

How do you build a children's home out of flip-flops?

British brothers Rob and Paul Forkan have experienced tragedy and success in their short and unusual lives. When they were still children, their parents took them out of school in the UK and moved the family to India to travel and do charity work. The experience taught them about life in other places and made them confident and independent.

Tragedy struck in 2004 when the Asian tsunami hit the coast of Sri Lanka, where the Forkans were staying. The giant wave killed their parents, but Rob (17), Paul (15) and their younger brother and sister survived. The children, now orphans, managed to hitchhike across Sri Lanka to the airport. From there, they flew back to Britain, where friends and family were waiting.

Six years later and now adults, the brothers decided to do something in memory of their parents. Their idea was simple. Make and sell attractive casual footwear and use the profits to help other orphans. Their company *Gandys* and their charity *Orphans for Orphans* were born.

After a lot of hard work and with the support of celebrity customers such as Richard Branson and Jamie Oliver, the comfortable rubber flip-flops became a hit. Customers love *Gandys*' stylish and fashionable designs and that the brothers give ten percent of the profits to their charity. In 2014, three years after *Gandys* began, *Orphans for Orphans* opened its first children's home in Sri Lanka.

Gandys' head office now employs a large team and is possibly the only office in London where you can wear flip-flops to work! Rob and Paul's charity work has even gotten them an invitation to meet British princes William and Harry. Normally of course, you must wear dress clothes at Buckingham Palace, but the brothers ignored the dress code and looked cool in their colorful flip-flops!

Rob and Paul's story shows that positive can follow negative and that you don't have to wear a business suit to be successful in business!

Glossary

hitchhike (v) to have people give you a ride in their car, usually by standing on the side of the road and holding out your thumb or a sign

in memory of someone (phrase) in honor of someone who has died, so that people will remember them

tragedy (n) a very sad event that causes people to suffer or die

GRAMMAR

Obligation, necessity and permission: *must*, *have to* and *can*

A **WORK IT OUT** Look at the last two paragraphs of *How do you build a children's home out of flip-flops?* and complete the sentences.

1 You ______________ wear flip-flops to work.

2 You ______________ wear a business suit to be successful in business.

3 You ______________ wear dress clothes at Buckingham Palace.

B Match the modal verbs (1–4) with the meanings (a–d).

Obligation, necessity and permission: *must, have to* and *can*

1 *don't have to*	**a** This is necessary or is a rule.
2 *must / have to*	**b** This is not necessary but allowed.
3 *can*	**c** This is allowed but not necessary.
4 *can't / must not*	**d** This is not allowed.

C Choose the correct word to complete the rule.

Obligation, necessity and permission: *must, have to* and *can*

Modal verbs, such as *have to, can* and *must* are followed by the ***base form*** / ***simple present*** form of a verb.

D Go to the **Grammar Hub** on **page 130**.

PRONUNCIATION

can / can't and *must / must not*

5.4 **A** Listen to the pairs of sentences. Can you hear the differences?

1 **a** You can wear casual clothes.
b You can't wear casual clothes.

2 **a** Staff must not wear sportswear.
b Staff must wear sportswear.

5.5 **B** Listen and check (✓) the sentence you hear.

1 **a** You must wear large earrings. ☐
b You must not wear large earrings. ☐

2 **a** You can wear a baseball cap. ☐
b You can't wear a baseball cap. ☐

3 **a** You must leave your coat downstairs. ☐
b You must not leave your coat downstairs. ☐

4 **a** You can hang your coat on your chair. ☐
b You can't hang your coat on your chair. ☐

VOCABULARY

Adjectives for appearance

A **SPEAK** Work in pairs. Make a list of adjectives to describe appearance. You have one minute.

cool, casual …

B Match the adjectives (1–7) with the definitions (a–g).

1 attractive	**a** show good judgement about how to dress well
2 casual	**b** relaxed and comfortable
3 colorful	**c** pleasant to look at
4 cool	**d** impressive and modern
5 fashionable	**e** clean and neat
6 well-dressed	**f** popular at a particular time
7 stylish	**g** has bright or many different colors

C Choose the words that you agree with most. Then work in pairs and explain why.

1 I ***do*** / ***don't*** think it's important to wear dress clothes to work.

2 I think that flip-flops are ***too casual*** / ***perfect*** for wearing around town.

3 I prefer clothes with ***colorful*** / ***cool and simple*** designs.

4 I think it ***is*** / ***isn't*** important to wear fashionable clothes.

5 You ***can*** / ***can't*** be stylish without wearing expensive clothes.

6 People ***spend too much*** / ***don't spend enough*** time and money trying to look attractive.

SPEAKING

A Work in groups. Think about the place where you work or study. Answer the questions.

1 What are the most important rules?

2 What annoying or unnecessary rules are there?

3 What rules would you add to make it a better place to work or study?

B Work in groups. Write ten rules for the perfect workplace or classroom. Think about what is/isn't allowed and what is/isn't necessary. Use these ideas:

Workplace: rules for workers, managers and directors; working hours; pay; dress code, etc.

Classroom: rules for students and teachers; during classes; homework; tests and exams, etc.

C Look at the rules written by other groups. Which are the most useful? Why? Are there any you do not agree with? Why?

Decide on the rules for a workplace or classroom

5.3 Don't call us

Answer questions on topics in which you are an expert

G present perfect with *for* and *since* **P** *has, have, for, since* **V** *work* + preposition **S** listening for inference

LISTENING

A Work in groups. Complete the tips for job interviews with *do* or *don't*.

1 __________ eat smelly food or smoke before the interview.

2 __________ arrive ten minutes before your appointment.

3 __________ listen carefully to introductions and try to remember names.

4 __________ answer your phone or check messages during the interview.

5 __________ be negative about yourself or your last job.

6 __________ ask one or two questions at the end.

5.6 **B LISTEN FOR GIST** Barry has a job interview with Gemma. Listen and choose the summary (1–3) that best describes the interview.

1 The interview goes well. Gemma and Barry have a good conversation. Barry will probably get the job.

2 The interview goes fairly well. Barry has a lot of experience working on a team. Barry might get the job.

3 The interview does not go well. Barry lies. Gemma is annoyed. Barry will definitely not get the job.

Glossary

call center (n) a place where a large number of people are employed to deal with customers by telephone, either in order to sell something or to answer questions

résumé (n) a document giving details of your certifications and the jobs you have had in the past that you send to someone when you are applying for a job

teamwork (n) work that you do together with other people

telemarketing (n) the activity or job of using the telephone to sell goods or services

5.6 **C** Test your memory! Check (✓) the things Barry has done and put an ✗ on the things he has not. Listen and check.

1 worked in a call center ☐

2 worked on a team ☐

3 worked for a telemarketing company ☐

4 been skydiving ☐

5 read French poetry ☐

5.7 **D** Listen to three extracts from the interview. Then answer the questions about each extract. Use the information in the box to help you.

Listening for inference

When you listen to a foreign language, use vocabulary and context clues and your wider knowledge to figure out the meaning of what you hear.

Think about the speaker's tone and attitude, as well as what they don't say.

Extract one

1 Does Barry check whether he needs to tell the truth? *yes / no*

2 Does he give a real example? *yes / no*

3 Do you think he has ever worked as part of a team? *yes / no*

Extract two

4 Is Barry interested in skydiving? *yes / no*

5 Does he think it's exciting? *yes / no*

6 Do you think he has ever actually done it? *yes / no*

Extract three

7 Does Barry remember what he wrote on his résumé? *yes / no*

8 Does he tell the truth about what he wrote on his résumé? *yes / no*

9 Do you think he enjoys French poetry? *yes / no*

E SPEAK Work in groups. Have you ever had an interview for a job, course or scholarship? Tell your group about it.

GRAMMAR

Present perfect with *for* and *since*

A WORK IT OUT Look at the sentences from Barry's interview and answer the questions.

I left my old job in June.

1 Does Barry still do his old job?
2 Is the action *leave* finished or unfinished?
3 What tense is the verb *leave* in?

I've worked at the call center for six weeks.

4 Does Barry still work at the call center?
5 Is the action *work* finished or unfinished?
6 What tense is the verb *work* in?

B Choose the correct words to complete the rules.

Present perfect and simple past

1 We use the ***present perfect / simple past*** to talk about actions or situations that started and finished in the past.
2 We use the ***present perfect / simple past*** to talk about actions or situations that started in the past, but are unfinished and so continue until the present.

C Look at the words in **bold** in the sentences from Barry's interview. Complete the rules with *how long*, *for* or *since*.

***How long** have you worked there?*

*Actually, I've been here **since** 9 am.*

*You've been here **for** three hours?*

Present perfect with *how long*, *for* and *since*

1 We use ________ + present perfect to ask about the duration of an action.
2 We use ________ to talk about the point in time when something started, e.g. *yesterday*, *I was young*.
3 We use ________ + present perfect to talk about a length of time until the present time, e.g. *three hours*, *two weeks*.

D Look at the sentence from Barry's interview and choose the correct words to complete the rule.

I've liked skydiving since I was a teenager.

since

After *since* we usually use a verb in ***present perfect / simple past***.

E Go to the **Grammar Hub** on **page 130**.

PRONUNCIATION

has, have, for, since

.8 Listen and repeat.

1 How long has he lived there?
2 How long have you worked there?
3 He's lived there for three years.
4 I've worked there since last summer.

VOCABULARY

work + preposition

A Go to the **Vocabulary Hub** on **page 148**.

B SPEAK Work as a class. Talk to as many different people as possible in five minutes about their job or the job of someone they know. Write notes for each person you talk to.

Cassie: She works in IT for a software company. She's a computer programmer. She works in their office in the center of the city.

C SPEAK Work in pairs. Compare your notes. Which jobs were the most unusual or interesting?

SPEAKING HUB

A You are going to talk about a topic in which you are an expert. Consider the following areas:

- your profession and/or studies
- a skill you've learned, e.g. cooking, skiing, car mechanics, piano

B PLAN Think of some questions you could ask your classmates about their topics.

How long ...?
What can/can't you do?

C DISCUSS Work in a group. Interview each student in your group about their expertise. What were the most interesting things you learned about your classmates?

Answer questions on topics in which you are an expert

Café Hub

5.4 The cat

F– give information about your work experience in a job interview
P– singular and plural forms

COMPREHENSION

A SPEAK Work in pairs. Look at the pictures above from Neena's job interview. What do you think goes wrong in the interview? Watch the video and check.

B 03:09–05:00 Watch the last part of the interview again. Answer the questions.

1 Whose cat was it?
2 What was the cat's name?
3 What is Neena doing on Monday?

C 00:27–03:06 Complete the job interview form for Neena. Then watch part of the video again and check your answers.

JOBS, JOBS, JOBS AND JOBS

Job interview

Name: *Neena Patel*
Current job: Working for a 1__________ firm.
Responsible for international 2__________.
Time in current job: 3__________ years.
Reasons for changing job: Is looking for a 4__________ challenge.
Strengths: Is good at working 5__________ pressure. Can 6__________ her time. Is very organized. Is good at 7__________ management. Works well on a 8__________.
Weaknesses: Is a perfectionist – enjoys getting everything 9__________.
A good candidate for the job: 10 Yes / No

MILLY

SAM

NEENA

ZAC

GABY

FUNCTIONAL LANGUAGE

Give information about your work experience in a job interview

A Cross out the word that is NOT possible to complete the sentences.

1 Currently, I'm working for *a law firm* / *Citibank* / ~~*architect*~~.

2 I have to manage *a team* / *five sales representatives* / *a company car*.

3 I've worked there for *last year* / *a long time* / *four years*.

4 People say I'm good at *working under pressure* / *manage my time* / *my job*.

5 I've learned how to *manage my time* / *working on a team* / *deal with clients*.

6 I work well *on a team* / *under pressure* / *my job*.

B Look at Exercise A. Think of another word for each sentence to replace the one you crossed out.

USEFUL PHRASES

A Complete the conversations with the useful phrases in the box. Then watch the video again and check your answers.

Go on. How did it go? It was going so well … Just go! Let me think. Please take a seat. Tell me about yourself. That's a good question.

Gaby: [1] ______________
Neena: Oh, Gaby, it was awful.
Gaby: What happened?
Neena: [2] ______________
Interviewer: Good afternoon, Neena. [3] ______________
So Neena, [4] ______________
What have you learned from your current job?
Neena: [5] ______________
Interviewer: And any weak points?
Neena: [6] ______________
Well, I have one question.
Interviewer: [7] ______________
Neena: So, will you call me?
Interviewer: [8] ______________

B How do you say these useful phrases in your language?

PRONUNCIATION

Singular and plural forms

5.9 **A** Listen and repeat the singular and plural forms of the nouns in the box. Which noun has an extra syllable in the plural form?

account(s) challenge(s) job(s) perfectionist(s) pressure(s) project(s) question(s) strength(s)

B **SPEAK** Work in pairs. Practice saying the words in Exercise A. Listen and check your partner's pronunciation.

SPEAKING

A Think about the things you are good at. Write down three strengths and one weakness. Then work in pairs and compare your ideas.

B Work in pairs. Write down three important skills for each of the jobs in the box.

accountant soccer team manager teacher website manager

C Role-play a job interview. Use the job interview form in Comprehension Exercise C to help you. Include at least two useful phrases. Take turns.

Student A: Choose a job from Exercise B and interview Student B for the job.

Student B: Answer Student A's questions.

Student A: Decide if Student B is suitable for the job.

Give information about your work experience in a job interview

➤ Turn to **page 162** to learn how to write a cover email.

Unit 5 Review

VOCABULARY

A Match beginnings of the sentences (1–5) with the ends of the sentences (a–e).

1 What advantages are there to a job where you work
2 How important do you think it is to earn
3 What are the disadvantages of being
4 When did you last take
5 Do you think people should get

a a day off from work or school and what did you do?
b shifts, so sometimes you start at night or early in the morning?
c a pay raise every year or only when they have done well at work?
d your own boss?
e a high salary in your job?

B Write the missing words to complete the sentences.

1 My brother is very c___ ___ ___; he always looks good.
2 She's not allowed to wear c___ ___ ___ ___ ___ ___ clothes to work.
3 I love those high-heeled shoes – they have a very s___ ___ ___ ___ ___ ___ ___ design.
4 I don't like that T-shirt. I don't think those colors look a___ ___ ___ ___ ___ ___ ___ ___ ___ ___ .
5 In our country, you must wear d___ ___ ___ ___ ___ clothes to a wedding.

C Choose the correct prepositions. In three examples, both are possible.

1 They work ***at / for*** the IT department.
2 He works ***in / at*** marketing.
3 She works ***at / for*** Bluemoon Software Services.
4 She works ***at / for*** an advertising firm.
5 I work ***at / in*** a library.
6 We work ***in / for*** a telemarketing company.

GRAMMAR

A Choose the best words to complete the sentences.

1 When I was young, I ***can / could*** stay up late, but these days I get tired early.
2 I really enjoy ***being able to / can*** work for myself.
3 Johann ***able to / can*** speak four languages.
4 I ***was able to / could*** speak to my boss last Friday about getting a pay raise.
5 I'd like ***can / to be able to*** speak perfect English one day.

B Match the rules (1–8) with the meanings (a–d).

Memo: Information for palace staff

1 ___ You can park your car in the staff parking lot.
2 ___ You must not bring your own cell phone inside the palace.
3 ___ You can't take any pictures while at work.
4 ___ You have to be nicely dressed at all times.*
5 ___ You must call the Queen 'Your Majesty'.
6 ___ You must not mention anything you see or hear at work to anyone.
7 ___ You can smoke in the staff smoking area.
8 ___ *If the Royal family are away, you don't have to wear the full uniform.

a This is necessary or is a rule.
b This is not necessary but allowed.
c This is allowed but not necessary.
d This is not allowed.

C Complete the conversations with the simple past or present perfect form of the verbs in parentheses.

Erin: How long [1] ________________ (*you / work*) here?
Paulie: Oh, not long. [2] ________________ (*I / start*) work last December. But, you see that lady there? Well, [3] ________________ (*she / be*) here for 20 years. [4] ________________ (*she / become*) a cook when she was only 17.

Karl: I thought you worked for a newspaper? When [5] ________________ (*you / change*) jobs?
Crystal: Years ago! [6] ________________ (*I / not work*) in journalism since about 2004.

Pippa: [7] ________________ (*I / want*) to be a doctor when I was a child, but now I'm a vet.
Gianni: A vet? That's so cool. [8] ________________ (*I / love*) animals since I was little.

FUNCTIONAL LANGUAGE

A Complete the phrases to use in job interviews with the words in the box.

enjoy	learned	problem	question	responsible	team

1 I've ________________ how to motivate other people.
2 Well, I have one ________________ I'd like to ask.
3 I'm ________________ for customer service.
4 I ________________ working in a busy office.
5 I work well on a ________________.
6 Well, I have a ________________ with the weekend hours.

6 HEALTH

> Health is not valued until sickness comes.
>
> Thomas Fuller

Yoga enthusiasts take part in the annual Times Square event celebrating the Summer Solstice, the longest day of the year, New York.

OBJECTIVES

- give a presentation on health dos and don'ts
- plan an exercise event for your local community
- encourage people to make a lifestyle change
- talk about your symptoms at a pharmacy
- write a product review

Work with a partner. Discuss the questions.

1 What do you do to stay healthy?
2 Read the quote. Do you agree with it?
3 Would you like to take part in an event like the one in the picture? Why/Why not?

6.1 Health myths

Give a presentation on health dos and don'ts

G quantifiers *too* and *enough* **V** minor illnesses **P** /ʌ/, /ɔː/, /uː/, /eɪ/ and /ɜː/

LISTENING

A Match the definitions (1–7) with the words in the box.

a balanced diet antibiotics confused expert liquid myth reality

1 something that people wrongly believe to be true
2 someone who has a particular skill or who knows a lot about a particular subject
3 a fact, event or situation as it really exists
4 a range of food that a person eats to provide all the good things their body needs
5 drugs that cure illnesses and infections caused by bacteria
6 unable to understand something or think clearly about it
7 a substance (such as water) that can flow, has no fixed shape and is not a solid or a gas

B SPEAK Work in pairs. Check (✓) the sentences about health you have heard before. Which ones do you think are true and which ones are myths? Give reasons.

1 Everyone should drink eight glasses of water per day. ☐
2 Eating fatty food makes you fat. ☐
3 Eggs are bad for your heart. ☐
4 Cold weather causes colds. ☐
5 Take antibiotics when you have a cold. ☐

6.1 **C LISTEN FOR GIST** Look at the glossary. Then listen to the introduction of *Live with Pippa* and answer the questions.

Glossary

calorie (n) unit for measuring how much energy you get from food
carbohydrate (n) a substance found in foods such as sugar, bread and potatoes. Carbohydrates supply your body with heat and energy.
fatty (adj) containing a lot of fat
virus (n) a thing that can enter your body and make you sick

1 How many experts does Pippa speak to?
2 Choose the best summary of Pippa's message in the introduction to the show.
  a It is better to ask a medical professional than look online for information about health.
  b It is difficult to know which online information about health is true.
  c Bad online advice about health is making healthy people sick.

6.1 **D LISTEN FOR DETAIL** Listen again and choose a, b or c.

1 Doctor Singh says that …
  a most headaches are due to a lack of water.
  b we get some of the water we need from our food.
  c more than eight glasses of water per day is dangerous.
2 Michael says that …
  a everyone needs some fat in their diets.
  b most people get fat because they eat too much sugar.
  c we shouldn't eat fatty food.
3 Dr. Tremblay says you are more likely to catch a cold or flu …
  a if you spend time outside in cold weather.
  b if you don't get enough vitamins in your diet.
  c if you spend time indoors with a lot of people.
4 Lia says that …
  a advice on eating eggs changes regularly.
  b advice on eating eggs is not the same as it was in the past.
  c advice on eating eggs is the same as it has always been.

GRAMMAR

Quantifiers *too* and *enough*

A WORK IT OUT Complete the sentences from the radio show (1–5) using the audio script on page 173. Then match the sentences with the rules (a–c).

1 You drink too ________ coffee. rule ___
2 You don't sleep ________. rule ___
3 It's because you go to bed ________ early. rule ___
4 Make sure you are getting ________ vitamins. rule ___
5 Too ________ eggs are bad for your heart. rule ___

Quantifiers *too* and *enough*

a We use *too* + adjective or adverb, *too much* and *too many* to mean more than the right amount.
b We use *enough* to mean the right amount.
c We use *not enough* to mean less than the right amount.

B Look at the sentences from the radio show in Exercise A and complete the rules.

too much and *too many*
1 We use *too much* / *too many* with countable nouns.
2 We use *too much* / *too many* with uncountable nouns.

C Go to the **Grammar Hub** on **page 132**.

D **PRACTICE** Complete the sentences so they are true for you.

1. I spend too much time ______________ and not enough time ______________.
2. I eat too much/many ______________ and not enough ______________.
3. I don't ______________ enough and I ______________ too much/often.
4. I find ______________ too difficult.
5. I have enough ______________, but not enough ______________.

E **SPEAK** Work in pairs. Discuss your answers to Exercise D.

VOCABULARY

Minor illnesses

A Read Dr. Tremblay's audio script on **page 173** and underline six health problems he talks about.

B Label the pictures (1–10) with the health problems in the box.

a broken bone ~~a cold~~ a cough
a headache a temperature a sore throat
flu stomachache sunburn toothache

PRONUNCIATION

/ʌ/, /ɔː/, /uː/, /eɪ/ and /ɜː/

A 6.2 Listen and repeat.

1. /ʌ/ but
2. /ɔː/ caught
3. /uː/ do
4. /eɪ/ pay
5. /ɜː/ fur

B 6.3 Each word contains one of the sounds in Exercise A. Listen and match the words with the sounds. Then underline the letter(s) that make the sounds.

1	burn	a	/ʌ/
2	ache	b	/ɔː/
3	stomach	c	/uː/
4	flu	d	/eɪ/
5	sore	e	/ɜː/

C **SPEAK** Work in pairs. What do people usually do for each of the problems in Vocabulary Exercise B? Use ideas below to help you and your own ideas.

- go to bed
- take medicine
- go to the doctor
- take painkillers
- put on lotion
- stay home from work

SPEAKING

A Work in pairs. Plan and give a short presentation called *The dos and don'ts of staying active and healthy*.

B Write a list of dos and don'ts for each of the topics:

- food and drink
- sleep
- exercise
- stress
- avoiding and recovering from illness

C Present your advice to the class. Ask them to guess which piece of advice is a myth or bad advice.

1

a cold

2
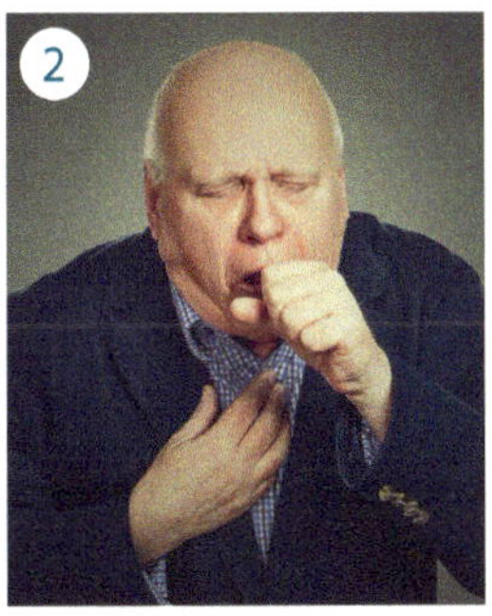
____

3

____

4

____

5

____

6

____

7
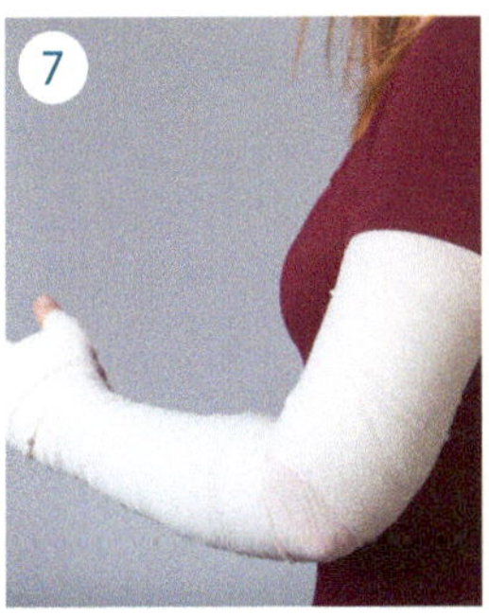
____

8

____

9
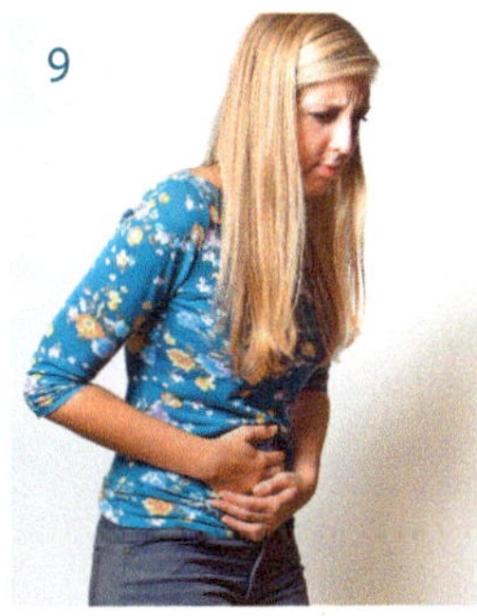
____

10
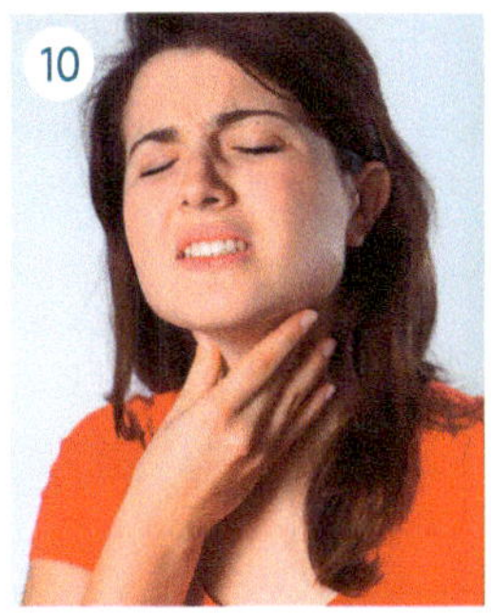
____

Give a presentation on health dos and don'ts

6.2 Keep fit

Plan an exercise event for your local community

V exercise **P** /ŋ/, /n/ and /m/ **G** *-ing* forms

VOCABULARY

Exercise

A Work in pairs. Make a list of different ways of exercising. You have one minute.

Walking, swimming …

B Go to the **Vocabulary Hub** on **page 148**.

C **SPEAK** Look at the **Vocabulary Hub** Exercise B on **page 149**. Go around the class and ask the questions. If someone answers *yes*, write their name and ask a follow-up question.

A: Do you hate working out at the gym?

B: Yes, I do.

A: Why?

B: I like to exercise outdoors and I don't like to exercise with so many other people watching me. I find most gyms too busy.

PRONUNCIATION

/ŋ/, /n/ and /m/

6.4 **A** Listen to these sounds. Do they sound the same or different?

1 /ŋ/ biking **2** /n/ run **3** /m/ team

6.4 **B** Listen again and repeat the sounds.

6.5 **C** Listen and complete the table with the words you hear. Do the words have an /ŋ/, /n/ or /m/ sound? Some words have more than one of the sounds.

/ŋ/	/n/	/m/

READING

A Check (✓) the sentences you agree with. Then work in pairs and explain your choices.

- Running is great exercise and great fun. ☐
- I'd like to run a marathon one day. ☐
- I prefer team sports, like racquetball or field hockey. ☐
- Jogging is exercise, not fun. ☐
- Running is boring. ☐
- The only time I run is to catch the bus. ☐

B **SCAN** Read texts 1–3. What is the purpose of each?

Text ___: to inform Text ___: to persuade

Text ___: to entertain

1

Funny fitness

Did you know that laughing for 15 minutes can burn up to 40 calories? We hope these jokes and quotes will keep you smiling as you walk to the store, jog around the park or run your next marathon.

Q What is a runner's favorite school subject?
A Jog-raphy

'If you are in a bad mood, go for a walk. If you are still in a bad mood, go for another walk.'
Hippocrates

Patient: Doctor, can you give me something to stop sleepwalking?
Doctor: I'm afraid I can't, sir. You need the exercise!

2

Parkrun

Are you looking for an easy way to stay in shape and lose weight? Would you like to run 5 km in a family-friendly atmosphere? Would you like to compare your results with other runners from all over the world? If so, then check out *Parkrun*.

Parkrun organizes free weekly timed runs in parks all over the world. The 5 km runs take place on weekend mornings and are open to everyone. After each race, runners receive detailed results via email.

Parkrun is an international community of over one million runners in 17 countries and there is always space for more! So come and join the *Parkrun* family and get fit for free!

Glossary

atmosphere (n) the mood or feeling in a place

3

MARATHON MAN

What do you think it takes to become a running master? Fauja Singh, from east London, finished a 10 km race in Hong Kong in one hour and 32 minutes – and he did it at the age of 101.

In 2011, Singh became the oldest person to run a marathon. At 100 years of age, he completed the Toronto Marathon in just over eight hours.

As a young man, Mr. Singh was a farmer in Punjab, India. Then in the 1960s, he went to live in Britain and only began running when he was 89 years old.

Mr. Singh plans to run again for charity, but the Hong Kong 10 km was his final competitive race. 'I will remember this day. I will miss it,' Mr. Singh said after the event.

C READ FOR DETAIL Read again and answer the questions. Write *Funny fitness* (FF), *Parkrun* (PR), *Marathon man* (MM) or none of the texts (N).

Which text …

1 tells the story of an individual? ______
2 offers readers the chance to read more online? ______
3 tries to sell readers something? ______
4 reports the results of a research project? ______
5 tries to make readers laugh? ______
6 describes the purpose of a particular organization? ______

D SPEAK Work in pairs. Discuss the questions.

1 Why is running such a popular form of exercise?
2 Would you like to do a parkrun? Why/Why not?

GRAMMAR

-*ing* forms

A Look at the examples of different -*ing* forms used in the texts. Then complete the rules with the words in the box.

1 Did you know that **laughing** for 15 minutes can burn up to 40 calories? (gerund)
2 Are you **looking** for an easy way to stay in shape and lose weight? (present participle)
3 What do you think it takes to become a **running** master? (adjective)

adjectives gerunds present participle

-*ing* forms

1 We use the ______________ -*ing* form with the verb *to be* to talk about things that are happening now or around now, and are not finished.
2 We use -*ing* form as ______________ to describe nouns.
3 We use -*ing* form as ______________ to make nouns.

B Go to the **Grammar Hub** on **page 132**.

C SPEAK Work in pairs. Discuss the questions.

1 What is your favorite form of exercise?
2 Do you like working out? Why/Why not?

SPEAKING

A Work in groups. Plan an event to encourage local people to start doing more exercise. Think about:

- who your event is for
- how it will help people get in shape or start exercising
- what people need to bring to the event
- how you will promote the event

B Describe your event to the rest of the class. Which event is the most popular. Why?

Plan an exercise event for your local community

6.3 We may never 'meat' again

Encourage people to make a lifestyle change

G– present perfect with *just, already* and *yet* V– food groups P– /s/ and /ʃ/ S– scanning for key words

READING

A Match the words in the box to pictures (1–6).

avocado broccoli fur
grain kale wheat

B **READ FOR GIST** Read *A fresh start*. Which three reasons for going vegetarian or vegan are given in the article?

A fresh start

Large numbers of people are saying 'never again!' to meat and becoming vegetarian or vegan. For some it's about health, for others it's about concern for the environment. Whatever the reason, many people are changing the way they eat forever.

Research by the Vegan Society states that in 2016 there were around 542,000 vegans in the UK alone. Veganism is also on the rise thanks to celebrity supporters including Ellie Goulding, Liam Hemsworth and Venus and Serena Williams.

There are various reasons why people decide to go vegetarian or vegan. Some do it for their health. Vegans get all the vitamins, minerals and other things they need for a balanced diet from grains, fruits, seeds, nuts and vegetables such as kale, broccoli, beans and avocados. A vegetarian diet can help people lose weight because it is low in fat. High-fat diets are linked to serious health problems including diabetes, heart disease and cancer.

Some people give up meat because they are worried about the environment. A 2006 FAO (The Food and Agriculture Organization of the United Nations) study reported that 18 percent of greenhouse gases come from farm animals such as cows, sheep and chickens. That's more than all of the world's cars, trains and planes put together. We use over 36 percent of the world's grain to feed farm animals, yet a quarter of the people in the world do not have enough food. If we made food for people from the grain instead, there would be enough for everyone.

Other people go meat-free because they feel it is wrong to kill animals. Animals feel pain and fear. Many farmed animals are kept in poor conditions with little space and no time outdoors. In the UK, around 990 million farmed animals are killed for food each year.

With so many grocery stores and restaurants now offering vegetarian and vegan goods, it's easier than ever to give up or reduce the amount of meat we eat. Why not try a few meat-free days a week – you could help reduce world hunger and even help with climate change!

Are you vegan or vegetarian?

We want your comments!

Nora_27: **I've just changed to a vegetarian diet after years of eating meat.** It's only been a week, but I feel much healthier and I highly recommend it!

M-M-Maxine: I feel bad about killing animals, but I really enjoy meat. **I've already eaten two sausages and a chicken sandwich today, and it's only lunchtime!** I don't think I'd last very long without meat.

Cool_keith2: **I've been vegetarian for a while, but I haven't managed to go vegan yet.** It seems like a lot of work to plan and prepare the food. Any advice?

Kellykale: Great article. Vegan food is great! **Have you tried kale chips yet?** They are really tasty and great as a healthy snack.

Glossary

billion (number) the number 1,000,000,000

greenhouse gas (n) a gas that stops heat from escaping the atmosphere and causes the greenhouse effect, the gas that makes global warming worse

mineral (n) a natural substance in some foods that you need for good health, for example, iron and calcium

vitamin (n) natural substances found in food that are necessary to keep your body healthy

C SCAN Read again. Are the sentences true (T) or false (F)? Use the information in the box to help you.

Scanning for key words

When you are reading to find specific information, such as names, dates and statistics, move your eyes quickly over the text and look for titles, numbers, symbols and names. Read around these items to find the information you are looking for. This is called scanning.

Scanning helps save time in exams and is useful for previewing texts to decide whether to read them in more detail.

1 There are about half a million vegetarians in the UK. *T / F*
2 A fair number of famous people are vegans. *T / F*
3 Vegans need to take extra vitamins to stay healthy. *T / F*
4 Vehicles produce less air pollution than farming animals for meat. *T / F*
5 If we produced less meat, there would be more food for those people who do not have enough. *T / F*
6 It is difficult to buy vegan products. *T / F*

D SPEAK Work in pairs. What are the arguments for and against farming and killing animals for food?

GRAMMAR

Present perfect with *just*, *already* and *yet*

A WORK IT OUT Look at the sentences in **bold** in the comments section of *A fresh start*. Then complete the rules with *just*, *already* or *yet*.

Present perfect with *just*, *already* and *yet*

1 We use the present perfect with ______________ in positive statements to say something happened very recently.
2 We use the present perfect with ______________ in positive statements to say that something happened before now or earlier than expected.
3 We use the present perfect with ______________:
- in negative statements to say that something hasn't happened, but it still might.
- in questions to ask if something has happened.

B Look again and choose the correct words to complete the rules.

1 *Just* comes ***before* / *after*** the past participle in a sentence.
2 *Already* usually comes ***before* / *after*** the past participle in a sentence.
3 *Yet* comes at the ***beginning* / *end*** of a sentence or question.

C Go to the **Grammar Hub** on **page 132**.

D SPEAK. Work in pairs. Have you done any exercise today? Make true sentences with present perfect and *just*, *already* or *yet*.

VOCABULARY

Food groups

A Work in pairs. Make a list of different food items. You have one minute.

B Go to the **Vocabulary Hub** on **page 149**.

C SPEAK Work in pairs. Have you eaten any healthy food today? Who has been kinder to their body?

I had two oranges with my breakfast, and I've just eaten an apple and two kiwis, so I've had five pieces of fruit today already.

PRONUNCIATION

/s/ and /ʃ/

A SPEAK Work in pairs. Write the words in the box in the correct place. Use the examples to help you.

chefs fish fresh lettuce ~~lobster~~ rice sandwich sauce spinach sushi ~~sugar~~

/s/	/ʃ/	/s/ and /ʃ/
lobster	*sugar*	

6.6 **B** Listen and check. Then listen again and repeat the words.

C SPEAK Work in pairs. Student A – point to a word in Exercise B. Student B – say the word. Take turns.

SPEAKING HUB

A Work in groups. You are going to design a leaflet to help other students make a lifestyle change. Choose one of the following:

- eat less meat
- stop drinking bottled water
- use more fresh ingredients when cooking
- eat less sugar

B PLAN What information will you include on the leaflet? Think about the areas below and then design your leaflet.

- health benefits
- environmental benefits
- how your school or college will help
- how you or someone you know changed their lifestyle in this way and how they benefited

C REFLECT Read the other groups' leaflets. Which do you think would be most successful and why?

Encourage people to make a lifestyle change

6.4 Painful experience

F – talk about your symptoms at a pharmacy

P – vowel sounds

COMPREHENSION

A 00:00–02:13 **Watch the first part of the video without sound and answer the questions.**

1 How does the pharmacist feel?

2 How does Gaby feel?

3 Check (✓) the parts of their bodies that hurt.

arm	☐	back	☐	ears	☐	eyes	☐	foot	☐
hand	☐	head	☐	leg	☐	nose	☐	throat	☐

B 00:00–02:13 **Watch the first part of the video again with sound and check your answers to Exercise A.**

C SPEAK **Work in pairs. What advice would you give Gaby? What advice would you give the pharmacist?**

D 02:26–04:54 **Watch the second part of the video and check your answers to Exercise C.**

FUNCTIONAL LANGUAGE

Talk about your symptoms at a pharmacy

A Write the headings in the box in the correct place (a–c).

Explain symptoms | Ask about health | Give advice

Useful language

a ______________

Are you OK?
Are you [1] ______________?
What's painful?
What are your symptoms?
Do you have anything for a sore throat / a [2] ______________?
Do you have sore eyes / [3] ______________?
Are you allergic to anything?

b ______________

It's very painful.
My nose / [4] ______________ hurts.
I'm not feeling very well.
I have a terrible cold.
You don't have a cold, you have hay fever / [5] ______________.

c ______________

I suggest these tablets / [6] ______________.
Take one every eight hours.
You could try drinking a hot lemon and honey.
I think you should rest / [7] ______________.

MILLY

SAM

NEENA

ZAC

GABY

B Write the words and phrases in the box in the correct place in Exercise A.

back flu a temperature headache relax sure you're OK this medicine

USEFUL PHRASES

A Match the useful phrases (1–6) with similar phrases which show the meaning (a–f).

1 I know how you feel.
2 We are both not very well today.
3 It's common at this time of year.
4 I'll be fine.
5 Is one enough?
6 That usually makes me feel better.

a A lot of people get this in the summer.
b Don't I need more?
c I have the same symptoms as you.
d It's my favorite cure.
e You and I are sick today.
f Don't worry about me.

B How do you say these useful phrases in your language?

PRONUNCIATION
Vowel sounds

A Match the words which have the same vowel sound.

1 cough
2 hurt
3 pain
4 sore
5 throat

a allergic
b door
c nose
d same
e wrong

B Listen and check. Then listen again and repeat the words.

.7

C **SPEAK** Work in pairs. Practice saying the words. Listen and check your partner's pronunciation.

SPEAKING

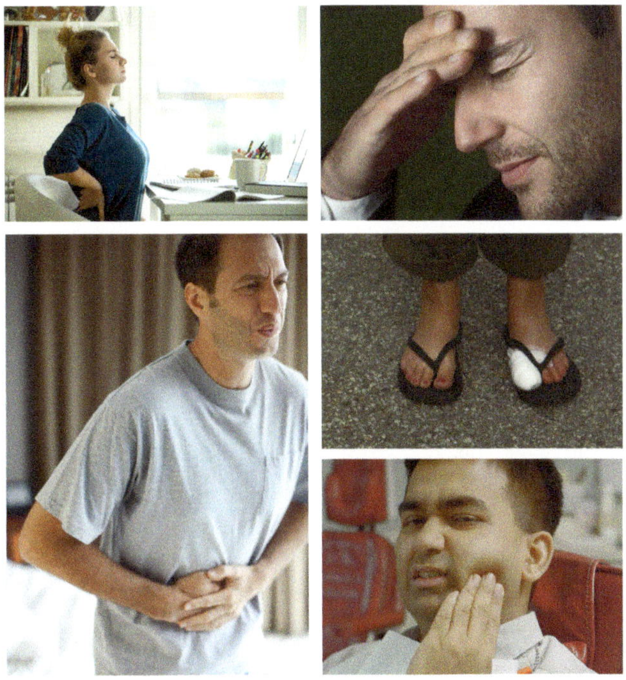

Work in pairs. Role-play a conversation about health. Take turns being Student A and Student B.

Student A: Choose an ailment from the pictures and explain the symptoms.

You must use the following words: *feeling*, *have*, *hurt(s)*, *painful*.

Student B: Ask questions and give advice.

You must use the following words: *allergic*, *take*, *temperature*, *try*.

Talk about your symptoms at a pharmacy

➤ Turn to **page 163** to learn how to write a product review.

Unit 6 Review

VOCABULARY

A Complete the crossword.

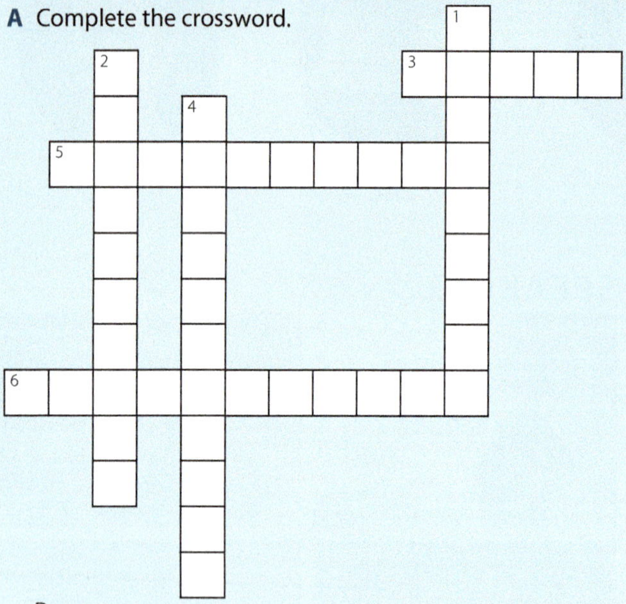

Down

1 See the dentist with this problem.
2 Leg, arm, finger? Go to the hospital. (two words)
4 You are warmer than you should be.

Across

3 Cover your mouth with your hand when you do this.
5 Try not to talk. Drink hot drinks. Suck a candy. (two words)
6 Did you eat too much?

B What are the missing words? Choose a, b or c to complete the survey.

WELCOME TO *SUNNY'S GYM*

Check (✓) your fitness goals.

1 __ weight ☐
2 get or __ in shape ☐

Do you …

3 __ at a gym? ☐
4 __ jogging? ☐
5 __ a team sport? ☐
6 __ yoga? ☐

	a	b	c
1	get	put	lose
2	stay	work	go
3	work it	work out	work on
4	run	do	go
5	go	play	join
6	play	go	do

C Choose the correct words to complete the sentences.

1 Pasta is made from ***nuts*** / ***wheat***.
2 You can eat the shell of ***shrimp*** / ***lobster***, but a lot of people choose not to.
3 Pizza is made with bread, cheese and ***avocado*** / ***tomato*** sauce.
4 British-style fish and chips usually includes ***tuna*** / ***cod***.
5 One of the main salad ingredients is ***rice*** / ***lettuce***.

GRAMMAR

A Complete the sentences with *too many*, *too much* and *not enough*.

1 We can't make a cake today. There are ______________ eggs in the fridge.
2 There are ______________ flavors of ice cream – I can't decide!
3 There are ______________ chairs here. I'll get two more from the kitchen.
4 We shouldn't eat ______________ sugar in our diets. It's unhealthy.
5 I've eaten ______________ pie. I don't feel well.

B Write the word in parentheses in the correct place. Then circle the correct *-ing* form. Choose gerund (G), adjective (A) or present participle (PP).

1 She left the gym because of the rising prices. (*rising*) *G / A / PP*
2 Lucien is very fit these days. (*becoming*) *G / A / PP*
3 He isn't any exercise right now. (*doing*) *G / A / PP*
4 My brother loves marathons. (*running*) *G / A / PP*
5 I want to try yoga by myself. (*practicing*) *G / A / PP*

C Complete the comments from a health website with *just*, *already* or *yet*.

HART_27: I became vegetarian about two weeks ago. I feel lighter and I have clearer skin [1]______________. I've [2]______________ weighed myself but I haven't lost any weight [3]______________.

KENNYKEN: This morning, I finally decided to go vegan. I've [4]______________ come back from the store with vegan ingredients and a cookbook. Actually, I have one vegan cookbook [5]______________, but I haven't made anything from it [6]______________.

FUNCTIONAL LANGUAGE

A Complete the words in the conversation at a pharmacy.

Pharmacist: Good morning. [1]H__ __ can I h__ __ __ ?
Customer: Oh, good morning. [2]I f__ __ __ terr__ __ __ __ .
Pharmacist: [3]Wh__ __ are your sym__ __ __ __ __ ?
Customer: [4]I ha__ __ a s__ __ __ thr__ __ __ and a cou__ __ . [5]It really hu__ __ __.
Pharmacist: Oh, dear. Anything else?
Customer: Well, I think [6]I ha__ __ a tem__ __ __ __ __ __ __ __, too, because I feel hot all the time.

7 MIND

The greatest thing in life is to keep your mind young.

Henry Ford

A little boy tries to solve the Sunday crossword puzzle, Lancashire, United Kingdom.

OBJECTIVES

- discuss what makes you happy
- write an online comment about the effects of the internet
- talk about intelligence and achievements
- describe an object and say what you use it for
- write a survey report

Work with a partner. Discuss the questions.

1 How can people 'stay young'?
2 Look at the picture. Who is helping whom?
3 What do you do to keep your mind healthy?

7.1 Smile

● Discuss what makes you happy

G articles **P** /ə/ (schwa) in *a* / *an* **V** feelings

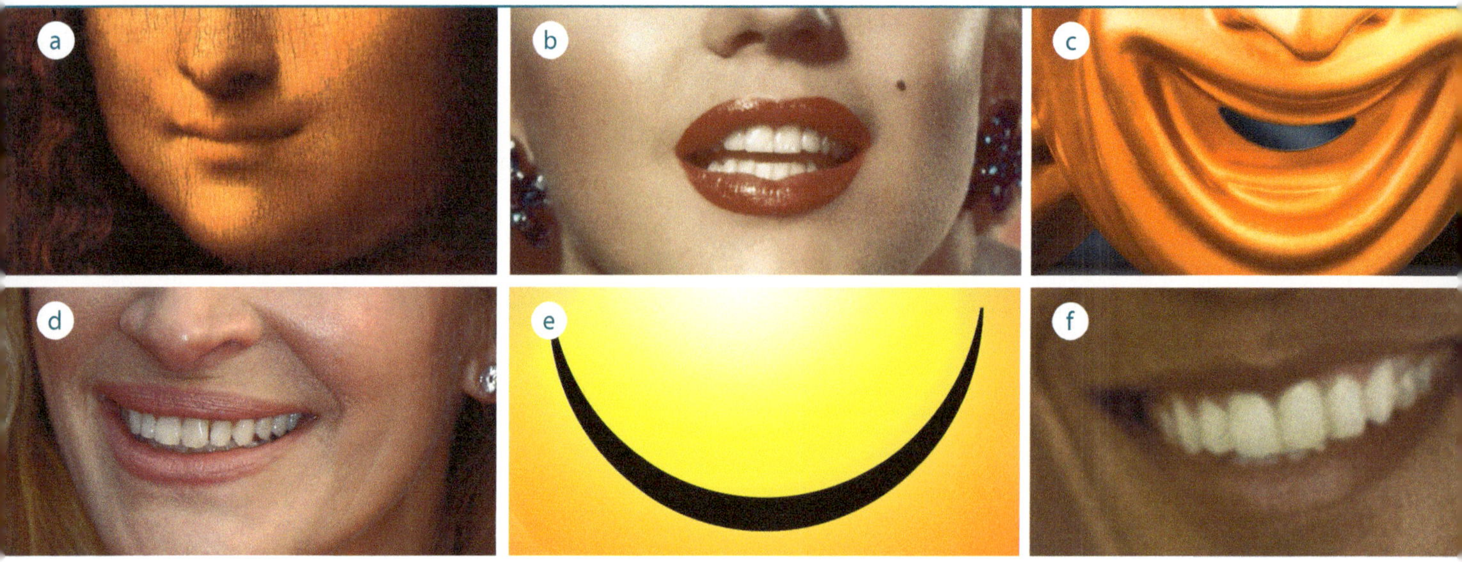

READING

A Work in groups. Discuss the questions.

1 Do you recognize these famous smiles? What do you know about them?

2 'Laugh and the world laughs with you.' What does this saying mean? Do you agree with its message? Do you have a similar saying in your language?

3 How many times a day do you think a person laughs on average?

4 How is laughing good for our health?

5 How do smiling and laughing help social relationships?

B READ FOR GIST Read *A smile a day …* quickly and check your answers to questions 3, 4 and 5.

C READ FOR DETAIL Are the following statements true (T) or false (F)? Correct the false sentences.

1 Happy people are likely to live to an older age. *T / F*

2 Laughing can have a similar effect to working out in the gym. *T / F*

3 Laughing slows our heartbeat and blood flow. *T / F*

4 Laughing can prevent small health problems. *T / F*

5 The production of chemicals in our brain causes laughter. *T / F*

6 Smiling and laughter began in humans to show there was danger. *T / F*

D SPEAK Work in pairs. Discuss the questions.

1 How many times do you think you laugh each day? When did you last laugh? What did you laugh at?

2 What everyday things make you feel good and put you in a positive mood? (For example, good food, music, new clothes)

A *smile* a day …

We all know that a cheerful state of mind makes us happy but it could also help us to live longer.

Laughing out loud, something we do on average 17 times a day, is particularly good for you. Laughter is a short sound which is repeated, on average, five times a second. It is widely believed that laughing 100 times is equal to ten minutes' light exercise in the gym. In addition, a 2005 study by the University of Maryland School of Medicine showed that laughter lowers blood pressure and there is a healthy increase in heart rate and blood flow. This can lead to a healthier heart and also make you less likely to catch colds and other minor illnesses. The research also suggests that people who are happy are likely to live longer. Laughing also produces chemicals in the brain that make us feel pleased and puts us in a positive mood. Smiling and laughing are also important for social relationships. Experts believe that smiling and laughing in humans began as a way to show relief when danger had passed. It helped the mind and body to feel relaxed and therefore showed trust between people. This stopped people from feeling scared of each other and helped people to connect. So the next time you want to connect with someone, why not start with a smile? It will help them to feel at ease and you might even make a new friend!

Glossary

minor (adj) not very important in comparison with things of the same type

relief (n) a relaxed, happy feeling that you get because a bad situation has ended

state of mind (phrase) the way that you are thinking and feeling at the present time

trust (n) a feeling of confidence in someone that shows you believe they are honest, fair and reliable

GRAMMAR
Articles

A WORK IT OUT Look at the sentences from *A smile a day …* Then complete the rules with *a/an*, *the* or – (no article).

The research also suggests that people who are happy are likely to live longer.

*Laughter is **a short sound** which is repeated, on average, five times a second.*

*Smiling and laughing are also important for **social relationships**.*

Articles

1 We use ________________ to refer to something indefinite when it is one of many. We usually use it when we refer to something for the first time.

2 We use ________________ to refer to something definite and which we know. This is usually because it has already been mentioned.

3 We use ________________ to refer to a plural or uncountable noun or something in a general sense.

B Go to the **Grammar Hub** on **page 134**.

C PRACTICE There are two mistakes in each question. Correct the mistakes.

1 The smiley face is a famous image all over world. Why do you think an image is so successful and popular?

2 Do you own or have you ever owned anything with smiley face on it, such as the T-shirt? Where else do we see it?

3 Do you use an emojis or icons in your online messaging? Do you have a favorite emoji? Are there the emojis for your country or culture?

D SPEAK Work in pairs. Ask and answer the questions in Exercise C.

PRONUNCIATION
/ə/ (schwa) in *a* / *an*

7.1 **A** Listen and repeat. What do you notice about the pronunciation of *a* and *an*?

1 Have **a** nice day.

2 We had **a** great time.

3 She's **an** old friend.

4 A smile **a** day keeps the doctor away.

B SPEAK Work in pairs. Student A – go to the **Communication Hub** on **page 156**. Student B – go to the **Communication Hub** on **page 153**.

VOCABULARY
Feelings

A WORK IT OUT Look at the sentences from *A smile a day …* Then choose the correct words to complete the sentences (1–3).

*We all know that a **cheerful** state of mind makes us happy …*

*It helped the mind and body to feel **relaxed** and therefore showed trust between people.*

*This stopped people from feeling **scared** of each other and helped people to connect.*

1 The words in bold are *adjectives* / *nouns*.

2 They describe *opinions* / *feelings and states of mind*.

3 Words like these *are always positive* / *are always negative* / *can be positive or negative*.

B Go to the **Vocabulary Hub** on **page 149**.

C SPEAK Work in pairs. When was the last time you felt anxious, confused, pleased, relaxed? Tell your partner.

SPEAKING

A Work in pairs. Do a class survey about what everyday things make people happy. Think of three everyday things that make you happy. Write them down and tell your partner about them.

A: I feel happy when I have a cup of tea in the morning. How about you?

B: Me, too, but I prefer coffee. And going for a walk on a sunny day with a clear blue sky makes me feel good.

A: I agree. A nice day makes everyone feel good!

B Go around the class and ask your classmates what three everyday things make them happy. Write down their answers.

A: Getting into bed after a long day.

B: When I find a bargain in the stores.

C: Relaxing with a good book.

C Work in pairs. Compare your findings. What were the most common answers? What were the most interesting or unusual answers? Work with other pairs and share your answers.

Discuss what makes you happy

7.2 The internet and the brain

Write an online comment about the effects of the internet

G used to P used to V shortened words

READING

A Work in pairs. Discuss the questions.

1 Look at the picture on the opposite page. What are the people doing?
2 How much time do you spend online? Which devices do you use?
3 What do you like or dislike about the internet?

B Match definitions (1–4) with the words in the box.

addicted attention span distracted memory

1 the length of time that you can pay attention to one thing without becoming bored or thinking about something else ________
2 the ability to remember things ________
3 not able to concentrate on something ________
4 enjoying a particular activity very much and spending as much time as you can doing it ________

C **READ FOR MAIN IDEA** Work in pairs. Look at the title of the show and think of three ways the internet could be killing or damaging our brains. Then read the blog and check your answers.

D **READ FOR DETAIL** Read the comments. Match the comments with the person.

Who …

1 doesn't think the internet is a negative thing?
Tom6 / JennyH / Sue123
2 is losing the ability to concentrate on something for long periods?
Tom6 / JennyH / Sue123
3 thinks the internet has many negative effects on people?
Tom6 / JennyH / Sue123
4 can't remember some things as well as in the past?
Tom6 / JennyH / Sue123
5 thinks it's normal to change the way we use our memory?
Tom6 / JennyH / Sue123

E **SPEAK** Work in pairs. What does 'use it or lose it' mean? What other skills could 'use it or lose it' apply to?

Glossary

adapt (v) to change your ideas or behavior so that you can deal with a new situation
approval (n) a positive opinion that you have towards someone or something that you think is good or suitable
impress (v) if someone or something impresses you, you admire them

Did you see …?

The TV blog for the TV lover *by Anna Frese*

Show: *Is the internet killing our brains?*

Did anyone see that TV show last night, *Is the internet killing our brains?* It was really interesting! First, it looked at the human memory in the 21st century and at how the internet is destroying our memory. This is because today most information is instantly available online and we don't need to remember things. And it said that over time, this could have a negative effect on the brain's memory system – a case of use it or lose it. The show then focused on how the human attention span is decreasing. It said that the brain is naturally easily distracted, and on the internet there is a lot of opportunity for this distraction. Evidence suggests that this is negatively affecting our attention spans and our ability to concentrate.

Finally, the show examined how the 'likes' and other positive comments and approval we receive on social media can be addictive. As a result, people are constantly trying to impress, and social network addiction is becoming a serious issue.

What do you think? Add your comments below:

Tom6 I don't agree with all the points. But, as soon as I start using the net, I find myself looking at site after site. It's very addictive. I can spend hours online and I suddenly realize it's dark outside! I didn't use to be like that. I really do think my attention span is decreasing because of the net. However, they used to say the same thing about the radio and TV when they became popular.

JennyH The Greek philosopher Socrates said that writing would destroy memory because we would not have to remember things. However, Einstein believed that remembering facts was not a good use of our brains or our time. He said we had books to do that for us. What's different about the internet? Humans will adapt to it as they have in the past. I don't see a problem.

Sue123 I disagree with JennyH. I read somewhere that more than 70 percent of people don't know important phone numbers. I used to know all my friends' numbers. Now, I don't know any. We rely on our devices and the internet too much. So I do think it's killing our brains, and in a lot of ways, not just our memories.

PRONUNCIATION
used to

7.2 **A** Listen and repeat. What do you notice about the pronunciation of *used to*?

1 used to
2 I used to play video games.
3 Phones used to be much bigger.

7.3 **B SPEAK** Work in pairs. Practice saying the sentences. Then listen and check your pronunciation.

1 We used to speak on the phone a lot more.
2 Computers used to be much bigger.
3 I didn't use to go online much.

GRAMMAR
used to

A WORK IT OUT Look at the sentences from *Did you see …?* Find the missing words and complete the sentences. Then choose the correct words to complete the rule.

1 I can spend hours online, and I suddenly realize it's dark outside! I ________________ be like that.
2 However, they ________________ say the same thing about the radio and TV when they became popular.
3 I ________________ know all my friends' numbers. Now, I don't know any.

used to

We use *used to* to talk about past situations that ***do not exist now / continue now***. The negative form is *didn't use to*.

- I used to work in a phone store.
- She used to have long hair.
- I didn't use to like chatting online.

B Go to the **Grammar Hub** on **page 134**.

C PRACTICE Write five sentences that are true for you with *used to* or *didn't use to*. Use the verbs in the box or your own ideas.

be be able to buy drive eat go have like listen to live play read smoke watch

I used to read comic books a lot when I was younger.
I didn't use to enjoy learning English.

D SPEAK Work in pairs. Discuss your answers to Exercise C.

VOCABULARY
Shortened words

A Look at the words in **bold** in the sentence from *Did you see …?* They are shortened words. What are the words short for?

But, as soon as I start using the ***net****, I find myself looking at* ***site*** *after* ***site****.*

B Go to the **Vocabulary Hub** on **pages 149** and **150**.

C SPEAK Work in pairs. Discuss the questions.

1 Why do you think we shorten some words?
2 Is it better to use shortened words in an informal or a formal situation?
3 Can you think of any other shortened words in English?

SPEAKING

A Read *Did you see …?* again. Comment on the blog or one of the comments.

B Write notes. Include at least one example of *used to* or *didn't use to*.

C Write about 50 words. Read your comment carefully and check for spelling and grammar.

D DISCUSS Work in pairs. Swap your comments and say whether you agree or disagree with your partner then add a further point.

E Display the comments for your classmates to read. Which ideas and opinions are the most common?

Write an online comment about the effects of the internet

7.3 Intelligence

Talk about intelligence and achievements

V phrasal verbs **G** no article (*school, the school*) **P** practicing *the*: /ðiː/ or /ðə/ **S** listening for the order of events

Wolfgang Amadeus Mozart

Pablo Picasso

Venus Williams

William James Sidis

Garry Kasparov

LISTENING

A SPEAK Work in pairs. Look at the pictures. What do you know about these people? What do they all have in common?

B Match the words (1–2) with the correct definitions (a–b).

1 intelligence
2 knowledge
a all the facts that someone knows about a particular subject
b the ability to understand and think about things

C LISTEN FOR KEY WORDS 7.4 Listen to the podcast about William James Sidis. Check (✓) what the presenter talks about.

1 Sidis's IQ ☐
2 where he was born ☐
3 his grandparents ☐
4 his language skills ☐
5 his college studies ☐
6 his jobs ☐
7 his friends ☐
8 how he died ☐

Glossary

child prodigy (n) a child who is extremely skillful at something that usually only adults can do
in/out of the public eye (phrase) well known or not well known to people in general
IQ = intelligence quotient (n) a number that represents a person's intelligence, based on the results of a particular type of test
turning point (n) a time when an important change takes place in a situation

D 7.4 Number the events (a–h) in William James Sidis's life in the order they happened (1–8). Use the information in the box to help you. Then listen again and check.

Listening for the order of events

Listen for words and phrases to help you follow the order of events in a story.

- Words and phrases that tell us when something happened:
  when he was nine by four years old at 11
  at age 16 in 1898
- Words and phrases that tell us that something happened before, at the same time or after something else:
  before before that earlier previously
  while during at the same time
  after after this soon after then next
- Words and phrases that tell us that one thing was a consequence of another:
  as a result therefore

a He received a prison sentence. ___
b He became interested in politics. ___
c He taught math at Rice University. ___
d He studied math at Harvard University. ___
e He went to Harvard University to study law. ___
f He gave a lecture in math at Harvard University. ___
g He traveled around the US doing different jobs. ___
h He learned seven languages and also invented one. ___

E SPEAK Work in pairs. Discuss the questions.

1 What were the key events and turning points in William James Sidis's life?
2 Sidis didn't go to school, his mother taught him at home. What are the advantages and disadvantages of this?

VOCABULARY
Phrasal verbs

A Look at the phrasal verbs in **bold** from the podcast about William James Sidis. Match the phrasal verbs (1–6) with the correct meanings (a–f).

1 He was born in 1898 and **grew up** in New York.
2 They **brought** him **up** to have 'a love of knowledge'.
3 His mother **gave up** her job and taught him at home.
4 He also **made up** his own language.
5 He **dropped out** of the university before he finished his degree.
6 He had a **falling out** with his parents and lost contact with them.

a invented
b spent his childhood
c stopped doing something
d left something before finishing it
e stopped being friendly because he had had a disagreement with them
f took care of him until he became an adult

B PRACTICE Complete the sentences with the correct form of a phrasal verb from Exercise A. Use each phrasal verb once.

1 Where did you ________________? What is the neighborhood like? Do you still live there?
2 Who ________________ you ________________? Do you have a big family or a small family?
3 Name something you have ________________. When and why did you stop doing it?
4 When you were a child, did you play traditional games or did you ________________ your own games?
5 Do you know anyone who ________________ of school or college? Why didn't they finish?
6 Have you ever had a ________________ with someone? Did you become friends again?

C SPEAK Ask and answer the questions in Exercise B.

GRAMMAR
No article (*school*, *the school*)

A WORK IT OUT Look at the sentences from the podcast. Then choose the correct words to complete the rules.

No article (*school*, *the school*)

Sometimes we use an article (*a*, *the*) with the words *school*, *college*, and *prison*. But sometimes we use no article.

- *He didn't go to school.*
- *News reporters followed him everywhere at the college.*
- *At 11, he went to college to study math.*
- *He didn't go to prison and instead he spent a year in a hospital.*

1 When we are referring to the *activity* associated with the place (studying / being a student, being a prisoner) we use *an article / no article*.
2 When we are referring to the *physical* place, we use *an article / no article*.

B Go to the Grammar Hub on page 134.

C PRACTICE Choose the correct words to complete the texts.

Most people go to [1]*the college / college* at age 18 or 19. However, in 1981, at the age of just 12, Ruth Lawrence became the University of Oxford's youngest ever student. She didn't go to [2]*the school / school* and her father gave up his job to teach her at home. He also accompanied her everywhere at [3]*the college / a college*.

Nelson Mandela was president of South Africa from 1994 to 1999. Before that, he spent 27 years in [4]*the prison / prison* for crimes against the government. Eighteen years of this was in [5]*the prison / prison* on Robben Island, which is seven kilometers out in the ocean from Cape Town.

D SPEAK Work in pairs. Close your books. Tell your partner a story from Exercise C.

PRONUNCIATION
Practicing *the*: /ðiː/ or /ðə/

A SPEAK Work in pairs. Practice saying the sentences.

1 Have you ever been to the East Coast of the United States?
2 No, but I've been to the West Coast.

7.5 **B** Listen and compare your pronunciation. What do you notice about the pronunciation of *the* in each sentence? Why is there a difference?

SPEAKING HUB

A You are going to give a short presentation about a child prodigy. Student A – go to the Communication Hub on page 152. Student B – go to the Communication Hub on page 157.

B PLAN Read the biography and write notes about:

- the person's early life and education
- his/her talents and abilities
- any key moments or turning points in his/her life
- achievements he/she is famous for
- what he/she did later in life

C ORGANIZE Work in groups. Decide who is going to present which topics and practice your presentation. Use words and phrases from the Listening box to help you.

D PRESENT Give your presentation to your classmates.

Talk about intelligence and achievements

Café Hub

7.4 Neena's dinner

F – describe an object and say what you use it for   P – objects

COMPREHENSION

A SPEAK Work in pairs. Look at the picture. Who do you think says the following, Zac (Z), Gaby (G) or Neena (N)? What do you think happens and who cooks Neena's dinner?

1 Gaby, what's wrong? ___
2 And we promised to cook dinner for her tonight. ___
3 And it's 6:30! ___
4 Who's going to cook? ___
5 I can make pizza! ___
6 I can't think of the word in English. ___
7 A knife? ___
8 You used to work at Pizza Roma? ___
9 Yeah, but I ate too much pizza. ___
10 It looks like Pizza Roma! ___

B ▶ Watch the video and check your answers to Exercise A. What is *rallador* in English?

FUNCTIONAL LANGUAGE

Describe an object and say what you use it for

A Complete the phrases with the verbs in the box. You need to use two verbs twice.

forgotten know made think use

Find out the English word for something
Problem
I've [1] ________ the name of it.
I can't [2] ________ of the word in English.
It's *rallador* in Spanish.
Oh, what's it [3] ________ of?
Description
You [4] ________ it to …
It's a thing you [5] ________ to …
It's [6] ________ of metal.
Check understanding
Do you [7] ________ what I mean?

B ▶ 01:09–02:43 Watch part of the video again and check your answers to Exercise A.

USEFUL PHRASES

A ▶ Match the useful phrases (1–5) with the phrase that comes before or after it (a–e). Then watch the video again and check your answers.

1 Let me think …
2 Who's going to cook?
3 You can be my assistant chef.
4 You know! 'Un rallador'.
5 Neena says she'll be home soon.

a I'm sorry, I don't understand Spanish.
b Oh, no! We have no time!
c Who's going to cook?
d Cool, good plan.
e Me, for sure.

B How do you say these useful phrases in your language?

MILLY

SAM

NEENA

ZAC

GABY

PRONUNCIATION

Objects

7.6 **A** Match the pictures (a–c) with the conversations (1–3). Then listen and repeat the conversations.

a

b

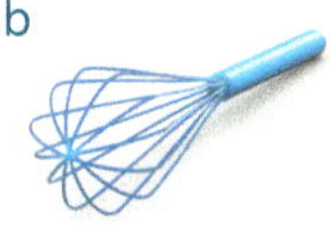

c

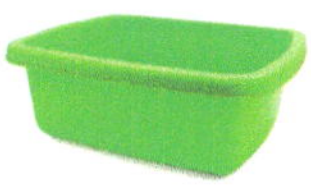

1 **A:** What's it made of?
B: It's made of metal. You use it to beat eggs.

2 **A:** What's it made of?
B: It's made of wood. You use it to roll pastry.

3 **A:** What's it made of?
B: It's made of plastic. You use it to wash the dirty dishes.

B SPEAK Work in pairs. Choose another object and write a conversation. Practice saying your conversation.

SPEAKING

1

2

3

4

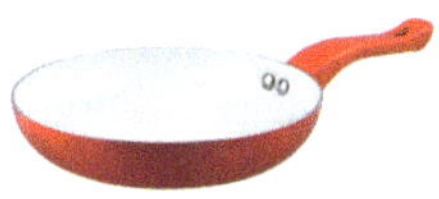

5

6

7

8

Work in pairs. Take turns being Student A and B.

Student A: Look at the pictures and choose an object. Tell your partner:

- the word in your language
- what it's made of
- what you use it for

Student B: Listen and guess the object your partner describes. Tell him/her the number of the object and the name in English.

Describe an object and say what you use it for

➤ Turn to **page 164** to learn how to write a survey report.

Unit 7 Review

VOCABULARY

A **Choose the best adjective to complete the sentences. Use the information in parentheses to help you.**

1 I feel really ***anxious*** / ***cheerful*** now that the holidays have started. (*positive*)

2 Lola is a little ***nervous*** / ***glad*** about the interview tomorrow. (*negative*)

3 I always feel ***scared*** / ***happy*** when I get a lot of 'likes' for my posts on Twitter. (*positive*)

4 I'm really ***nervous*** / ***glad*** that you liked the cake I made. (*positive*)

5 Casper didn't go to the top of the building because he was too ***relaxed*** / ***scared***. (*negative*)

B **Look at the shortened words. Write the missing letters to complete the full words.**

1 cell *p h o n e*

2 info_ _ _ _ _ _ _

3 lab_ _ _ _ _ _ _

4 _ _ _plane

5 _ _ _ _ _net

6 mic_ _ _ _ _ _ _

7 _ _ _ _case

8 _ _ _site

C **The phrasal verbs are in the wrong places in the texts. Write them in the correct place. Change the tense if necessary.**

I [1]**brought up** in Sheffield. It was just me and my mom, so she [2]**made** me **up** on her own. We had a good relationship, although we argued sometimes and had a [3]**gave up** from time to time. Because I was an only child, I played on my own a lot of the time. This was OK because I had a good imagination and I used to [4]**grew up** my own games. To be honest, I had a really good childhood.

I didn't enjoy college. I found it really difficult. Studying took up all of my time and I had to [5]**drop out** a lot of my hobbies and other activities. I just went to lectures in the day and then studied all evening. So, I decided to [6]**falling out** and get a job instead. It was the best decision I ever made.

GRAMMAR

A **Choose the correct article or no article to complete the text.**

Humans are not [1]***the*** / – only animals that laugh. Other animals such as [2]***the*** / – gorillas, chimpanzees and orangutans also laugh. [3]***A*** / ***The*** main reason for laughter in [4]***the*** / – animals is when they are playing. [5]***A*** / ***The*** laughter indicates that it is [6]***a*** / ***the*** game and that no one is going to get hurt. [7]***A*** / – Laughter has also been observed in [8]***the*** / – rats.

B Think about everyday life forty years ago. For each pair of words or phrases, write what we *used to* and *didn't use to* do. Use the verbs in the box.

chat ~~use~~ use watch write and send

1 online maps and GPS / paper maps

We didn't use to use online maps and GPS. We used to use paper maps.

2 on social media / on the phone

3 videos / movies online

4 emails / letters

C Complete the questions about school and college with *a*/*an*, *the* or – (no article).

SCHOOL AND COLLEGE QUESTIONNAIRE

1 Where did you go to ___ school as a child? Was ___ school close to where you lived?

2 Did you enjoy ___ school? What were your favorite subjects at ___ school?

3 Did you, do you or will you go to ___ college? If so, is ___ college well known for anything?

4 Is there ___ college in the town or city where you grew up? Do most cities in your country have ___ college?

FUNCTIONAL LANGUAGE

Write the missing letters to complete the words. Then match the conversations (1–3) with the pictures (a–c).

a 
b 
c 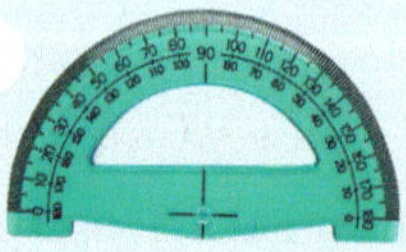

1 **A:** What's a protractor?

B: It's a thing you **u**_ _ to measure and draw angles. It's shaped like half a circle and usually **m**_ _ _ of plastic.

2 **A:** I can't **t**_ _ _ _ of the English word for *agrafeuse*. Do you know?

B: Yes, it's stapler, I think.

3 **A:** What's this for?

B: You **u**_ _ it to draw circles. It's **c**_ _ _ _ _ a compass.

8 ART

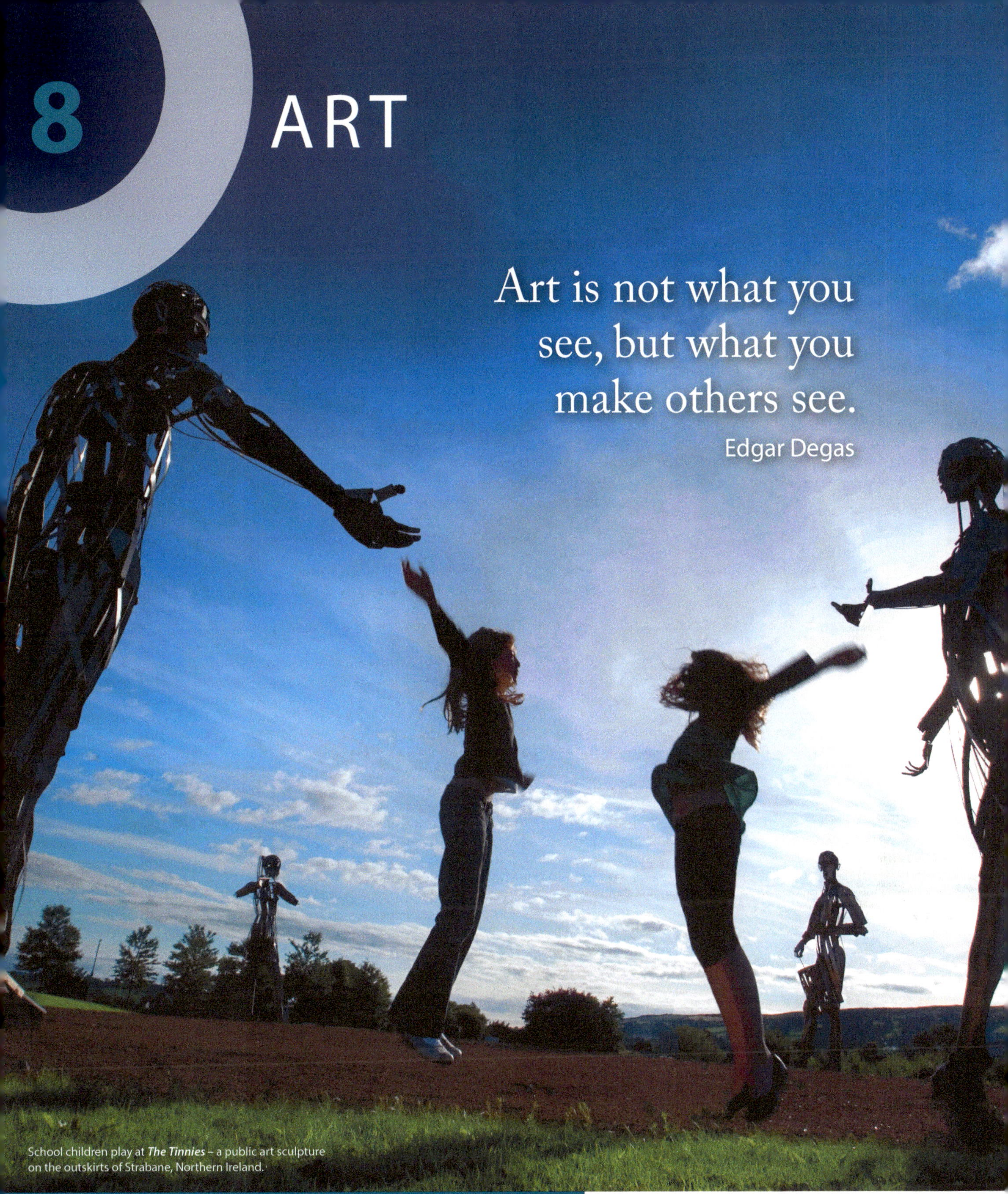

> Art is not what you see, but what you make others see.
>
> Edgar Degas

School children play at ***The Tinnies*** – a public art sculpture on the outskirts of Strabane, Northern Ireland.

OBJECTIVES

- talk about taste in music and your favorite songs
- talk about art and artists
- describe movies and books
- show interest in a topic
- write a review

Work with a partner. Discuss the questions.

1 What different types of art can you name?

2 Look at the picture. Would you like to visit this place?

3 Do you think museums and art galleries should be free? Why/Why not?

8.1 Musical taste

Talk about taste in music and your favorite songs

G reflexive pronouns **V** music **P** consonant clusters in words

LISTENING

8.1 **A** Listen to the music extracts (1–7) and match them with the different types of music (a–g).

a rap ___
b jazz ___
c rock ___
d disco ___
e blues ___
f reggae ___
g classical ___

B SPEAK Work in pairs. Discuss the questions.

1 Can you think of any other types of music?
2 What types of music do you like? What don't you like? Why?
3 Who are your favorite bands or musicians?
4 Why do we like certain types of music? Think of three reasons.

8.2 **C LISTEN FOR MAIN IDEA** Listen to the podcast *Music matters* with Professor Suzy Harrison. What are the three things which explain our taste in music?

Glossary

comforting (adj) making you feel less sad, worried or disappointed
energize (v) to make someone feel excited and enthusiastic
influence (v) to affect the way someone thinks or behaves, also *be influenced by*

8.2 **D LISTEN FOR DETAIL** Choose the correct answer a, b or c, to complete the sentences. Then listen again and check your answers.

1 When we are older, the music from our childhood makes us feel …
  a old.
  b sad.
  c happy.
2 Our first big music influence is generally …
  a our younger brothers and sisters.
  b our older brothers and sisters.
  c our school friends.
3 Music brings people together because we can share …
  a music files and records.
  b our opinions of the music.
  c the mood it creates.
4 We sometimes choose a particular type of music …
  a to create the right conditions for an activity.
  b to give us a break from an activity.
  c to help us forget about an activity.
5 Compared with the past, people today generally like …
  a fewer kinds of music.
  b more kinds of music.
  c the same variety of music.

E SPEAK Work in groups. Discuss the questions.

1 Who has influenced your taste in music, your parents, brothers and sisters, friends or someone or something else?
2 Do you generally like the same kinds of music as your friends? Do you think music is an important part of your friendships?
3 Do you tend to play different kinds of music at different times and when you are in different moods? Give some examples.

GRAMMAR

Reflexive pronouns

8.3 **A** Complete the sentences from the podcast *Music matters* with the pronouns in the box. You need to use one of the pronouns more than once. Then listen and check.

ourselves (x2) themselves yourself

1 **We** don't choose this music ___________, of course.
2 So, when **we** start to discover music by ___________, it is influenced by what we listened to when we were growing up.
3 In contrast, for **other people**, musical taste is a way to make ___________ different from other people.
4 And when you're preparing for a night out, **you** might want to energize ___________ and play something loud and full of energy.

B WORK IT OUT Match the sentences in Exercise A (1–4) with the rules (a–c).

Reflexive pronouns

There are several ways we can use reflexive pronouns. The most usual are:

a We use a reflexive pronoun as the object of a verb. This is when the subject and the object are the same person or thing. ___ ___

b We also use a reflexive pronoun after the object of a verb. This is to emphasize the person or thing that does the action. ___

c We use *by* + reflexive pronoun to say we do something alone or with no help. ___

C Go to the **Grammar Hub** on **page 136**.

D SPEAK Work in pairs. Have you ever …

1 taught yourself to do something (for example, play a musical instrument, play a sport, learn a skill)?
2 designed and/or built something yourself?
3 bought yourself something special?

VOCABULARY

Music

A Go to the **Vocabulary Hub** on **page 150**.

B Replace the words in **bold** with words in the box with the same or similar meaning.

album band members catchy cover songs gig live lyrics on tour

1 It's a great song. I love the **words**. ________
2 It's the best **concert** I've been to. ________
3 They play their own songs and **songs by other bands**. ________
4 This song is **very easy to remember**. ________
5 They are **doing a series of concerts** soon. ________
6 Their first **collection of songs** is their best. ________
7 I would love to see them **performing a concert**. ________
8 They have some great **people in the group**, who are excellent musicians. ________

C SPEAK Work in pairs. Replace the pronouns in Exercise B to make true sentences. Tell your partner.

PRONUNCIATION

Consonant clusters in words

8.4 **A** Underline the consonant clusters in each word. Then listen carefully. Are all the letters in the consonant clusters pronounced?

1 background
2 electric
3 individual
4 influenced
5 keyboards
6 ourselves

8.4 **B** Listen again and repeat the words.

SPEAKING

A Read the text about a radio show. Do you have a similar show in your country?

DESERT ISLAND DISCS

Desert Island Discs is a BBC Radio 4 show in the UK. It was first broadcast in 1942 and since then 3000 episodes have been recorded. Each week, a guest is asked to choose eight songs or other pieces of music they would take if they had to go on a desert island. The guest explains the reasons for their choices.

B Choose three songs or pieces of music to take to a desert island. Which is your number one song?

C Think about how to describe the songs and what you like about them, for example, the lyrics. Write notes about:

- what type(s) of music the songs are
- where the singers or bands are from
- the instruments they play
- what other songs or music the singers or bands are famous for

D Work in pairs. Tell each other what songs you have chosen. Describe the songs and say what you like about them.

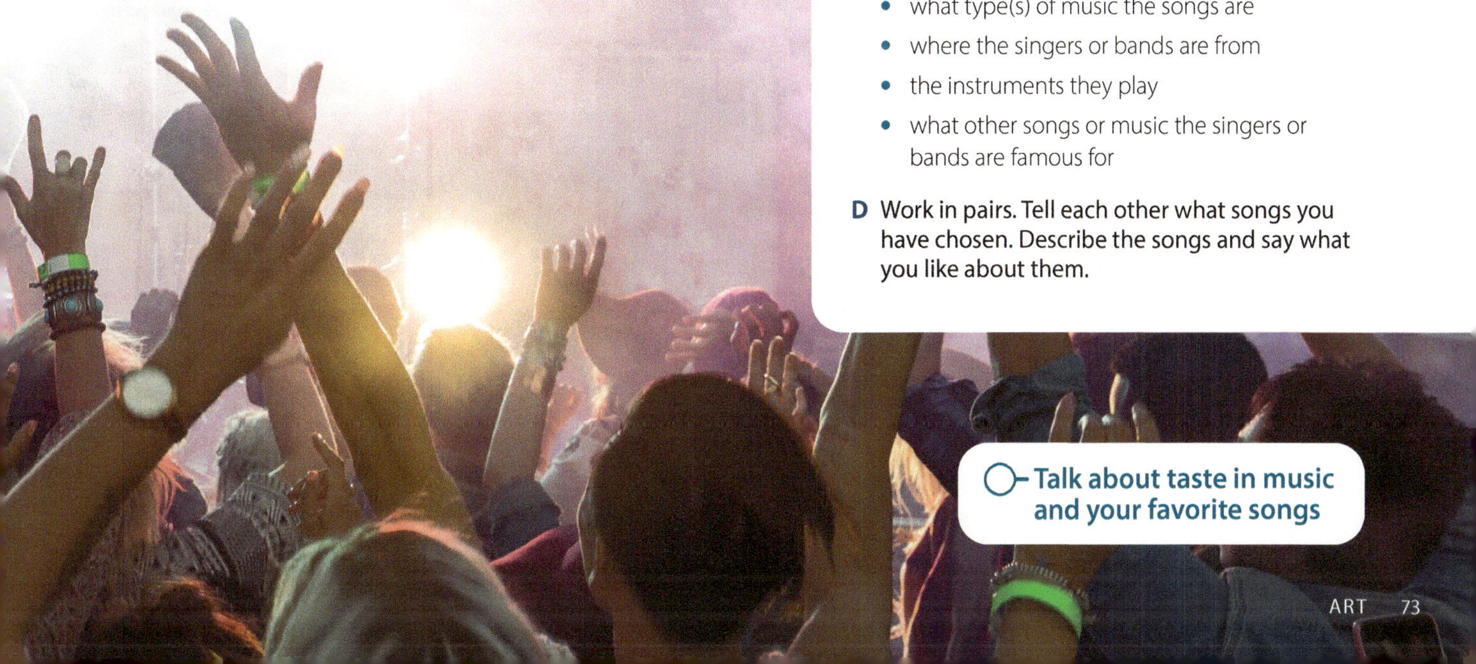

Talk about taste in music and your favorite songs

8.2 Unusual art

Talk about art and artists

V – types of art   P – /ɪ/ and /iː/   G – infinitive of purpose

VOCABULARY

Types of art

A SPEAK Work in pairs. How many artists can you name? What do you know about them or their paintings? Who are the most famous artists from your country?

B Go to the **Vocabulary Hub** on **page 150**.

PRONUNCIATION

/ɪ/ and /iː/

8.5 Listen to the sounds /ɪ/ and /iː/. Then listen and underline the word you hear.

	/ɪ/	/iː/		/ɪ/	/iː/
1	slip	sleep	4	sit	seat
2	ship	sheep	5	pitch	peach
3	live	leave	6	bit	beat

READING

A Work in pairs. Look at the works of art (a–d). What material do you think the artist uses in each one? Tell your partner.

UNUSUAL ART

1 Art and artists come in many forms. In this post, we look at four artists who use unusual materials to produce their art.

2 French artist Anastassia Elias uses toilet paper rolls and paper to create everyday scenes of life. She cuts out the image from paper and places it inside the roll. She then illuminates the images from the back, which creates a silhouette.

3 Max Zorn uses brown packing tape to create his works of art. He sticks the tape on glass sheets and illuminates them from the back. He creates dark and light by using thick or thin layers of tape. Originally, he used street lights in Amsterdam in the Netherlands, which is where he is from.

4 Russian artist Stanislav Aristov uses burned matchsticks to create his art. First, he photographs a match after it has finished burning. He then photographs a separate burning flame. Aristov then combines these two images to produce the final picture using picture software. He produces images from nature, such as flowers and animals, as well as everyday objects.

5 Scott Wade creates works of art on the dirty windows of cars. He usually uses artificial dirt to make the car dirty. Wade creates his own images and also recreates famous paintings, such as landscapes and still life. He also produces portraits of famous people. Wade has displayed his work at car shows and other automotive events around the world. He believes that 'dirt is beautiful'.

Glossary

artificial (adj) made by people and used instead of something natural
illuminate (v) to shine a light on something
layer (n) an amount or sheet of a substance that covers a surface
silhouette (n) the dark shape of something

B SCAN Read *Unusual art* quickly and check your answers to Exercise A. Then match the works of art (a–d) with the correct paragraphs (2–5).

C READ FOR DETAIL Read again. Are the following sentences true (T) or false (F)?

1 Anastassia Elias cuts up toilet paper rolls to produce her works of art. T / F
2 Max Zorn uses different colored tape to produce light and dark. T / F
3 Stanislav Aristov uses more than one picture to create his art. T / F
4 Scott Wade mostly creates images of cars and things connected with the automotive industry. T / F

D SPEAK Work in pairs. Which of the works of art do you like best? Why?

a

b

c

d

Little Dancer by Edgar Degas

The Scream by Edvard Munch

Self-Portrait by Vincent Van Gogh

Girl with Balloon by Banksy

GRAMMAR

Infinitive of purpose

A Complete the sentences from *Unusual art*. Write two words in each blank.

1 Max Zorn uses brown packing tape ______________ his works of art.

2 Aristov then combines these two images ______________ the final picture.

3 He usually uses artificial dirt ______________ the car dirty.

B **WORK IT OUT** Look at the sentences in Exercise A and complete the rule. Then find and underline three more examples in the article.

Infinitive of purpose

We use ______________ + ______________ to express the purpose or reason for doing something.

C Go to the **Grammar Hub** on **page 136**.

D **SPEAK** Complete the sentences with your own ideas to express purpose or reason. Then work in pairs and compare your ideas.

1 I go to museums and galleries …

2 We take pictures …

3 People go on vacation …

SPEAKING

A Look at the pictures above. What do you know about the works of art and the artists (1–4)? Which do you like the best? Why? What other famous works of art do you know?

B Choose one of the works of art or the artist who produced it (1–4) or use your own ideas. Write notes about:

Work of art

- What is the title?
- Who painted or made it? When?
- Is it in a museum or gallery? Where?
- What does it show?
- What materials are used?
- How does it make you feel?
- Have you seen the original?
- Any other information?

Artist

- What is his/her name?
- Where is he/she from?
- When was he/she alive?
- What is his/her style?
- What are his/her famous works of art?
- Do you have a favorite picture by him/her?
- Do you like this artist? Why/Why not?
- Any other information?

C Work in groups. Give your presentation to the group.

Talk about art and artists

8.3 Telling stories

Describe movies and books

V movie and book genres; adjectives for describing movies and books **P** word stress in longer words
G first conditional **S** identifying contrasts

VOCABULARY

Movie and book genres

A Match the pictures (1–6) with the genres in the box. Then work in pairs to think of movies and books which match the other genres in the box.

action adventure animated autobiography biography biopic comedy costume drama fairy tale fantasy historical horror musical romantic comedy (rom-com) science fiction (sci-fi) thriller western

1

2

3
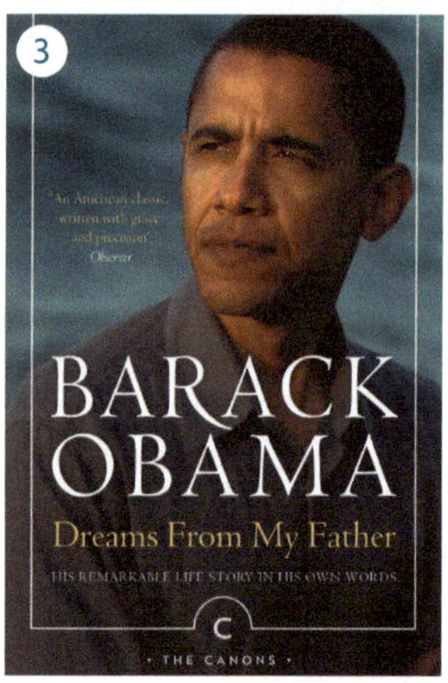

4

5

6

PRONUNCIATION

Word stress in longer words

A Write the movie and book genres in the box in the correct place.

adventure animated biography comedy fantasy historical musical romantic comedy science fiction

1 •●•	2 ●•••	3 •●••
adventure		
4 ●••	**5 •●•●••**	**6 ●•●•**

B Work in pairs. Compare your answers. Then listen and check. 8.6

C SPEAK Work in pairs. What genres of movies and books do you enjoy?

LISTENING

A Match the definitions (1–5) with the words in the box.

engaging gripping memorable sense visualize

1 easy to remember because of being special in some way ______
2 attracting and keeping someone's attention ______
3 to form a picture of something in your mind ______
4 one of the natural abilities most people have to see, hear, smell, taste and feel things ______
5 very exciting and interesting ______

B PREDICT Do you think the following statements refer to movies (M) or books (B)?

1 They allow us to imagine and see things in our own way. ___
2 We get to know the characters more. ___
3 They connect with our different senses at the same time. ___
4 It is an experience we usually share with friends. ___

C LISTEN FOR GIST Listen to a podcast comparing movies and books and check your answers to Exercise B. 8.7

Glossary

book club (n) a group of people who meet regularly to discuss books
chapter (n) one of the sections into which a book is divided; a chapter usually has a number or a title
character (n) a person in a book or movie
dialogue (n) the words that characters speak in a book or movie

.7 **D** Match the sentences (1–5) with their contrasting ideas (a–e). Then listen again and check your answers. Use the information in the box to help you.

Identifying contrasts

Listen for linking words and phrases that express a contrast between two ideas:

but, though, however, although	*(but) at the same time*
on the other hand	*compared to*

Listen for phrases that introduce a further contrast:

another (important) difference is	*and one more thing*

1 Books allow the reader to use their imagination.
2 With books, the story generally moves more slowly.
3 We generally watch a movie with other people.
4 Reading is a less sociable activity.
5 People usually say they are disappointed by the movie.

a Book clubs are very popular these days.
b In many cases people actually prefer the movie.
c Reading a book is more individual and personal.
d With a movie the whole story needs to start and finish in 90 minutes.
e With movies we see what the director and the actors want us to see.

.8 **E LISTEN FOR KEY WORDS** Listen to the extracts. Which linking words or phrases express the contrasting ideas in Exercise D? Make a list.

VOCABULARY

Adjectives for describing movies and books

A Look at the sentences from the podcast. Complete the adjectives with the missing vowels (*a, e, i, o, u*).

1 I think this makes the experience more personal and _e_ng_a_g_i_ng.
2 A movie can be much more __xc__t__ng and gr__pp__ng than a book.
3 Music can also make the movie more __nt__r__st__ng and m__m__r__bl__.
4 Compared to the book, people usually say they are d__s__pp__ __nt__d by the movie.

3.9 **B** Read the information in the box and choose the correct option in the sentences below. Listen and check.

Adjectives for describing movies and books

We use adjectives ending in *-ing* to talk about what caused the feeling.

- *The movie was disappoint**ing**.*

We use adjectives ending in *-ed* to talk about how we feel.

- *I was disappoint**ed**.*

1 It was totally ***engaged / engaging*** and the acting was ***amazed / amazing***.
2 I was, well, a little ***bored / boring*** by the end. It isn't very memorable I'm afraid.
3 You won't be ***disappointed / disappointing***. The singing was incredible.
4 It's really ***gripped / gripping***. And it's very ***moved / moving*** and sad, too.

GRAMMAR

First conditional

A WORK IT OUT Look at the first conditional sentences below. Then choose the correct words to complete the rules.

*If you **want** a great night out, you **should see** this movie.*

*If you **remind** me, **I'll lend** it to you.*

*If you **like** musicals, **you'll love** it.*

First conditional

1 We use the first conditional to talk about ***impossible / possible*** situations in the future.
2 Conditional sentences usually have two clauses: the *if*-clause and the main clause. To make a first conditional sentence, we use:
   - *If* + ***present tense / will*** and ***present tense / will*** + base form.
3 We ***can / can't*** use other modal verbs (for example, *can, could, might, should*) instead of *will* in the main clause.

B Go to the **Grammar Hub** on **page 136**.

SPEAKING HUB

8.10 **A** Listen to Salli recommending a movie. What does she talk about?

1 the movie type or genre
2 the main story
3 the actors, the director, the writer
4 what she likes about it
5 how it made her feel

B PLAN You are going to recommend a movie or book. Decide which movie or book you are going to talk about and write notes about the topics in Exercise A.

C ORGANIZE Use adjectives for describing movies or books and at least one first conditional sentence (*If you like …, you'll love …*).

D DISCUSS Work in groups. Recommend the movie or book you chose to your group.

Describe movies and books

Café Hub

8.4 First date

F– show interest in a topic   P– intonation

COMPREHENSION

A SPEAK Work in pairs. Which topics do you think Milly and Zac will talk about on their first date? Then watch the video and check your answers.

children culture family food home
marriage money music the weather work

B Are the sentences true (T) or false (F)? Correct the false sentences. Then watch the video again and check your answers.

1 Zac arrives first at the park. T / F
2 Milly knows the band Zac is listening to. T / F
3 Zac and Milly have tickets to the same show. T / F
4 It's Milly's birthday today. T / F
5 Zac loves English food. T / F
6 Milly likes English culture. T / F
7 Zac thinks Milly is shy. T / F
8 Milly wants to go home. T / F

FUNCTIONAL LANGUAGE

Show interest in a topic

A Complete the replies (1–11) with the words in the box.

are believe did do for kidding
neither no really so too

Comment	Reply
	Show surprise
[music playing]	1 ________ way! Is this Gold Sounds?
It's their new record.	2 ________ real?
I have tickets to their show.	You're 3 ________ ! I don't 4 ________ it!
I'm going with my sister.	5 ________ you?
She got the tickets for my birthday.	She 6 ________ ?
It's today.	7 ________ ? It's your birthday today?
I like that about you.	You 8 ________ ?
	Show you understand
I miss my family.	9 ________ do I.
I'm not crazy about English food.	10 ________ am I.
I feel like I can be myself here.	Me, 11 ________ .

B Watch the video again and check your answers.

MILLY

SAM

NEENA

ZAC

GABY

Glossary

Really? **(interjection) (British)** = For real? **(phrase) (American)**
You're joking! **(phrase) (British)** = You're kidding! **(phrase) (American)**

PRONUNCIATION

Intonation

.11 **A** Listen to the replies from Functional language Exercise A. Write them in the correct place. Then listen again and check your answers.

Rising intonation	Falling intonation
	No way!

.11 **B** Listen again and repeat the replies. Copy the intonation.

SPEAKING

A Write a short sentence about the following topics:

1 something surprising
I have tickets for Rihanna!
2 something shocking
______
3 something that isn't true
______
4 something about the past
______
5 something about the future
______
6 something you like
______
7 something you don't like
______

B Work in pairs. Take turns. Student A – read out your sentences. Student B – show interest and reply.

Show interest in a topic

➤ Turn to **page 165** to learn how to write a review.

Unit 8 Review

VOCABULARY

A Rearrange the letters of the words in **bold**. The first and last letters are in the correct place.

1. Do you listen to whole **ablmus** or do you usually listen to individual songs?
2. Do you pay much attention to the **lriycs** of a song or do you mostly listen to the music?
3. Do you have a favorite **sigenr** or musician (**giuristat, dmruemr**)?
4. Do you go to many **ggis**? What was the last band you saw **lvie**? Was there a good **lhgit sohw**? Where were you in the **aduenice** – near the **satge** or far away from it?

B Complete the quiz questions with the words in the box. There is one word you do not need. Then take the quiz.

abstract exhibit gallery landscape portrait sculpture still life

ART QUIZ
How much do you know?

1. **Which is the world's most visited art ________?**
   a The British Museum, London
   b The Metropolitan Museum of Art, New York
   c The Louvre, Paris
2. **It toured the world in the 1970s and is the most visited ________ of all time. What was it?**
   a *The Treasures of Tutankhamun*
   b The *Art of the Aztecs*
   c *The Visions of Van Gogh*
3. ***David* by Michelangelo is perhaps the most famous ________ in the world. How tall is it?**
   a 5.17 meters
   b 7.15 meters
   c 1.75 meters
4. ***Sunflowers* is one of the world's most famous collections of ________ paintings. Who painted them?**
   a Leonardo da Vinci
   b Vincent van Gogh
   c Pablo Picasso
5. ***Girl with a Pearl Earring* by Johannes Vermeer is a famous ________ painting. When did Vermeer paint it?**
   a 1465
   b 1665
   c 1865
6. **Pablo Picasso was most famous for his ________ art. Where was Picasso born?**
   a France
   b Italy
   c Spain

C Match the movie and book genres (1–5) with the descriptions (a–e). Then choose the correct adjectives. Which of the descriptions are positive (P) and which are negative (N)?

1. comedy
2. thriller
3. biography
4. fantasy
5. horror

a It isn't scary at all and I was pretty *bored / boring* for most of it.
b It's really funny. Go see it, you won't be *disappointed / disappointing*.
c It has a lot of strange creatures in it. The visuals are *amazed / amazing*.
d The story of his life was very *engaged / engaging* and very *moved / moving*.
e It's very *excited / exciting* and *gripped / gripping*. I couldn't stop reading it.

GRAMMAR

A Complete the conversations with the correct reflexive pronouns.

1. A: Great gig! Who's the last song by?
   B: We wrote it ________.
2. A: I like Jenny's website. Who designed it for her?
   B: I think she designed it ________.
3. A: Did you have guitar lessons or teach ________?
   B: I taught ________.

B Complete the sentences with the best verb to express purpose. Use *to* + infinitive.

1. We're going to the museum ________ the Picasso exhibit.
2. I mostly use my laptop ________ movies.
3. I started a hobby ________ new people.
4. Can I use your phone ________ my friend?

C Complete 1–3 with the correct form of the verbs in parentheses.

1. If you ________ (*see*) Janice this evening, ________ (*you / say*) hello from me?
2. A: If we ________ (*miss*) the bus, we ________ (*get*) a taxi.
   B: OK, or if it ________ (*stop*) raining, we ________ (*walk*). It isn't far to the movie theater.
3. If you ________ (*like*) reggae, you ________ (*love*) this band. I ________ (*get*) you a ticket if you ________ (*like*).

FUNCTIONAL LANGUAGE

A Complete the conversations with the words in the box.

believe did do real so too

1. A: Alice got a place in the art course.
   B: She ________? That's great news.
2. A: Jimmy's band has a record contract.
   B: For ________?
3. A: Did you know that the movie won three Oscars?
   B: Really? I don't ________ it! It was terrible.
4. A: I'm going see Jake's new band tonight.
   B: Yeah. Me, ________.
5. A: I want to go to the Damien Hirst exhibit.
   B: You ________ ? I didn't think you liked his stuff.
6. A: I love musicals.
   B: ________ do I!

9 MONEY

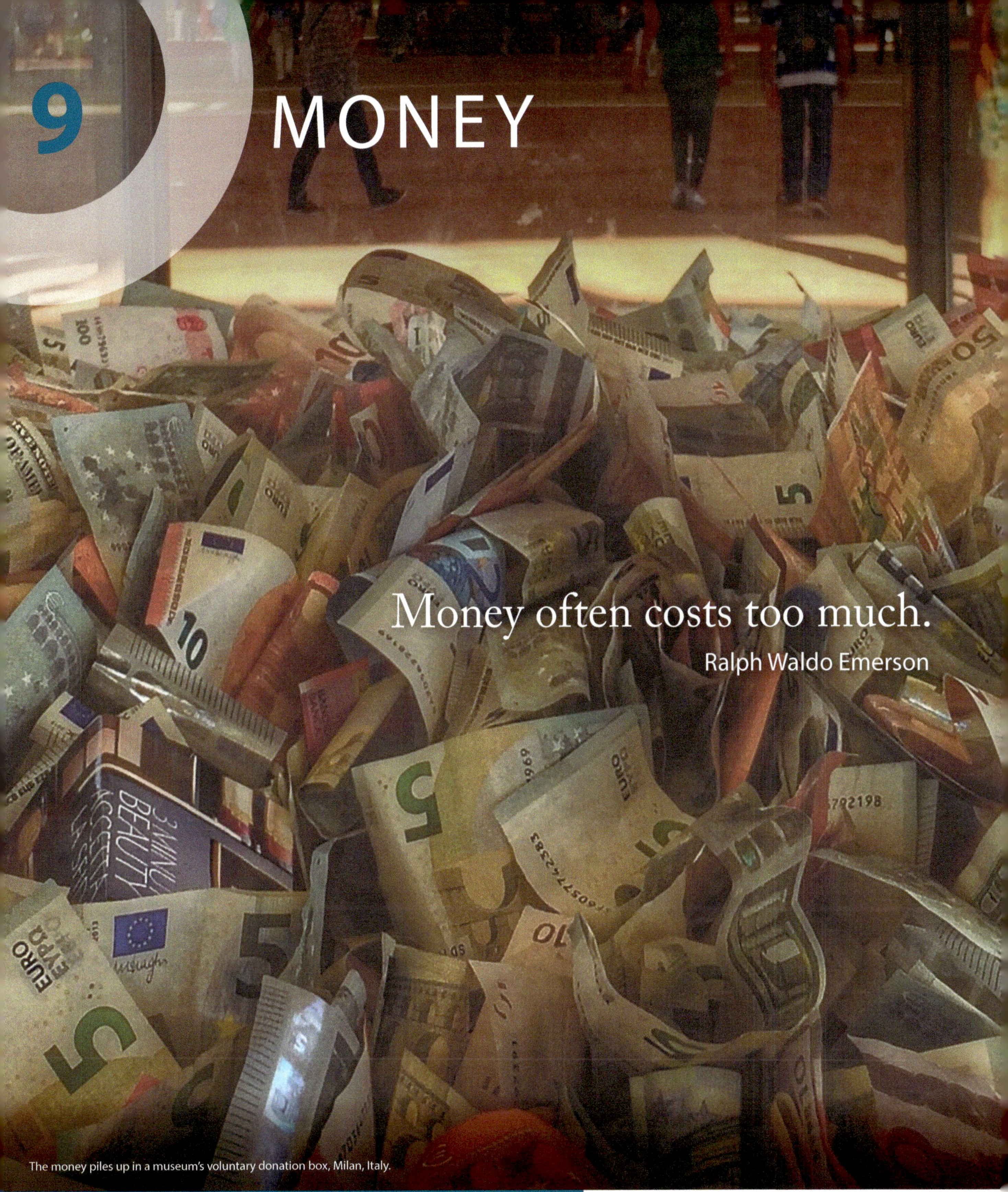

Money often costs too much.
Ralph Waldo Emerson

The money piles up in a museum's voluntary donation box, Milan, Italy.

OBJECTIVES

- talk about attitudes toward money and about spending money
- talk about philanthropy and charities
- discuss your skills and how they could help others
- go shopping for clothes and ask for a refund
- write a 'for sale' advertisement

Work with a partner. Discuss the questions.

1 Is money important?
2 Read the quote. What do you think Emerson meant? Do you agree?
3 Do you spend money every day? What do you buy?

9.1 Spending money

Talk about attitudes toward money and about spending mor

P /ɑː/, /ʌ/ and /æ/ G second conditional V prepositions in money phrases

READING

A Match the words (1–4) with the definitions (a–d).

1 obsessed
2 gain
3 inspire
4 possession

a something that you own
b to get something
c to give someone the enthusiasm to do something
d considering something so important that you are always thinking about it

B READ FOR MAIN IDEA Read *How to buy happiness*. Write the paragraph headings in the correct place. There is one heading you do not need.

a Try something new
b Discover yourself
c Take your time
d Open your mind

C READ FOR DETAIL Read again and answer the questions.

1 Which makes us feel better for longer, possessions or experiences?
2 In what three ways does Julie benefit from traveling?
3 What does Carmen learn from meeting people?
4 According to Carmen, how can traveling improve our character?
5 What does Hugo think can make us lazy?
6 Why does Hugo think experiences inspire us to do more?

D SPEAK Work in pairs. Discuss the questions.

1 Do you agree with the article? Why/Why not?
2 Have you spent money on experiences such as travel? What did you do? Were the experiences positive or negative? Why?

HOW TO BUY HAPPINESS

We live in a society that is obsessed with spending money – a society that is obsessed with materialism. When we buy things, it gives us happiness. But this feeling usually lasts only for a short time. Experiences, on the other hand, stay with us for a long time after they have finished. Therefore, if we spent more of our money on experiences, we would gain something that can last a lifetime. Here are three more reasons we should spend more time and money on experiences and three people who agree with this advice.

1 ______________________

Julie from the UK believes travel is an important experience. She says, 'Traveling helps us to discover our interests. I'm always saving up so I can go away at least once or twice a year. It helps me to discover what I like and what I don't like. It helps me to understand who I am. I think we wouldn't find out these things if we didn't spend money on experiences.'

2 ______________________

Carmen from Italy also believes that travel is important. She says, 'I spend a lot of my money on traveling. It helps us to see different points of view. As you travel, you meet new people with different ideas and opinions to your own. This teaches us some important life lessons and helps us to understand the world.' Carmen also believes that traveling helps you to become more independent and more confident.

Glossary

materialism (n) the belief that money and possessions are the most important aspects of human existence

3 ______________________

According to Hugo from Brazil, our experiences can inspire us. He says, 'It's always good to do something that is new. If we didn't do anything different, we might become lazy. We don't have to climb Mount Everest, but we can do things like learn to play a musical instrument, start a new sport or simply do something new for the first time. This will make us feel good and give us a sense of achievement. This will then inspire us to try more things in life. So, my attitude toward money is to spend it on experiences as much as possible!'

So, before you buy your next possession, ask yourself 'Is there an experience I can spend my money on instead?' This could be a night out with friends, a concert or a sporting event, or maybe a weekend away or a vacation. Whatever we choose, it will make us rich with memories and life lessons.

PRONUNCIATION
/ɑː/, /ʌ/ and /æ/

A Look at the underlined letters in each word. What sound do they make? Write the words in the correct place.

after discover happiness last money much ~~past~~ travel up

/ɑː/	/ʌ/	/æ/
past		

B Listen and check. Then listen again and repeat the words.

C SPEAK Work in pairs. Practice saying the sentences. Listen to your partner and check their pronunciation.

1 Happiness usually lasts only for a short time.
2 Traveling helps us to discover our interests.
3 Is there an experience I can spend my money on instead?

GRAMMAR
Second conditional

A WORK IT OUT Look at the second conditional sentences from *How to buy happiness*. Write the missing words. Then choose the correct words to complete the rules.

1 If we ________ more of our money on experiences, we ________ something that can last a lifetime.
2 We ________ these things if we ________ money on experiences.
3 If we ________ anything different, we ________ lazy.

Second conditional

1 We use the second conditional to talk about *real / unreal or impossible* situations in the present or future.
2 Conditional sentences usually have two clauses: the *if*-clause and the main clause. To make a second conditional sentence, we use:
- *If + simple past / would* and *simple past / would + base form*.

3 We *can / can't* use other modal verbs (for example, *can, could, might, should*) instead of *would* in the main clause.

B Go to the **Grammar Hub** on **page 138**.

VOCABULARY
Prepositions in money phrases

A Complete the sentences with the correct prepositions. Then read *How to buy happiness* again and check your answers.

1 I'm always saving ________ so I can go away at least once or twice a year.
2 I spend a lot of my money ________ traveling.
3 My attitude ________ money is to spend it on experiences as much as possible.

B Complete the sentences with the prepositions in the box.

by for from in out out of to

1 I usually take money ________ the ATM once or twice a week. I take ________ 20 or 30 dollars each time.
2 For things under, say, five dollars, I generally pay ________ cash. I usually pay ________ things over five dollars ________ card.
3 I occasionally borrow money ________ my friends and I also sometimes lend it ________ them. But it's never usually more than 10 or 20 dollars.

C SPEAK Work in pairs. Change the sentences in Exercises A and B so they are true for you. Ask your partner questions to find out more information.

A: I'm always saving up so I can go to concerts and music festivals.
B: My attitude toward money is spend a little and save a little.

SPEAKING

A Work in groups. Think about different situations and make choices. Group A – go to the **Communication Hub** on **page 157**. Group B – go to the **Communication Hub** on **page 153**.

B Work in pairs. Ask your partner your new questions and make a note of their answers.

C Work in groups. Compare your findings. How similar or different are they? What are the most common or unusual answers?

Talk about attitudes toward money and about spending money

9.2 Getting and giving

Talk about philanthropy and charities

V verbs connected with money P /s/ and /z/ G essential adjective clauses

VOCABULARY

Verbs connected with money

A Complete the facts below with the correct form of the verbs in the box.

donate	~~earn~~	give away	lose
make	owe	raise	support

MONEY facts

1 In 1979, baseball player Nolan Ryan became the first professional athlete to *earn* $1 million a year.

2 Microsoft's Bill Gates, businessman Warren Buffet and Facebook's Mark Zuckerberg have all said they will ____________ 95 percent of their money to charity. A number of other philanthropists have also made the same promise.

3 Spanish actress Penélope Cruz ____________ many charities (organizations that give money and help to people who need it). In fact, she gave all of her salary from her first Hollywood movie to charity.

4 On September 16, 1992, Hungarian-born businessman George Soros ____________ $1 billion. This is the biggest single-day profit in history.

5 Eike Batista was once Brazil's richest person with $30 billion. However, unfortunately he ____________ it all. In fact, in 2014, he ____________ $30 billion to the banks.

6 The London Marathon ____________ more money for charity than any other sports event. In 2016, this was almost £60 million.

7 Philanthropy is about giving money to people who need it. Philanthropists across the world ____________ around $500 billion a year to charity and other organizations. The main givers include the United States, China, United Kingdom, Russia, Australia and Switzerland.

B Complete the questions with the correct verbs. Use the *Money facts* to help you.

1 Have you ever **d**____________ money to a charity? If so, what does the charity **r**____________ money for?

2 If you could give a lot of money to charity, which charities or organizations would you **s**____________? Why?

3 Do you agree that all people who **e**____________ a lot of money or who have **m**____________ a lot of money should **g**____________ some of it **a**____________ to charities? Why/Why not?

C **SPEAK** Ask and answer the questions in Exercise B.

PRONUNCIATION

/s/ and /z/

A **SPEAK** Work in pairs. Look at the words in the box. Do the letters in **bold** make a /s/ or a /z/ sound? Underline the /s/ sounds and (circle) the /z/ sounds.

across	also	baseball	Facebook	givers	promise
raises	salary	same	supports	Switzerland	visit

9.2 **B** Listen and check. Then listen again and repeat the words.

LISTENING

A Work in pairs. Discuss the questions.

1 What you know about the people in the pictures? What do you think they have in common?

2 Which other philanthropists do you know?

Andrew Carnegie

John D. Rockefeller

Bill Gates, Melinda Gates, Warren Buffet

Oprah Winfrey

9.3 **B LISTEN FOR KEY WORDS** Listen to Part 1 of a lecture about philanthropists. Complete the first column with the people in the pictures on page 84.

Names of philanthropists	Numbers	What the numbers mean
John D. Rockefeller	$540m, 1937	John D. Rockefeller gave away about $540 million. He died in 1937.
	$350m, 90 percent	
	half a billion dollars	
	tens of billions of dollars, 2010	

9.3 **C LISTEN FOR KEY INFORMATION** Listen again. What do the numbers mean? Write your answers in the third column in Exercise B.

9.4 **D LISTEN FOR GIST** Listen to Part 2 of the lecture. Which is the best explanation of the Giving Pledge? Choose a, b or c.

The Giving Pledge asks people to give at least 50 percent of their wealth to charity …

a when they die.

b before they die.

c in the next ten years.

9.4 **E LISTEN FOR MAIN IDEA** Listen again. Check (✓) the names of the philanthropists who have joined the Giving Pledge. Put an ✗ in the box for the ones who have not.

1 Mark Zuckerberg ☐

2 Richard Branson ☐

3 Ann Gloag ☐

4 Carlos Slim ☐

5 Sara Blakely ☐

6 Li Ka-shing ☐

7 Meg Whitman ☐

8 Azim Premji ☐

9.4 **F LISTEN FOR DETAIL** Listen again. Write the names of the philanthropists.

1 Azim Premji has set up a university.

2 ________________ has given away one quarter of his or her wealth.

3 ________________ would refuse to join the Giving Pledge if he or she was invited.

4 ________________ believes that there should be more women in powerful positions.

5 ________________ believes the best way to end poverty is through education and jobs.

6 ________________ is mostly concerned with education and health in his or her own country.

GRAMMAR

Essential adjective clauses

A WORK IT OUT Underline the adjective clauses in the sentences from the lecture. Then complete the rules with *who, which* or *that.*

1 And today, there are many celebrities who have given money to charity.

2 Let's now look at five modern-day philanthropists that you may or may not have heard of.

3 Instead she has her own charity that focuses on the environment and education.

4 He has also set up a university which promotes educational thinking.

Essential adjective clauses

1 An essential adjective clause gives information about and identifies a noun (a person or thing). It comes after the noun and starts with a relative pronoun.

We use [a] ________________ when the noun is a person.

We use [b] ________________ when the noun is a thing.

We can use [c] ________________ for a person or a thing.

2 We can leave out the relative pronoun when the word following the noun is a subject (*I, you, people, the charity*).

- *Let's now look at five modern-day philanthropists ~~that~~ you may or may not have heard of.*

B Go to the **Grammar Hub** on **page 138**.

C You are going to write some definitions. Student A – go to **page 152**. Student B – go to **page 154**.

D SPEAK Complete the sentences with the correct relative pronouns and your own ideas. Leave out the relative pronoun if possible. Then, work in groups and share your ideas.

1 A famous person ________ I admire is …

A famous person I admire is Michelle Obama.

2 A charity ________ does a lot of good is …

3 Someone ________ has influenced me a lot is …

4 A global issue ________ I think is important is …

5 A person ________ has positively influenced society is …

SPEAKING

A Work in groups and discuss the questions.

1 Which charities do you know?

2 What do you know about them?

3 Why do people give to charity?

4 Do you think it is better to give time or money? Why?

Talk about philanthropy and charities

9.3 Who needs money?

Discuss your skills and how they could help others

G gerunds V *make* and *do* expressions P /ʒ/ and /dʒ/ S using context to guess unknown words

READING

A Did you exchange anything with other people when you were younger, for example, toys, books or soccer cards? What about later in life?

B PREDICT Look at the title of the article and at the glossary. What do you think the article is about?

C SCAN Read *Bartering is back* and complete the notes.

1 Kyle McDonald started a website, and after one year exchanged a ________________ for a ________________.
2 Websites such as Craigslist.org: People can exchange ________________ with each other.
3 Antonio Puri exchanged a ________________ for ________________.
4 Time banks: For every ________________ you work, you earn ________________.
5 Basic rule: Ask a ________________ for what you are offering. Need to agree what is ________________.

BARTERING IS BACK

Back in 2005, Canadian Kyle MacDonald was making a living delivering pizzas, but he dreamed of owning his own house. So, one day he set up a website and offered a red paper clip in exchange for 'something bigger and better'. One year later, and after 14 exchanges, he had swapped the paper clip for a house! First, he swapped the paper clip for a pen. After that, the trades included a snowmobile, a van, an afternoon with rock star Alice Cooper and a role in a Hollywood movie. Finally, he swapped the movie role for a house.

But trading or bartering one item for another is nothing new. It was how people 'shopped' before the invention of money. And today, bartering is back. The number of people who use websites such as Craigslist.org, where you can exchange one item or service for another, is increasing. Some websites, such as babysitterexchange.com, provide just one service, while other sites cover a range of items and services. People have exchanged yoga lessons and language lessons for decorating, offered dog-walking and rides to the airport in exchange for theater and concert tickets, and some people will offer to do your shopping, cleaning or ironing in exchange for items they need. People also offer to trade professional services such as legal advice and accountancy. Antonio Puri, an artist based in Philadelphia in the US, was in his dentist's chair when he noticed there were no paintings on the walls. He told his dentist 'You need art. How about doing a trade?' Puri made him an offer and swapped a $1200 painting for his dental treatment.

Glossary

barter (v) to exchange goods or services for other goods or services instead of using money

Time banks are another recent development. You register at your local *Time Bank*'s website and list the services you have to offer or like doing. For each hour of work you provide to another member, you earn a certain number of 'time credits'. You can then spend your 'time credits' on another service on the site that someone else enjoys doing.

Doing your research and suggesting realistic prices are the basic rules with both barter sites and time banks. It's important not to try to make a profit. At the same time, if someone does you a favor, don't give them something below its value. If you do this, the system will break down and stop working. If you are bartering, it is important to agree with the other person what is a fair exchange. So, for example, you might agree that a driving lesson is equal to two haircuts or that fixing someone's washing machine is equal to a half-hour guitar lesson.

So, next time you need something, don't reach for your wallet or bankcard. Who needs money when you can trade?

D Do you know the meaning of the words and phrases in the box? Find them in the text and use the information in the box to work out or check their meaning.

break down dental favor making a living set up swapped treatment

Using context to guess unknown words

If there is a word or phrase in a text that you don't know or understand, try to guess the meaning from context. Read the sentence before and the sentence after to help you.

Think about the wider context, for example, the topic and message of the paragraph.

Identify the word's grammatical form and function to help give it meaning.

If you can't work out the meaning, keep reading. You may read something later which helps you to understand the word.

E Guess the meaning of the words in **bold** (1–3). Then match them with their definitions (a–c).

Bartering is about communities. It connects people. It [1]**fosters** human contact. For something [2]**tangible**, like a couch or a bike, it is easy to decide a price. But to work out a price for a service is more [3]**tricky**.

a difficult to do

b helps something to develop over a period of time

c something that you can touch

F SPEAK Work in groups. Do you think bartering items and services is a good idea? What are the pros and the cons?

GRAMMAR

Gerunds

A Look at the gerunds in **bold** in the phrases from *Bartering is back*. Then choose the correct words to complete the rules.

... but he dreamed of ***owning*** *his own house.*

... that someone else enjoys ***doing****.*

Doing *your research and suggesting realistic prices are the basic rules ...*

... the system will break down and stop ***working****.*

Gerunds

1 Gerunds are types of *nouns / verbs*.
2 We use gerunds *after / before* prepositions.
3 We can use gerunds directly after *some / all* verbs.
4 We can use gerunds as *subjects only / objects only / subjects or objects*.

B Go to the **Grammar Hub** on **page 138**.

C SPEAK Work in pairs. Discuss the questions.

- What are you looking forward to doing this weekend?
- What do you like/dislike spending your money on?
- Are you good at saving money? Why/Why not?

VOCABULARY

make and *do* expressions

A Complete the sentences from *Bartering is back* with the correct form of *make* or *do*. Then check your answers in the article.

1 Back in 2005, Canadian Kyle MacDonald was *making* **a living** delivering pizzas.

2 Some people will offer to ________ your **shopping, cleaning** or **ironing** in exchange for items they need.

3 Puri ________ him **an offer** and swapped a $1200 painting for his dental treatment.

4 ________ your **research** and suggesting realistic prices are the basic rules with both barter sites and time banks.

5 It's important not to try to ________ **a profit**. At the same time, if someone ________ you **a favor**, don't give them something below its value.

B Go to the **Vocabulary Hub** on **page 151**.

PRONUNCIATION

/ʒ/ and /dʒ/

9.5 **A** Listen to the sounds /ʒ/ and /dʒ/. They are very similar. Then listen and say whether you hear the sound /ʒ/ or /dʒ/ in each word.

1 exchange
2 language
3 decision
4 Asia
5 suggest

9.6 **B** Listen, check and repeat the words.

SPEAKING HUB

A You are going to swap skills and services with your classmates. Follow the instructions.

- Think about two or three skills and services that you can offer (music, language or driving lessons; help with cleaning, gardening; accounting advice).
- Decide on the price of your service. For example, a one-hour driving lesson = $30, or an hour's ironing = $10.

B SPEAK Walk around the class and find out what skills and services your classmates are offering and how much they cost.

C PLAN When you have spoken to at least five people, decide which three skills and services you would like.

D DISCUSS Try to exchange skills or services with your classmates. For example, you could offer a one-hour driving lesson in exchange for three hours of ironing.

Discuss your skills and how they could help others

Café Hub

9.4 Difficult customer

F– go shopping for clothes and ask for a refund

P– adding emphasis

COMPREHENSION

A SPEAK Work in pairs. Think of a time when you bought something in a clothing store (or any store) and then returned it. Discuss the questions.

1 What was the item?

2 What was the problem?

3 What happened in the end?

B ▶ Watch the video and answer the questions in Exercise A.

C How would you describe Milly? How would you describe the customer? Choose adjectives from the box or use your own ideas.

anxious dishonest friendly kind relaxed scared shy

FUNCTIONAL LANGUAGE

Go shopping for clothes and ask for a refund

A Work in pairs. Change the highlighted words for more polite words in the box.

Can you enter Here's your refund I'd like a refund I'd like to I'll take it I'm looking for kind of thing would you like

Sales clerk	Customer
Can I help you?	I want [1] ______ a gift for my nephew. He's 15.
What exactly [2] ______ are you looking for?	A blue sweater.
	How much is this sweater?
$15	Great. I want it [3] ______.
How do you want [4] ______ to pay, cash or card?	Card, please.
Put in [5] ______ your pin?	
Would you like me to gift wrap it for you?	Yes, please.
OK.	
Two weeks later	
	I want to [6] ______ return this, please. It doesn't fit my nephew. It's the wrong size.
	I want my money back [7] ______, please.
Do you have your receipt?	It's in here somewhere.
Don't worry about it. Take your money. [8] ______	

B ▶ Watch the video again and check your answers to Exercise A.

MILLY SAM NEENA ZAC GABY

USEFUL PHRASES

A Complete the useful phrases. Who says them, Milly (M) or the customer (C)?

about be must only over right

1 You're a yoga teacher, ________? M / C
2 The sweaters are ________ there. M / C
3 It says 'hand wash ________' on the label. M / C
4 I have to ________ quick. M / C
5 It ________ be here! M / C
6 Don't worry ________ it. M / C

B How do you say these useful phrases in your language?

PRONUNCIATION

Adding emphasis

9.7 **A** To emphasize a point, you can change the stressed word. Listen and underline the stressed word in each sentence.

1 a He is so special to me.
  b He is so special to me.
2 a My niece is really tall.
  b My niece is really tall.
3 a These shoes are very comfortable.
  b These shoes are very comfortable.
4 a You've been extremely helpful.
  b You've been extremely helpful.

9.7 **B** Listen again and repeat the sentences.

C SPEAK Work in pairs. Student A – say a sentence from Exercise A. Student B – point to the sentence. Take turns.

SPEAKING

A Work in pairs. Role-play buying a gift for your mother, father or best friend. Take turns being the customer and the sales clerk. Use the Functional language box to help you.

- Customer: Tell the sales clerk you want to buy a gift. Choose one of the items in the pictures. Ask for the price and for gift-wrapping.
- Sales clerk: Answer the customer's questions and sell the item.

B Role-play returning the gift you bought in Exercise A.

Customer: Tell the sales clerk you want to return something. Choose one of the following problems:

- it is the wrong size
- it is damaged
- the person you bought it for doesn't like it

Sales clerk: Listen to the customer and give them a refund.

Go shopping for clothes and ask for a refund

➤ Turn to page 166 to learn how to write a 'for sale' advertisement.

Unit 9 Review

VOCABULARY

A Complete the questions with the prepositions in the box.

by for from in ~~on~~ out of to up

1 What do you **spend** most money ___on___?
2 Do you ever **lend** money ________ your friends? Or **borrow** it ________ them?
3 How often do you **take money** ________ the ATM?
4 Do you **pay** ________ things mostly ________ **card**, cash or do you use your phone?
5 What kind of things do you pay for ________ **cash**?
6 What kind of things do you **save** ________ for?

B Complete the sentences with the correct form of *make* or *do*. Then finish the sentences so they are true for you.

1 I need to ___make___ **a decision** about *what to do on the weekend.*
2 I usually ____________ **mistakes** when ...
3 I ____________ **a mess** when I was ...
4 I usually ____________ **my homework** ...
5 I'd love to be able to ____________ **a living** as a ...
6 I ____________ my friend **a favor** when ...

GRAMMAR

A What would you do in these situations? Write sentences using the second conditional.

If I were you ...

Get answers to your dilemmas.

1 The other day, I found a $100 bill in the street. What would you do? Would you keep it or take it to the police?

If I found a $100 bill in the street, I'd take it to the police.

2 I bought a phone from an online company, but they sent me two by mistake. What would you do? Would you tell them or keep both phones?

____

3 I am the best at math in my class. Some of my classmates want to give me money to copy my homework. What would you do? Would you accept the money or tell the teacher?

____

4 I saw someone who looked homeless steal some food from the local store that I shop at regularly. Would you offer to pay for the food for them or tell the store manager?

____

B Complete the news report with the adjective clauses in the box.

that Matt has hidden / that is useful / who finds one / who has received a favor / who needs food / you don't know / you spend it on

Man hiding money in Cardiff

A man from Cardiff in South Wales has hidden twenty £10 notes around the city (£10 is roughly $15). Anyone [1] ____________ has to use the £10 to do something good for someone else. And this has to be someone [2] ____________. The man behind the idea, Matt Callanan, says that you could give it to a person [3] ____________ or, if it's raining when you find the note, you could buy something [4] ____________, like an umbrella, and give it to someone! Callanan believes that a person [5] ____________ will then do something good for someone else, and so on. So, if you find £10 [6] ____________, you could be helping more than just the person [7] ____________.

FUNCTIONAL LANGUAGE

Put the words in the correct order to complete the conversations.

Sales clerk: [1]I / help / you / can / ? *Can I help you?*
Customer: [2]for / I'm looking / for / a gift / my mother ____________. It's her birthday.
Sales clerk: [3]thing / kind / what / of / are you looking for / ? ____________
Customer: Well, maybe a scarf or some gloves ... I like these gloves. [4]much / they / are / how / ? ____________
Sales clerk: Let me see. They're $20.
Customer: Great. [5]them / I'll / take ____________
Sales clerk: [6]for / would you like me to / gift-wrap / you / them / ? ____________
Customer: Yes, please.
Sales clerk: [7]like / you / how / would / pay, / to / cash or card / ? ____________
Customer: Card, please.
Sales clerk: Thanks a lot!

10 SCIENCE AND TECHNOLOGY

Be less curious about people and more curious about ideas.

Marie Curie

Engineers of the future – two young Serbians work together to repair a robot.

OBJECTIVES

- describe and compare personal possessions
- describe types of technology
- discuss the requirements for a job
- make and receive formal and informal phone calls
- write a recommendation

Work with a partner. Discuss the questions.

1 Look at the picture. What were you curious about when you were a child?

2 What was your dream job when you were younger? Is it different now or the same?

3 What would you like to learn more about?

10.1 Devices

Describe and compare personal possessions

V electronic devices G comparatives and superlatives P /ɪst/ and superlative adjectives

VOCABULARY

Electronic devices

A SPEAK Work in pairs. Make a list of words to name or describe electronic devices. You have one minute.

A: Can you think of anything?
B: OK, a tablet and a cell phone.

B Go to the **Vocabulary Hub** on **page 151**.

LISTENING

10.1 **A LISTEN FOR MAIN IDEA** Listen to four people talking about devices. What question are they answering?

a Which device do you use every day?
b What is the most useful device you own?
c What device do you most regret buying?

Glossary

package (n) an object or set of objects wrapped in a box or in paper and sent or given to someone
regret (v) to feel sorry or sad about something that has happened or about something you have said or done
reliable (adj) a reliable vehicle, piece of equipment or system always works well

10.1 **B LISTEN FOR DETAIL** Listen again and match the speakers (1–4) to the devices (a–h) they are describing. There are four devices you do not need.

a drone	___	e power bank	___
b e-reader	___	f tablet	___
c fitness tracker	___	g USB drive	___
d GPS	___	h laptop	___

C SPEAK Work in groups. Discuss the questions.

1 Which of the devices in the list in Exercise B do you own or would you like to own?
2 Which do you think is most useful and why?

GRAMMAR

Comparatives and superlatives

A Underline the comparative and superlative adjectives and adverbs in the sentences from the radio show.

1 My bag is a lot lighter than it used to be.
2 It's the best gadget I've ever bought.
3 I bought the cheapest one.
4 You can check words so much more quickly than in a paper dictionary.
5 This is definitely the most useful piece of technology I own.
6 It was more expensive than an old-fashioned paper map.
7 We spend a lot of time arguing about which turns the most quickly.

B WORK IT OUT Write the words you underlined in Exercise A in the correct place.

Comparatives and superlatives				
	Comparative	Example	Superlative	Example
one syllable adj	adjective + *-er* (+ *than*)	cheaper 1 ______	*the* + adjective + *-est*	the 4 ______ the lightest
adj with two + syllables	*more* + adjective (+ *than*)	more useful 2 ______	*the most* + adjective	the 5 ______ the most expensive
adj with two + syllables ending in *-y*	we cut the *-y* and add *-ier*	heavier easier	we cut the *-y* and add *-iest*	the heaviest the easiest
irregular adj	adjective (+ *than*)	better worse	*the* + adjective	the 6 ______ the worst
regular adv	*more* + adverb	more slowly 3 ______	*the most* + adverb	the most slowly 7 ______

C Look at the sentences and answer the questions.

1. 'My bag is a lot lighter than it used to be.'
   Which two words make the comparative adjective *lighter* stronger?
2. 'You can check words so much more quickly.'
   Which two words make the comparative adverb *quickly* stronger?
3. 'Mine is a little heavier than some of the others because it has a camera.'
   Which two words make the comparative adjective *heavy* weaker?

D Go to the **Grammar Hub** on **page 140**.

PRONUNCIATION

/ɪst/ and superlative adjectives

A Listen and repeat. (10.2)

/ɪst/ heaviest, strongest, fastest

B Listen and underline the sound /ɪst/ in the sentences. Then listen and repeat. (10.3)

1. The cheapest devices aren't the best.
2. The lightest laptop is better than the rest.
3. It's the fastest phone in our product test.

SPEAKING

A Work in groups. Show and describe your cell phone to the rest of the group. Use the questions to help you.

- When did you buy your phone? How old is it? How much was it? (If you don't mind saying!)
- How is it different from any other phones you have owned?
- What do you like about it?
- What don't you like about it?

B Use comparatives to compare your phones.

A: Jenny's phone is a little heavier than Marvin's.
B: Carly's phone was a lot more expensive than Mohammed's.

C Talk to the other groups in the class. Use superlatives to tell them about your group's phones.

A: Lucia's phone is the newest.
B: Fa's phone is the most interesting.

Describe and compare personal possessions

10.2 It's only good when it works

Describe types of technology

V using devices and the internet **G** more comparative structures **P** /əz/ in comparative structures

READING

A Complete the definitions (1–6) with the words in the box.

> advertise (v) annoying (adj) mix (n)
> rely on (phr verb) security (n) symbol (n)

1 ________________ = making you feel slightly angry

2 ________________ = to trust someone or something to do a job or task for you

3 ________________ = a combination of different types of people who form a group, for example: *There was a good ________________ of people at the party.*

4 ________________ = to try to persuade people to buy a product or service by announcing it on television, on the internet, or in newspapers

5 ________________ = a picture or shape used to represent something: &*+@

6 ________________ = safety from attack, harm or damage

B Read the posts on the online forum *Is it just me?* Do you agree or disagree with the users' opinions?

	Agree	Disagree	Not sure
User 1			
User 2			
User 3			
User 4			

C Read again. Match the sentences to the users.

Which user …

1 says that other people might not have the same problem as they do? ____User 2____

2 regularly forgets important personal information? ________

3 feels that technology is often unreliable? ________

4 thinks that people waste money on technology? ________

5 feels that it is important to protect your money online? ________

6 gets annoyed when trying to communicate online? ________

7 finds it hard to concentrate when using the internet? ________

D SPEAK Work in groups. What would you post on the site? Are the other students in your group annoyed by the same thing?

Is it just me? Tell the internet what annoys you and find out who agrees and who doesn't!

You say: People say technology and the internet have made life better. Sure, there are benefits, but there are also lots of annoying things. Does anyone agree?

The internet says:

(User 1) Dancingmaggie
I agree! The worst thing is how often things go wrong. Many times, when I try to make a video call, for example, the screen freezes. Video calls seem to fail as often as they work! Other things, too – you connect a drive and your computer crashes. You install a new app and everything stops working. Technology is only good when it works.

(User 2) RossM8
We rely on the internet, but we also waste time because of it. I'm usually searching for something online, but then I notice something interesting, click on a link and ten minutes later I'm reading about a cat that looks like Beyoncé or a man that married himself! Sometimes I forget what I was searching for in the first place. Some people are probably not as easily distracted as me.

(User 3) Aoneandatwo
The internet is amazing, and technology, too, in general. My problem is with the technology companies. They are always advertising new devices, so many people feel they have to own the latest model. If you ask me, the old models are usually just as good as the new ones, but, you know, 'your device is not as new as my device, so you're just not cool'. It annoys me that people stop using perfectly good phones and laptops.

(User 4) ABC123
I know online security is important, especially when it comes to your bank details, but trying to remember passwords is not as easy as it sounds. They usually have to be a mix of symbols, numbers and letters, and of course, you shouldn't write them down or use the same password on different websites. My memory is not reliable and I forget passwords as often as I remember them. I have blocked my accounts so many times!

Glossary

benefit (n) an advantage you get from a situation
distracted (adj) not able to concentrate on something
waste time (phrase) to spend time doing things that aren't important

VOCABULARY
Using devices and the internet

A **Read *Is it just me?* again. Complete the collocations with verbs from the posts.**

1 ___make___ **a video call** – use the internet to talk to and see someone else

2 ________ **your account** – if a bank or a social media provider does this, they stop your account from working because you have done something wrong

3 ________ **your password** – keep in your mind the secret word you chose to keep your email, bank or social media account safe

4 ________ **a drive** – add a small device with extra memory to your computer

5 ________ **on a link** – press the button on your mouse to connect quickly to a website

6 **your computer** ________ – your computer stops working; often you see a blue screen and a warning

7 **the screen** ________ – there's a problem that means the screen on your device won't change

8 ________ **an app** – add a new application to your phone or tablet

B **SPEAK** **Work in groups. Discuss the questions.**

1 What was the last really good app you installed on a device? Why do you like it?

2 How do you remember passwords? Have you ever blocked an account by entering the wrong password?

GRAMMAR
More comparative structures

A **WORK IT OUT** **Look at the sentences from *Is it just me?* and choose the correct words to complete the rules.**

If you ask me, the old models are usually ***just as good as*** *the new ones.*

Video calls seem to fail ***as often as*** *they work!*

Some people are probably ***not as easily distracted as*** *me.*

Comparative structures

1 To say that two things or people are ***the same*** / ***different*** in some way, we use (*just*) *as* + adjective/adverb + *as*.

2 To say that two things or people are ***the same*** / ***different*** in some way, we use *not as* + adjective/adverb + *as*.

B **Match the sentences (1–4) with the correct meanings (a–d).**

1 I don't get as annoyed with technology as my boyfriend does.

2 I get just as annoyed with technology as my boyfriend does.

3 I don't forget my passwords as often as my girlfriend does.

4 I forget my passwords just as often as my girlfriend does.

a We get equally annoyed with technology.

b He gets more annoyed with technology than me.

c She forgets her passwords more often than me.

d There is no difference in how often we forget our passwords.

C Go to the **Grammar Hub** on **page 140**.

PRONUNCIATION
/əz/ in comparative structures

10.4 **A** **Listen to the sentences. How does each speaker pronounce *as*?**

1 I don't think online banking is as secure as personal banking.

2 Sending an email is not as thoughtful as making a phone call.

10.4 **B** **Listen again and repeat the conversation.**

C **SPEAK** **Work in pairs. Make similar conversations about these topics. Use *as* … *as* in its weak form.**

1 going to the movie theater vs. watching movies online

2 paying in cash vs. paying by credit or debit card

3 shopping online vs. shopping in town

SPEAKING

Work in pairs. You are going to talk about different types of technology. Student A – go to the **Communication Hub** on **page 154**. Student B – go to the **Communication Hub** on **page 155**.

Describe types of technology

10.3 The best view in the universe

Discuss the requirements for a job

G *need to* **V** collocations: science and research **P** /ʊ/ and /uː/ **S** facts and opinions

READING

A Work in pairs. Describe the picture. Try to use all the words in the box.

astronaut Earth International Space Station (ISS) space spacesuit spacewalk view

B SPEAK Work in groups. Discuss the questions.

1 What do you know about the history of human space travel?

2 What do you think would be the best and worst parts about visiting the ISS?

C READ FOR GIST Read the glossary and quickly read the article. Then choose the best subtitle.

1 A bridge to Mars

2 The laboratory in the stars

3 Just another day in space

INTERNATIONAL SPACE STATION

There are more than seven billion human beings living on Earth, and then there are a very special group of people who live somewhere completely different. Four hundred kilometers above us and circling the planet at 7.7 km per second, there are between six and ten astronauts who call the International Space Station (ISS) home.

Since the first crew members arrived in November 2000, records confirm that over 200 people from 18 countries have visited the ISS. Many only need to stay for a short time, but others need to spend several months there. So, what is the average zero-gravity day like on the ISS?

Living in space may seem exciting, but in fact, the daily routine is fairly repetitive. The crew needs to follow a detailed schedule. Days begin each morning at 6 am when, instead of an alarm clock, a different song chosen by the crew's families back on Earth is played to wake them up. As on Earth, the first stop is the bathroom. Keeping clean is difficult because without gravity everything floats, including water. Residents of the ISS report that washing your hair is particularly difficult in space.

After a challenging start comes breakfast. Almost all the food on the ISS is either dried or canned. Most people would agree that the daily menu is not one of the highlights of life in space. Next, it's time to exercise. Research has shown that muscles and bones quickly become weak in space, so astronauts need to work out for at least two hours each day, using special zero-gravity gym equipment.

The ISS is a large floating laboratory and astronauts spend much of the day doing research. Crew members work with scientists on Earth to do experiments and collect data, usually about the effects of space travel on the mind and body. It is thought that one day humans will travel to Mars, so astronauts test new technologies and look for solutions to the challenges of spending large amounts of time in space.

ISS crews have made many important discoveries. For example, they have proved that it is possible to grow a range of different vegetables to provide food in space. They have also found new ways to develop drugs to help treat diseases.

Crews also need to repair equipment and solve any problems with the station itself. Sometimes this means going outside. Because of the obvious risks, the astronauts spend weeks making preparations. Incredibly, it takes four hours just to put on a spacesuit before going out for a 'spacewalk'.

When they don't need to do any other tasks, the astronauts usually use their free time to contact relatives, read or watch movies. However, there is no doubt that the most popular activity is simply looking out of the window at what is probably the best view in the universe.

Glossary

crew (n) the people who work on a ship, aircraft, or space station

float (v) to move slowly through air

gravity (n) the force that makes objects fall to the ground

laboratory (n) a building or large room where people do scientific research

D READ FOR DETAIL Read again. Are the sentences fact (F) or opinion (O)? Use the information in the box to help you decide.

Facts and opinions

With so much written information online these days, it is important to question what you read. To do this, you need to recognize the difference between facts and opinions.
Facts are clearly true and usually presented with support.
Opinions are things that people believe, but may not be true.

Language regularly used to present facts

report, confirm, show, prove, find

There is no doubt that …

Language often used to present opinions

seem, think, believe, feel, hope

Most people would agree that …

1. There have been more than 200 visitors to the ISS. *F / O*
2. Life in space is exciting. *F / O*
3. It is hard to wash your hair when there is no gravity. *F / O*
4. The food on the ISS is not particularly enjoyable. *F / O*
5. The human body quickly loses strength in space. *F / O*
6. People will travel to Mars in the future. *F / O*
7. Plants can grow successfully in space. *F / O*
8. Research on the ISS is helping people with serious illnesses. *F / O*
9. The astronauts' favorite free time activity is looking down at Earth. *F / O*
10. There is no better view than the one from the ISS. *F / O*

E SPEAK Work in groups. Discuss the questions.

1. Would you visit the ISS if you had the chance? Why/Why not?
2. What would you miss most from Earth if you lived on the ISS for several months?

GRAMMAR

need to

A Look at the sentences from *International Space Station*. Choose the correct words to complete the rules.

The crew needs to follow a detailed schedule.

Crews also need to repair equipment and solve any problems with the station itself.

When they don't need to do any other tasks, the astronauts usually use their free time to contact relatives, read or watch movies.

need to

1. We use *need* to say something is ***possible / necessary***.
2. When *need* is followed by a verb, we use ***-ing / to*** + *base form*.
3. We ***add / don't add*** *-s* to *need* when the subject is *he, she* or *it*.
4. We use the auxiliary ***do / have*** with negative and question forms of *need*.

B Go to the **Grammar Hub** on **page 140**.

VOCABULARY

Collocations: science and research

A Choose the correct verbs to complete the collocations in **bold** in the ISS schedule memo. Use *International Space Station* to help you.

ISS schedule memo 1174639 – Schedule number 4077

Good evening from Earth and the Control Center.
As always, please [1]***do / follow*** tomorrow's **schedule** carefully.
9:00 am – IMPORTANT [2]***repair / solve*** broken gym **equipment**. This must be fixed today. Exercise program must return to normal.
10:00 am – Live link with University of Beijing – Give a presentation to students on Chinese astronauts who have [3]***made / found*** important **discoveries** on the ISS.
11:00 am – Continue [4]***testing / making* new technologies** for long-distance communication.
1:00 pm – Meeting to [5]***look for / collect* solutions** to the recent computer problems.
2:00 pm – Continue [6]***making / doing* research** into growing fruit in space. [7]***Do / Test* experiments**, numbers 146 to 149 and [8]***collect / follow*** more **data** on water levels.
5:00 pm – [9]***Make / Do*** more **preparations** for the next spacewalk. Try to [10]***test / solve*** the **problems** with spacesuit number 4.

B SPEAK Work in pairs. Go to the **Communication Hub** on **page 155** and complete the survey. Then compare your results. Which of you would be best at working in space?

PRONUNCIATION

/ʊ/ and /uː/

10.5 **A** Listen to the word pairs. How is the pronunciation of the vowel sounds different?

1 foot food 2 woman routine

10.5 **B** Listen again and repeat the words.

10.6 **C** Write the words in the correct place in the table. Listen and check.

~~crew~~ group look move room would

/ʊ/	/uː/
	crew

10.6 **D** Listen again and repeat the words.

SPEAKING HUB

PREPARE You are going to talk about working in space. Go to the **Communication Hub** on **page 156** and follow the instructions.

Discuss the requirements for a job

10.4 Locked out

F – make and receive formal and informal phone calls
P – word stress and intonation

COMPREHENSION

A Cover the video screen. Listen to the video and put the events (a–j) in the correct order (1–10).

- **a** The front door closes and locks shut. ___
- **b** Gaby phones Neena's work. ___
- **c** The signal is bad. ___
- **d** Gaby is put on hold. ___
- **e** Gaby phones Zac's mobile. ___
- **f** Gaby leaves a voice message for Neena. ___
- **g** It starts raining. ___
- **h** Neena's phone is switched off. ___
- **i** Gaby phones Neena's mobile. ___
- **j** Gaby opens the front door to take the rubbish out. ___

Glossary

phones **(v) (British)** = calls **(v) (American)**
mobile **(n) (British)** = cell phone **(n) (American)**
rubbish **(n) (British)** = trash **(n) (American)**

B **SPEAK** Work in pairs. Predict the answers to the questions. Then watch the video and check your answers.

1. Where is Gaby?
2. How does Gaby get locked out?
3. Where is Zac?
4. Where is Neena?
5. What is the music we hear three times?
6. How does the video end?

MILLY

SAM

NEENA

ZAC

GABY

FUNCTIONAL LANGUAGE

Make and receive formal and informal phone calls

A Write the words in the correct order to make useful phrases. Then write each phrase in the correct place.

1 up / breaking / You're / .

You're breaking up.

2 you / hear / can't / I / .

3 me / Can / you / hear / ?

4 cut / out / You / again / .

5 that / What / was / ?

6 very / The / isn't / signal / good / .

Describe a phone problem	Ask for clarification
You're breaking up.	

B Complete the receptionist's replies with two of the words in the box.

just over soon through

Receptionist: Good morning. You're [1] ______ to Jobs, Jobs, Jobs and Jobs. How can I help?

Gaby: Hello, is it possible to speak to Neena Patel?

Receptionist: Yes, of course. I'll [2] ______ try to put you [3] ______. I'm afraid the line is busy. Would you like to hold?

Gaby: Yes, please.

[MUSIC ON HOLD]

Receptionist: Thank you for calling. [4] ______ putting you [5] ______.

C SPEAK Work in pairs. Practice the conversation in Exercise B with your own ideas.

PRONUNCIATION

Word stress and intonation

10.7 **A** Listen and repeat Amelia's voicemail greeting. Copy the word stress and intonation.

Amelia: Hi, this is Amelia Jones. I can't take your call at the moment. Please leave a message after the beep.

B SPEAK Work in pairs. You are going to record your own voicemail greeting in English.

- Practice your voicemail greeting.
- Record your voicemail greeting on your phone.
- Call your partner and listen to his/her greeting.
- Leave a message for your partner.

SPEAKING

Work in groups. Choose a problem from the box or use your own ideas. Then role-play calling two friends to ask for help. Use the Functional Language box to help you.

You've locked yourself out. You've lost your car keys. You've lost your house keys. You've missed the last bus home. You've forgotten your passport.

Student A: Call a friend (Student B). The signal is bad.

Student B: Answer Student A. The signal is bad.

Student A: Call another friend at Jones & Jones. You can't get through. You speak to Student C (the receptionist).

Student C: You are the receptionist at Jones & Jones. Answer Student A. The line is busy.

Student A: Answer Student C (the receptionist).

Make and receive formal and informal phone calls

➤ Turn to page 167 to learn how to write a recommendation.

Unit 10 Review

VOCABULARY

A Choose the correct words to complete the sentences.

1. My new ***drone*** / ***fitness tracker*** has arrived. Should we go to the park and fly it?
2. I'm so bad at directions – this ***USB drive*** / ***GPS*** is really useful!
3. I think a ***fitness tracker*** / ***tablet*** would make me exercise more.
4. I always take my ***e-reader*** / ***power bank*** on vacation with me. I love books.
5. My son wants a ***drone*** / ***tablet*** so he can watch his favorite TV shows.
6. A ***GPS*** / ***USB drive*** is very useful when I go on business trips. I can take my work everywhere!
7. I don't know what I would do without my ***power bank*** / ***e-reader*** – my phone battery is always running out.

B Complete the information with the verbs in the box. You need to use one of the verbs twice.

collect do look make test

Higgerfield University
SCIENCE DEPARTMENT

Why study science at Higgerfield?

We asked three first-year students why they chose science subjects.

Sergei: I want to 1 __________ data and 2 __________ for solutions to the problem of climate change.

Masha: I want to 3 __________ research on space travel and 4 __________ new technologies to help get us to other planets.

Melissa: I want to 5 __________ discoveries and 6 __________ experiments that will help save people's lives.

To find out more about studying Science at Higgerfield, join us at one of our open houses.

GRAMMAR

A Complete the article with comparative and superlative forms of the missing adjectives and adverbs.

Hi-fi & Wi-fi Magazine **Awards**

Cell phones

1st Chitchat 8
2nd Speakup 4 3rd Talkabout 2

Overall

The Talkabout 2 is a good phone, but the Speakup 4 is 1 ___better___. And this year, the Chitchat 8 is 2 ___the best___.

Is it reliable?

The Talkabout 2 is fairly reliable, but the Speakup 4 is 3 __________. Again, the Chitchat 8 is 4 __________.

Is it easy to use?

The Talkabout 2 is fairly easy to use, but the Speakup 4 is definitely 5 __________ to use. However, the Chitchat 8 is 6 __________ to use.

Does it charge quickly?

The Talkabout 2 charges quickly, but the Speakup 4 charges 7 __________. Again, the Chitchat 8 wins this year because it charges 8 __________.

B Add *as* … *as* to complete each sentence.

1. I get just *as* annoyed with pop-up ads *as* anybody else.
2. That messaging service is not private this one.
3. My wife doesn't forget passwords easily I do.
4. My dad's phone is just old-fashioned my mom's.
5. I don't learn how to use new devices quickly I used to when I was young.
6. This game is just good the other soccer games on the market.

FUNCTIONAL LANGUAGE

Complete the words in the phone conversation. The first letter of each word has been given to help you.

Derek: Hello, this is Derek Lebarge. 1Sorry, I can't **t**______ your call at the **m**______. 2Please leave a **m**______ after the **b**______.

Murray: Derek? Derek? It's Murray. 3Sorry, the **s**______ isn't very **g**______. 4What was **t**______? 5You're **b**______ up. Hello?

11 NATURAL WORLD

Everybody needs beauty as well as bread, places to play in where nature may heal and give strength to body and soul alike.

John Muir

An urban fox begins his nightly hunt for food, Twickenham, United Kingdom.

OBJECTIVES

- talk about natural wonders
- read and talk about wildlife photography
- talk about the causes and effects of plastic pollution
- tell a story
- write an email giving suggestions and advice

Work with a partner. Discuss the questions.

1 Do you find the city or the country more relaxing? Why?
2 Read the quote. Do you agree with Muir?
3 Look at the picture. What wildlife is there in your city?

11.1 Natural wonders

Talk about natural wonders

V natural features **P** /e/ and /iː/ **G** the passive voice (simple present and simple past)

VOCABULARY
Natural features

A Label the pictures (1–7) with the words in the box.

canyon harbor lights mountain reef volcano waterfall

B Go to the **Vocabulary Hub** on **page 151**.

C **SPEAK** Work in pairs. Name other examples of the natural features in Exercise A and in the Vocabulary Hub.

A: Well, there's Mount Fuji and The Great Barrier Reef. But I can't think of a famous canyon.

B: What about The Grand Canyon in Arizona?

PRONUNCIATION
/e/ and /iː/

11.1 **A** Listen to the vowel sounds /e/ and /iː/. What is the vowel sound in each word in the box? Write the words in the correct place.

be get leave met reef rest see ten

/e/	/iː/

11.2 **B** Listen and check your answers. Then listen again and repeat the words.

LISTENING

A The places in the pictures above have recently been named as the *Seven Natural Wonders of the World*. Match the names (a–g) with the pictures (1–7). What do you know about them?

a Mount Everest *4*
b Great Barrier Reef ___
c Grand Canyon ___
d Northern lights (aurora borealis) ___
e Rio de Janeiro harbor ___
f Victoria Falls ___
g Paricutin volcano ___

11.3 **B** **LISTEN FOR KEY WORDS** Listen to a radio travel show about the *Seven Natural Wonders of the World*. In which order did the travel writer visit the places?

1 *the Great Barrier Reef*
2 ___
3 ___
4 ___
5 ___
6 ___
7 ___

Glossary

coral (n) a very small ocean creature that lives in large groups that look like plants, in places where the water is warm
crater (n) the round hole at the top of a volcano
form (v) to make something exist
promote (v) to support something
unique (adj) not the same as anything else

.3 **C LISTEN FOR DETAIL** Listen to the radio show again and answer the questions.

1 What is the goal of the Seven Natural Wonders organization?

2 What three main factors were used to choose the Seven Natural Wonders?

3 Why did Mike decide to visit the Seven Natural Wonders?

4 Which of the seven natural wonders …

a is visible only at certain times of the year? ____________

b was formed the most recently? ____________

c is located in two countries? ____________

d is famous for its different colors? ____________

e is the highest? ____________

f is the most visited? ____________

D SPEAK Work in pairs. Which of the Seven Natural Wonders you would most like to visit and why?

GRAMMAR

The passive voice (simple present and simple past)

A WORK IT OUT Look at the sentences from the radio show about the seven natural wonders. Then complete the rules using the words in the box.

1 The decision **was based** on three main things.

2 The places **were chosen** according to how unique the place is …

3 It's **made** of over 400 different kinds of coral.

4 It **was** only **formed** in 1943.

5 The canyon **was created** by the Colorado River.

6 It's **visited** by about four-and-a-half million people a year.

be *by* do not say past participle

The passive voice (simple present and simple past)

1 We make the passive voice with the auxiliary verb ____________ + the ____________ of the main verb.

2 We most commonly use the passive voice when we ____________ who or what performs or causes the action. This is usually because the person or thing is not known, not important or obvious.

3 We sometimes use the passive voice with an agent (the person or thing that performs or causes the action). We use ____________ to introduce the agent.

B Go to the **Grammar Hub** on **page 142**.

C SPEAK Work in pairs. Test your general knowledge! Make sentences about these natural wonders using a word from each column. Discuss what you know about each place.

Jeju Island is located off the coast of South Korea.

1 Jeju Island	form	around 30 million people a year
2 The White Cliffs of Dover	locate	40–50 million years ago
3 The Himalayas	visit	as Ayers Rock
4 The Niagara Falls	make	off the coast of South Korea
5 Uluru in Australia	discover	of chalk and similar minerals
6 The Galapagos Islands	also/know	the Bishop of Panama in 1535

SPEAKING

11.4 **A** Listen to a presentation about the Gullfoss Waterfall in Iceland and answer the questions.

- Where is it located?
- When was it formed or created?
- What is it surrounded by?
- How is it reached?
- Who and how many people visit it?
- Why are people attracted to it?

B Work in pairs. Choose a natural wonder in your country or continent to give a presentation about. Use the questions in Exercise A to help you.

C Give your presentation to the class.

Talk about natural wonders

11.2 Animal images

Read and talk about wildlife photography

V animals G adjective + infinitive P *to* /tə/

VOCABULARY

Animals

A **SPEAK** Work in pairs. Make a list of animals. You have one minute.

B Go to the **Vocabulary Hub** on **page 151**.

C **SPEAK** Work in pairs. Write down your three favorite animals. Tell your partner what you wrote. Explain your choices.

D **SPEAK** Work in pairs. Go to the **Communication Hub** on **page 157** to see what your answers to Exercise C mean. Do you agree or disagree?

My first animal is a dolphin. I think I'm like a dolphin because it's smart, moves quickly, is very sociable and always in groups.

READING

A Match the words and phrases (1–5) with the definitions (a–e).

1 habitat
2 wildlife
3 make eye contact
4 facial expression
5 life cycle

a the series of changes that happen to an animal or plant during its life
b the look on someone's face that shows what their thoughts or feelings are
c animals, birds and plants that live in natural conditions
d the type of place that a particular animal usually lives in or a particular plant usually grows in
e situation in which two people look at each other's eyes

Behind the lens: Anthony Remy, wildlife photographer

You may not know Anthony Remy's name but you will almost certainly have seen one of his photos. He spoke to us about his 30-year career close-up with wildlife.

Where did your interest in wildlife photography come from?
I grew up in Canada with nature right on my doorstep. I just had to step outside and I could see all manner of mammals, reptiles, birds and amphibians. One day my older cousin, Julian, took me to see a grizzly fishing with her cub … from a safe distance, of course. Julian passed me his camera so that I could zoom in. It was great to watch them so closely, I never wanted to forget it. I pressed the shutter and that's when I decided what I wanted to do for the rest of my life.

Is it easy to find work? I imagine it's fairly difficult.
It is at first when no one knows your name and you don't have any contacts at magazines. Over time your reputation grows. You ask local stores to put up framed photos or sell some of your cards … you know, anything to make a living!

I guess you're asked this a lot but what's your favorite animal?
Well … I love dogs … I have four at home. In terms of photography though orangutans without a doubt. Their name literally means 'person of the forest' in Malay and you can see why. It's not just their body language and facial expressions that are so like ours, but also their social interactions. Over my career I've also taken a lot of photos of spiders, which you may not understand! But most people come to realize, like me, that up close they are unexpectedly fascinating.

And which animal don't you enjoy taking photos of?
Well some animals are so 'seen' there are hundreds of photographs of them … you know, elephants, eagles, tigers. It isn't easy to take something amazing that everyone would be interested in. Certain types of monkeys are challenging too as they don't want to make eye contact with people. Then there are lemurs which will look you in the eye, in fact they'll climb all over you, but they live deep in the Madagascan rainforest. Habitats like that are hard to get to, especially carrying camera equipment.

So any top tips for future wildlife photographers out there?
Don't rush out and spend a fortune on a new camera. It really isn't the most important thing. An interest in animals is obvious but essential. Unless you are incredibly lucky, be prepared for uncomfortable hours or even weeks waiting for the perfect shot. Researching habitats and life cycles can certainly help this. If you watch an animal for long enough, you can predict its behavior. For example, I always know when a grizzly will swipe for the salmon and so I am there ready to capture the moment.

Glossary

body language (n) the movements or positions of your body that show others what you are thinking or feeling
close-up (n) a picture of someone or something taken from a position very near them
make a living (phrase) to earn money from a job

B SCAN Read *Behind the lens* and answer the questions.

Which animal(s) …

1 did Anthony Remy first take pictures of?
2 is/are his favorite to photograph?
3 is/are difficult to get a good picture of?
4 does he think has/have predictable behavior?

C READ FOR DETAIL Choose the correct answers, a, b or c.

1 Anthony Remy started taking pictures of bears …
  a to show his cousin what he had seen.
  b to help him remember them.
  c to capture the beauty of where he is from.
2 He thinks orangutans are …
  a shy.
  b dangerous.
  c similar to humans.
3 He thinks his pictures of spiders usually …
  a surprise people.
  b frighten people.
  c disappoint people.
4 He thinks some animals, such as elephants …
  a are not interesting to photograph.
  b don't do anything surprising.
  c have been photographed too much.
5 He says monkeys …
  a don't like to look at humans.
  b try to hide from humans.
  c behave like humans.
6 In Anthony's opinion, it is <u>not</u> necessary …
  a to know about the animals you are photographing.
  b to spend time watching and have a lot of patience.
  c to have a lot of expensive camera equipment.

D SPEAK Work in pairs. Discuss the skills and characteristics you need to be a wildlife photographer.

GRAMMAR

Adjective + infinitive

A WORK IT OUT Look at the sentences from *Behind the lens*. Add the missing adjective + infinitive. Then complete the rule.

1 It was ______________________ them so closely …
2 It isn't ______________________ something amazing that everyone would be interested in.
3 Habitats like that are ______________________ to, especially carrying camera equipment.

Adjective + infinitive

When a verb comes after an adjective, we use the ______________ form of the verb.

B Go to the **Grammar Hub** on **page 142**.

C SPEAK Go to the **Communication Hub** on **page 153** and follow the instructions.

PRONUNCIATION

to /tə/

11.5 **A** Listen to the weak pronunciation of *to* /tə/ in the sentences.

1 It's easy to take a good picture.
2 It's important to be patient.
3 Are you ready to leave?

11.5 **B** Listen again and repeat the sentences.

SPEAKING

A Read the tips about what makes a good animal picture. Do you agree? Add a tip of your own.

✓ It's important to show the animal in its natural habitat.
✓ It's important to be able to see the animal's face and eyes. It gives an idea of how the animal is feeling or what it's thinking.
✓ It's good to photograph the animal doing something. It's even better to catch it doing something unusual or maybe something funny.
✓ A good animal picture shows detail and color that you don't normally see.
✓ A good picture is one where you see something new. You learn something about the animal.

B Look at the pictures (a–f) above and answer the questions.

- Which of the features in the tips above does each picture have?
- Choose the best animal picture in your opinion.
- Put the others in order of second favorite, third favorite.

C Work in groups. Compare your ideas. In your group, decide on the best animal picture.

Read and talk about wildlife photography

11.3 Throw-away world

Talk about the causes and effects of plastic pollution

P /l/ pronounced and silent **G** *even* **V** *somewhere, nowhere, everywhere, anywhere*
S looking for ways of expressing cause and effect

READING

A Work in pairs. Discuss the questions.

1 Do you recycle? What kind of things do you recycle? Is it easy to recycle things where you live? What happens to things you throw away that are not recycled?

2 Look at the picture. What can you see on the beach? How do you think it got there?

B READ FOR GIST Read *The nightmare of Plastic Island* and decide which is the best summary.

a Plastic is usually blown into the ocean and is carried around the world by ocean currents. The pictures of Henderson Island show how we should clean the beaches before the plastic enters the ocean.

b Plastic is carried to certain parts of the world by ocean currents, but it does not reach other parts of the world. The pictures of Henderson Island suggest that the situation is worse than it actually is.

c Plastic is carried around the world by ocean currents and reaches the most remote beaches and other places. The pictures of Henderson Island show how serious the problem is.

C READ FOR DETAIL Answer the questions. Use the information in the box to help you. Then read again and check your answers.

Looking for ways of expressing cause and effect

Look for verbs, linking words and nouns that express cause and effect:

- **verbs:** *This* ***means*** *there are … This has* ***led*** *to …*
- **linking words:** *This is* ***because*** *…* ***Because of*** *this, …* ***If*** *we do this, …*
- **nouns:** *And as* ***a result****, …*

1 Why is there plastic everywhere?

2 Why was plastic successful when it first appeared?

3 Scientists believe that there are five trillion pieces of plastic in the oceans. What is this number based on?

4 Some marine animals eat plastic. How can this affect humans?

5 Experts believe plastic pollution in the oceans is a serious problem. How have some governments responded to this?

6 What can individuals do to help reduce the amount of plastic pollution?

The nightmare of PLASTIC ISLAND

Plastic is everywhere. It is at the bottom of the oceans, on tropical beaches and at the top of Mount Everest. It is even on the surface of Mars. This is because each year, over 300 million metric tons of plastic is produced, used and then most of it is thrown away.

Plastic was invented over 100 years ago. When it first appeared, it was an instant success. It was cheap, convenient, had many uses and was long-lasting. And that is the problem. Plastic will not go away. It may break into smaller and smaller pieces, but every piece of plastic ever made still exists somewhere in the world.

Up to 12 million metric tons of plastic enters the world's oceans every year. This means there are around five trillion pieces of plastic currently in our oceans. Once there, it can be carried by the currents for many years and travel thousands of kilometers. Some of it is eaten by marine wildlife and enters the food chain. As a result, thousands of pieces of marine plastic are consumed by humans each year when they eat fish and other seafood. However, most of the plastic in the seas and oceans eventually washes up on beaches. Nowhere on Earth has as much plastic as the beaches of Henderson Island in the South Pacific. The remote island is the most polluted anywhere in the world, and 99.8 percent of this pollution is plastic. The island's beaches contain around 38 million pieces of plastic; most of this is from everyday consumer goods.

Henderson Island is a UNESCO World Heritage site and it is an important habitat for wildlife. Jennifer Lavers, of the University of Tasmania, says that the situation on Henderson Island shows that 'nowhere is safe from plastic pollution'. She even believes that marine plastic pollution is 'as important as climate change'. Other experts describe the situation as 'a major ecological disaster' and 'an environmental emergency'.

Because of this, there is a global effort to reduce the amount of plastic pollution. For example, Indonesia has promised to spend up to $1 billion on reducing plastic and other waste products which pollute its waters. This has led to other governments making similar pledges.

However, the best way to prevent trash from washing up on beaches would be for us as individuals to use less plastic, especially things that we don't even need. These are single-use and 'disposable' items, such as cutlery and even toothbrushes. We should also buy products with less packaging and recycle more. If we do this, we will reduce the amount of plastic that ends up in our oceans and on our beaches. We will also be less likely to find plastic returning to us on our dinner plates.

Glossary

consumer goods (n) things you buy for personal or home use, such as food and clothing
current (n) a strong movement of water in one direction
marine (adj) living or happening in the ocean
remote (adj) far away from other cities, towns or people

PRONUNCIATION

/l/ pronounced and silent

A Listen to the words. Is the letter *l* pronounced in each word?

1 plastic 3 smaller 5 calm 7 should
2 travel 4 would 6 climate 8 folk

B Work in pairs. Write the words in the correct place. Listen and check.

l is pronounced	*l* is not pronounced

C SPEAK Work in pairs. Why is the letter *l* pronounced in some words and not in others?

GRAMMAR

even

A WORK IT OUT Look at the phrases from *The nightmare of Plastic Island*. Then choose the correct words to complete the rules.

It is even on the surface of Mars.

She even believes that marine plastic pollution is 'as important as climate change.'

... especially things that we don't even need.

These are single-use and 'disposable' items, such as cutlery and even toothbrushes.

even

1 We use *even* to suggest that something is ***surprising / obvious***.
2 We use *even* ***before / after*** verbs, but ***before / after*** auxiliary verbs (*be, have, can, don't*).
3 We ***can / cannot*** use *even* before nouns.

B Go to the **Grammar Hub** on **page 142**.

C SPEAK Work in groups. Tell your group three things that you think are surprising. You can talk about natural wonders, animals or pollution. Use *even* and *don't even*.

VOCABULARY

somewhere, nowhere, everywhere, anywhere

A Complete the sentences from *The nightmare of Plastic Island* with *somewhere, nowhere, everywhere* or *anywhere*. Then read again and check your answers.

1 Plastic is ______________.
2 Every piece of plastic ever made still exists ______________ in the world.
3 ______________ on Earth has as much plastic as the beaches of Henderson Island.
4 The remote island is the most polluted ______________ in the world.
5 Jennifer Lavers says that '______________ is safe from plastic pollution'.

B Complete the sentences with *somewhere, nowhere, everywhere* or *anywhere*.

1 I'd like to live by the ocean – ideally, ______________ near a big sandy beach and without too many people.
2 There is ______________ like India. It's unique. There's a lot of pollution and poverty, but it's an amazing place. ______________ you go, you see something incredible.
3 If I could visit ______________ in the world, I'd go to California. I've always wanted to go there. If not California, I'd like to go ______________ similar with big cities, lots of beaches and warm weather.
4 I was very impressed by Singapore. ______________ was so clean. There was no trash ______________.

C SPEAK Rewrite the sentences in Exercise B using your own ideas. Then work in pairs and share your ideas. Ask questions to find out more information.

I'd like to live in a town – ideally, somewhere with a few stores and surrounded by nice countryside.

SPEAKING HUB

A You are going to do the Plastic Challenge. Read about the Plastic Challenge, which is organized by the Marine Conservation Society.

The Plastic Challenge asks people to stop using plastic items for as long as they can. This could be for a day, a week or a month. Our message is 'reduce, reuse, recycle'. We're challenging people to give up their single-use plastics, such as prepackaged sandwiches, prepackaged meals, bottled drinks and so on. Do the Plastic Challenge and you'll never look at your grocery shopping in the same way again!

B PLAN Spend a few minutes thinking about the following.

1 Make a list of all the plastic you have used ...
  a today.
  b in the last week.
  c How much of this was single-use items?
2 Imagine you are going to do the Plastic Challenge.
  a Which items would be easier to stop using and which would be more difficult?
  b What changes would you need to make in your daily life to do the challenge?
  c How long do you think you could do the challenge for?

C DISCUSS Work in groups.

1 Compare and discuss your lists and your ideas about the Plastic Challenge.
2 Decide on a plan for doing the Plastic Challenge. You must agree to do the same things.

Talk about the causes and effects of plastic pollution

Café Hub

11.4 Power cut

Ⓕ – tell a story Ⓟ – showing interest

COMPREHENSION

A ▶ **00:00–03:33 Watch the first part of the video and answer the questions.**

1. What is a 'power cut'? What is the American English word for this?
2. What kind of story does Sam tell Neena and Gaby?
3. How do Neena and Gaby feel as Sam tells the story?
4. How do you think Sam's story ends?

B ▶ **03:33–04:29 Watch the second part of the video. Compare the end of Sam's story with your ideas in Exercise A. Is it a good story?**

C ▶ **Work in pairs. Put the events of Sam's story in the correct order (1–10). Then watch the video again and check your answers.**

- **a** After that, I tried to switch the lights on, but there was no power. ___
- **b** I wasn't alone. ___
- **c** It was stormy. Very stormy. ___
- **d** I arrived back at my uncle's house, got out of the car and walked up to the front door. ___
- **e** So anyway, I went inside and called out to see if my uncle was home. 'Uncle Mike' I shouted – there was no answer. ___
- **f** It all started on a stormy night when I was in Cornwall staying with my uncle. ___
- **g** I walked into the kitchen and sat down in the dark. My uncle was missing – I was scared. ___
- **h** I pushed the door and the wind blew it open. ___
- **i** In the end, I sat there alone in the dark. ___
- **j** Then the front door slammed shut behind me. ___

D **Match Sam's sentences (1–5) with the replies (a–e).**

1. This reminds me of a very scary experience I once had.
2. It all started on a stormy night when I was in Cornwall staying with my uncle.
3. Can I continue my story now?
4. I was scared.
5. My phone was dead.

- **a** Where is Cornwall?
- **b** You poor thing!
- **c** How awful!
- **d** So, tell us. What happened?
- **e** Sure. Go on.

MILLY

SAM

NEENA

ZAC

GABY

FUNCTIONAL LANGUAGE
Tell a story

A Look at the underlined words in Comprehension Exercises C and D. Complete the box with one of the words.

Tell a story and listen to a story
Give background information
It was [1] ______________ */windy/raining.*   *The sun was shining and it was hot.*
Use linking phrases
Beginning: *At first … / To start with … / It all* [2] ______________ …
Middle: *Then … / After* [3] ______________ … / *So* [4] ______________, …
End: *In the* [5] ______________, …
Say how you felt
I was excited/surprised/worried/relieved/frightened/ [6] ______________.
Keep the story going
Go on. / So, [7] ______________ us. *(Then) What happened?*
Respond to dramatic events
You [8] ______________ */lucky thing.*   *How* [9] ______________ */frightening/funny.*   *That's terrible/awful/funny.*

B SPEAK Work in pairs. You are going to practice responding to events.

1 Look at the responses in the box. Choose three responses you want your partner to give. Circle them.

> How awful/frightening/funny. That's terrible/awful/funny. You poor/lucky thing.

2 Write down three things you could tell your partner to get him/her to give those responses.

3 Tell your partner your ideas. How does he/she respond?

Student A wants Student B to say 'You lucky thing'.

A: I found $5 in the street this morning.
B: You lucky thing!

Glossary

power cut **(n) (British)** = power outage **(n) (American)**
torch **(n) (British)** = flashlight **(n) (American)**

PRONUNCIATION
Showing interest

11.8 **A** Listen and write how the responses sound in the correct place.

Very interested	Not very interested
That's awful.	

11.8 **B** Listen again and repeat the responses.

C SPEAK Work in pairs. Practice saying the responses. Listen to your partner and say whether he/she sounds very interested or not very interested.

SPEAKING

A Work in pairs. You are going to tell your partner a story. Choose one of the topics or use your own ideas. Include background information, linking phrases and say how you felt.

A time when … you got lost / you lost your keys / you met an old friend / you won a prize / something happened on vacation.

B Tell each other your stories and react and respond appropriately.

A: I lost some car keys once.
B: That's awful!
A: I was on vacation with the family in Menorca …
B: Where is Menorca?

Tell a story

➤ Turn to **page 168** to learn how to write an email giving suggestions and advice.

Unit 11 Review

VOCABULARY

A Complete the sentences using a word from box a and box b.

a Amazon Atlas Death Grand Lascaux Panama ~~Sahara~~ San Francisco

b Bay Canal Canyon Caves ~~Desert~~ Mountains Rainforest Valley

1 The *Sahara Desert* is 9.3 million square kilometers, which is almost the same size as China.

2 The ______________ stretch for 2,500 km in Morocco, Algeria and Tunisia.

3 The Golden Gate Bridge is 2,737 meters long and crosses the ______________.

4 The ______________ is 446 km in length and 29 km across at its widest point.

5 The ______________ is 9.3 million square kilometers and is located in nine countries in South America.

6 In 1913, a temperature of 56.7°C was recorded in ______________ in eastern California.

7 The ______________ connects the Atlantic Ocean with the Pacific Ocean.

8 The walls of the ______________ in southwestern France are decorated with 17,000-year-old paintings of animals, such as cows, horses and deer.

B Find 17 animals and write them in the correct place.

Mammals	Birds	Reptiles	Insects	Fish
bear				

C Choose the correct words to complete the sentences.

1 Plastic is ***anywhere / everywhere***. It has more forms and uses than any other material on the planet.

2 About 30 percent of all the plastic ever made is still in use ***anywhere / somewhere*** in the world today.

3 Recycling rates of plastic are not the same ***somewhere / everywhere*** in the world. For example, in Europe about 30 percent is recycled, in China around 25 percent and in the US the figure is just 10 percent.

4 There is almost ***anywhere / nowhere*** on Earth that does not have plastic pollution.

GRAMMAR

A Complete the text with the correct passive form of the verbs in parentheses. Add *by* where it is needed.

Ayers Rock [1] ______________ (*locate*) in the Uluru-Kata Tjuta National Park in central Australia. It [2] ______________ (*also / know*) as Uluru, which is its original Aboriginal name. The rock [3] ______________ (*form*) over 600 million years ago and it [4] ______________ (*originally / locate*) under the ocean. The summit is generally flat but, there are valleys and caves that [5] ______________ (*create*) the wind and rain over millions of years.

B Complete the conversations with the words in the box.

easy/use lucky/see necessary/have safe/drink unusual/see

1 **A:** Is your camera ______________?
B: Yes, it's very easy. Anyone can use it.

2 **A:** It isn't ______________ the water here.
B: OK, I'll get some bottled water.

3 **A:** It isn't ______________ expensive equipment to take good pictures.
B: I agree. A creative eye is all you need.

4 **A:** It's ______________ the northern lights at this time of year.
B: Yes, we were very ______________ them.

C Rewrite the sentences with the correct form of *even / don't even*.

1 I use plastic bags. (*not even*)

____

2 Ella does a lot of recycling; she recycles clothes. (*even*)

____

3 I never buy plastic. I let my children play with plastic toys. (*not even*)

____

FUNCTIONAL LANGUAGE

Add the missing words to complete the conversation.

A: It all [1]**s**__ __ __ __ __ __ when we decided to walk along the Samaria Gorge in Crete.

B: [2]**G**__ on.

A: Well, Sandy, my friend, didn't want to do it. It's a fairly long and steep walk to get down in the gorge. But she finally agreed to it.

B: So, what [3]**h**__ __ __ __ __ __ __ __?

A: After about two hours, Sandy fell over and hurt her leg.

B: Oh, no! [4]**H**__ __ awful! [5]**P**__ __ thing!

A: So, [6]**a**__ __ __ __ __, she took some painkillers and decided to go back to the hotel.

B: [7]**T**__ __ what happened?

A: Well her leg was broken …

B: [8]**T**__ __ __'__ terrible.

A: Yes, but in the [9]**e**__ __, everything was OK.

12 MEDIA

> I do not take a single newspaper, nor read one a month, and I feel happier for it.
>
> Thomas Jefferson

A printer works through the night to get out the news on time.

OBJECTIVES

- talk about the pros and cons of online news
- talk and debate about different TV viewing habits
- talk about advertising and what makes a good advertisement
- give and respond to opinions
- write a story

Work with a partner. Discuss the questions.

1 How often do you read the news?
2 Look at the picture. Do you think newspapers will exist in the future?
3 Do you think 24-hour news on TV and the internet is a positive thing? Why/Why not?

12.1 The news

Talk about the pros and cons of online news

V news expressions **G** reported speech **P** /ɒ/, /ɔː/ and /oʊ/

VOCABULARY

News expressions

A Replace the words in **bold** with the words and phrases with the same meaning in the box.

> breaking news follow ~~get~~ journalist news headlines report share

1 How do you generally ~~watch / listen to~~ ___*get*___ the news? TV? Radio? Online?

2 How closely do you **pay attention to** ______ the news?

3 What are the current **biggest news stories** ______?

4 How do you usually find out about **the very latest news** ______?

5 How often do you **repost** ______ news stories on social media?

6 What characteristics and qualities do you need to be a **person who writes about the news** ______?

7 Do different news organizations **communicate** ______ the news in different ways? How?

B Work in pairs. Ask and answer the questions in Exercise A.

READING

A READ FOR GIST Read the article and choose the best subtitle. Give reasons.

a here and now
b good or bad?
c past and present
d truth or lies?

B READ FOR DETAIL Read again and answer the questions.

1 Today, what are the main ways we get our news?
2 Do people trust newspapers, radio and TV news more or less than online news sites?
3 Why is there less control over the quality of journalism today than in the past?
4 What is fake news and what is the main reason for it?
5 Why is it usually difficult to know if something is fake news or not?
6 What can help us to decide if a news story is fake or not?

C SPEAK Work in pairs. Discuss the questions.

1 What are the pros and cons of online news?
2 Do you think fake news is a problem? Why/Why not?

The news: ______

Not long ago, television, radio and newspapers were the main ways of receiving the latest news. But the way we get our news today is very different. Most of us have mobile devices and the internet is available almost everywhere. As a result, online news sites and social media give us quick and easy access to what is going on in the world. Headlines change constantly, we get breaking news as it happens and we can follow the latest developments minute by minute.

Most people still believe traditional media more than news found online – stating that online articles tend to have a very one-sided view. When questioned further one person said they thought the news was usually unreliable or that they did not trust it. In contrast, those who get their news from the TV, radio or paper said that 'fake' or biased news was not really a concern. This lack of trust in online news is mostly because it is so easy for anyone to set up a website and report the news. This means there is less control over online journalism, and separating fact from fiction is becoming more difficult.

'Fake news' has become a familiar term. It describes invented news stories that are designed to seem real. Fake stories are usually used for political reasons or to support some other way of thinking. There were a number of famous fake news stories, for example, during the 2016 United States presidential election. Some fake news websites are designed to look like genuine news sites and have similar web addresses, for example ABCnews.nett. Also, the fake news stories are usually mixed in with real stories, which makes it difficult to notice them.

So, how do we know if a story is fake or not? First, check the source of the story. If the story comes from an unfamiliar organization, check the 'about' section to learn more. Look closely at the website address. When you are reading, notice how much information there is to support the story. Genuine stories will have a lot of supporting facts. Also, look carefully at the pictures – false news stories usually contain fake images. Finally, check to see if other reliable organizations are reporting the story. If not, it may mean that the story is false. Also most important of all, use your own common sense and think critically about the stories being reported – don't believe everything you read!

Glossary

balanced (adj) considering all arguments and opinions fairly and equally
fake (adj) made to look like something real in order to trick people
genuine (adj) real rather than false
source (n) someone who provides information for a journalist

GRAMMAR

Reported speech

A WORK IT OUT Look at the sentences from *The news*. Do they show direct speech or are they reporting speech and ideas? What tense are the verbs in **bold**? Why is this?

*When questioned further one person said they **thought** the news **was** usually unreliable or that they **did not trust** it.*

*In contrast, those who get their news from the TV, radio or paper **said** that 'fake' or biased news **was** not really a concern.*

B Read the rules and complete the example sentences (1–4) with the correct form of the verbs.

Reported speech

When we report what people say or report their thoughts or ideas, we use a reporting verb (*said, told, asked*) and we usually change the tense of the verb(s) in the sentence (simple present → simple past, present progressive → past progressive, *will* → *would*).

- *65 percent of people said they had a preferred news website.*
- *The survey asked how often people checked the news.*
- *Most people said they would think more carefully about the news stories.*

We also do this when we report someone's words directly. We also change the pronoun (*I → he/she, you → me*)

- *'Do you like your job?' → She asked me if I [1] __________ my job.*
- *'I'm doing some work.' → He said he [2] ______________ some work.*
- *'I don't think there's a lot of fake news.' → She said she [3] ____________ there [4] ____________ a lot of fake news.*
- *'I'll get back to you later.' → He said he [5] ______________ back to me later.*

C Go to the **Grammar Hub** on **page 144**.

D SPEAK Complete the questions with your own ideas. Then work in pairs and ask and answer each other's questions. Then work with another person and tell them what your partner's answers were.

1 What's your favorite …?
2 How often do you …?
3 Do you think you'll …?

Sara said her favorite TV show was Game of Thrones.

PRONUNCIATION

/ɒ/, /ɔː/ and /oʊ/

12.1 **A** Listen to the sounds /ɒ/, /ɔː/ and /əʊ/. They are easily confused.

1 /ɒ/ hot 2 /ɔː/ report 3 /oʊ/ hope

12.1 **B** Listen again and repeat.

12.2 **C SPEAK** Write the words in the correct place in the column. Be careful! One word contains two of the sounds. Listen and check.

box caught episode follow honest more online short show

/ɒ/	/ɔː/	/oʊ/

SPEAKING

A Work in groups. You are going to conduct a short survey about people's attitudes to the news. Write at least four survey questions to ask your classmates.

Where do you get most of your news?
Do you always use the same news source?
Do you think that news on the internet is generally reliable?

B Each of you interview one or two classmates and write down their answers.

C Work in groups. Discuss your findings and prepare a report of your results.

D Present your results to the class.

First, we asked where people got their news. Four people said they got it mostly from the internet, including social media. And two said they got it mostly from TV.

Talk about the pros and cons of online news

12.2 On the box

Talk and debate about different TV viewing habits

V television **G** past perfect **P** word stress in past perfect sentences

VOCABULARY
Television

A SPEAK Work in groups. Check you understand the words in **bold**. Discuss the questions.

1 Which TV **channels** do you watch the most often? What kind of **shows** do you generally watch?
2 Do you own any box sets? Do you watch on-demand TV or online streaming services?
3 Are there any **series** that you always try to watch on TV or online? How long is each **episode**? How many **seasons** of this show are there? Have there been any exciting **season finales**?

HOW BINGE-WATCHING HAS CHANGED TV FOREVER

Once upon a time
Not long ago, once a week, people regularly discussed what had happened in the previous night's episode of a certain television show. They knew that they had to wait seven long days to find out what happened next. If it was a season finale, the wait was even longer. Those days are gone.

What changed?
It all started with the DVD box set. And now, thanks to on-demand TV and internet streaming services such as Netflix (which actually started as a mail-order DVD rental service) and Amazon Prime, the way we watch television has changed forever. At the heart of this is binge-watching.

The 'now' generation
Thirty to sixty minutes of our favorite series is no longer enough. Instead, people spend hours and even whole weekends watching episode after episode. As a result, audiences are now watching more TV than ever, and around 75 percent admit to binge-watching. It is now the 'new normal'.

People want new content and they want it now. They don't want to wait to find out what happens next. Because of this, TV companies now release a complete series at one time, rather than releasing the shows episode by episode as they have done in the past.

Some of the most popular shows of all time became so successful because they could be binge-watched. As a result, a whole industry has built up around binge-watching and TV has been changed forever.

A new kind of show
Today, shows are made differently. Now, there is no need for a whole story to be contained in one episode. There is also less need for the traditional end-of-episode 'cliffhanger'. This is changing the familiar format of TV series, and show-makers now can be much more creative. For example, shows usually include actual real-world events that are happening at the same time.

TV is the new movie theater
Budgets for this new generation of TV shows are high and the shows have huge international audiences. Consequently, a lot of Hollywood stars are moving away from making traditional theater movies and appearing more on TV. At the same time, binge-watching is replacing going to the movie theater as a social occasion, with friends getting together for an evening of television. You don't actually need to be in the same physical place. Thanks to social media sites such as Twitter and Facebook, even watching alone can be a social event.

Is binge-watching here to stay?
In today's online world, people are becoming more demanding and more impatient. They want and expect everything to be immediately available. TV companies will therefore need to make more and more shows that meet this demand. As other media companies are starting to make their own TV shows, too, binge-watching will continue to be big business.

Glossary

binge-watching (n) the activity of watching TV for an extended period of time, for example, several episodes of a series
budget (n) the amount of money a person or organization has to spend on something
cliffhanger (n) an exciting end to a television show that makes you want to watch the next part
format (n) the arrangement, design or organization of something
release (v) to make a movie, TV show, etc. available for people to see or buy

READING

A Look at the title of the article and the glossary. How do you think binge-watching has changed TV? Read the article and check your answer.

B READ FOR DETAIL Read *How binge-watching has changed TV forever*. Are the sentences true (T) or false (F)? Correct the false sentences.

1 Netflix was originally a DVD manufacturer. T / F
2 We are now watching less TV than in the past. T / F
3 People binge-watch because they want to find out what happens next. T / F
4 Many shows have become successful because people could binge-watch them. T / F
5 Today, TV shows need to have a complete story in one episode. T / F
6 More and more famous movie actors are starring in TV shows. T / F

C SPEAK Work in pairs. Are you a binge-watcher? Are you addicted to TV? Go to the Communication Hub on page 154 and take the quiz! Compare your answers.

GRAMMAR

Past perfect

A WORK IT OUT Look at the verbs in **bold** in this sentence from *How binge-watching has changed TV forever*. Which action was first, 1 or 2?

*Not long ago, once a week, people regularly [1]**discussed** what [2]**had happened** in the previous night's episode of a certain television show.*

B Choose the correct words to complete the rules.

Past perfect

1 We make the past perfect with *had* / *have* + past participle.
2 When we are talking about two events in the past, we use the past perfect to show that one event happened *after* / *before* the other.
- *I found a ticket that someone had dropped.*
- *I'd seen a couple of episodes before the one last night.*
- *I was late, but the movie hadn't started.*

3 We usually use the past perfect with *already* and *just*.
- *The bus had already left when we got to the station.*
- *The meeting had just finished when we arrived.*
- *Had you already seen the movie?*

C Go to the Grammar Hub on page 144.

PRONUNCIATION

Word stress in past perfect sentences

12.3 **A** Listen and underline the stressed words. What happens to words that are not stressed?

1 I was late, but the movie hadn't started.
2 I found a ticket that someone had dropped.

12.3 **B** Listen and repeat.

C SPEAK Work in pairs. Underline the stressed words in the sentences. Practice saying them.

1 I'd seen a couple of episodes before the one last night.
2 The meeting had just finished when we arrived.
3 Had you already seen the movie?

D SPEAK Complete the sentences using the past perfect. Then work in groups and compare your sentences. Who has the most interesting or unusual idea for each sentence?

1 We arrived late because …
2 We didn't watch any more TV because …
3 We talked for a long time because …

SPEAKING

A Work in groups. You are going to hold a debate about which is better, box sets and on-demand viewing or more traditional weekly TV shows.

- Decide who will be in Group A and Group B.
- Group A are going to argue that box sets and on-demand viewing is better, and Group B are going to argue that more traditional weekly TV shows are better.
- Group A – go to the Communication Hub on page 153. Group B – go to the Communication Hub on page 154.

B Using the ideas in the Communication Hub and your own ideas, plan what you are going to say and prepare your argument. Also, think about what the other group's arguments might be and prepare to argue against this.

C Hold the debate. Can you convince the other group to agree with you or to agree with some of your points?

Debating language

Building an argument
- *First, …*
- *Also, …*
- *Furthermore, …*
- *On top of that, …*

Agreeing and disagreeing
- *I (don't) agree.*
- *Yes, but …*
- *I see what you mean, but …*
- *You have a point, but …*

Talk and debate about different TV viewing habits

12.3 Advertising

● Talk about advertising and what makes a good advertisement

G *should* **V** advertising **P** /æ/ and /e/ **S** identifying opinion and attitudes of speakers

LISTENING

A **SPEAK** Work in pairs. What do you think makes a successful advertisement?

B Look at the pictures of two different advertising campaigns. What is the product? How do you think each campaign works?

12.4 **C** **LISTEN FOR MAIN IDEA** Listen to two people discussing the advertising campaigns and check your answers to Exercise B.

Glossary

ad (n) an advertisement on television or radio, on the internet, in a newspaper or magazine, etc
billboard (n) a large board for advertisements in an outside public place
suck (v) to pull air or liquid somewhere

Campaign 1

1

2

3

Campaign 2

1

2

3

12.4 **D** Listen again. Match the sentences to *Alex*, *Kerry* or *both*. Use the information in the box to help you.

Identifying opinion and attitudes of speakers

Listen for expressions that people use to express their opinions and attitude and to agree or disagree.

Expressing opinion or attitude

I (don't) think …

In my opinion, …

… to be honest.

To agree

I agree.

Yes, … / Yes, and … / And yes, … / Yes, but …

To disagree

I don't agree. / I disagree.

Actually, …

I'm not (so) sure …

Which person (Alex, Kelly or both) think(s) …

1 the Reebok ad campaign is smart? ___
2 Alex is a fast runner? ___
3 the vacuum ad was a real billboard? ___
4 the best ads are simple and original? ___
5 an advertisement needs a clear message that you can connect with? ___
6 the most important thing about an advertisement is that you notice it? ___

E SPEAK Work in pairs. Discuss your opinion of the two ads. Which do you think is the more creative, smart or original ad? Why?

GRAMMAR
should

A Look at the sentences from the conversation between Alex and Kerry. Choose the correct words to complete the rules.

You know what, I think I might try it. ***Should*** *I?*

should

1 We usually use *should* to ***ask permission / make suggestions or offers.***
2 *Should* has ***a different meaning from / the same meaning as will.***
3 We use *should* with ***I and we / me and us.***

B Go to the **Grammar Hub** on **page 144.**

C SPEAK Work in pairs. Make two questions with *should*. Ask and answer the questions with your partner.

VOCABULARY
Advertising

A Complete the advice about advertisements with the words in the box.

attention brand connect eye logo message slogan

What makes a good advertisement?

A good advertisement must catch your 1 ______________. It needs to be original and needs to grab your 2 ______________. It needs to make you stop and look at it. The image should also be something the viewer can 3 ______________ with on a personal level. A good ad also needs to have a clear and simple 4 ______________ and also have a catchy 5 ______________, such as Nike's 'Just do it' or Microsoft's 'Where do you want to go today?' It should also have the company name or 6 ______________ on the ad somewhere. But above all, the advertisement needs to tell you that the product or 7 ______________ is the best there is and it needs to make you go and buy it.

B SPEAK Work in pairs. Discuss the questions.

1 How many famous logos and slogans can you think of?
2 What famous ads or advertising campaigns do you know? Do you have any favorites?

PRONUNCIATION
/æ/ and /e/

12.5 **A** Listen to the sounds /æ/ and /e/. Then underline the letters that represent /æ/ and circle the letters that represent /e/.

best brand can connect grab message

12.6 **B** Listen and check.

12.6 **C** Listen again and repeat the words.

SPEAKING HUB

A Work in groups. You are going to plan an advertising campaign for an everyday item. Go to **page 155** and choose the product for your campaign.

B PLAN Decide if your campaign will be an online, billboard, magazine or 'live' (like the Reebok) campaign. You may want to have a mix of these.

- Think about what makes a good advertising campaign. Consider all the points in the article *What makes a good advertisement?*
- Plan your campaign in detail. Think of a name, logo and slogan.

C PRESENT Present your advertising campaign to the class.

D REFLECT Take a class vote for the best advertising campaign.

Talk about advertising and what makes a good advertisement

Café Hub

12.4 Watch this

F – give and respond to opinions

P – agreeing and disagreeing

COMPREHENSION

A SPEAK Work in pairs. Make a list of ten different types of shows you can watch on TV. Then discuss how often you watch them.

I never watch …   I usually watch …

A: I watch dramas and movies, but I never watch documentaries. How about you?

B: I like documentaries, but most of the time I watch series.

B ▶ 00:00–01:04 Watch the first part of the video. What do Zac, Neena and Gaby want to watch?

C SPEAK Work in pairs. The roommates argue about the pros and cons of football. Predict some of the arguments.

In favor of football	Against football
	Players are paid far too much money

D ▶ 01:04–04:15 Watch the second part of the video. Do the roommates use any of your arguments in Exercise C? What do they watch in the end?

Glossary

football **(n) (British)** = soccer **(n) (American)**

MILLY

SAM

NEENA

ZAC

GABY

FUNCTIONAL LANGUAGE
Give and respond to opinions

A Write the phrases in the correct place.

I don't have a strong opinion. I'm not so sure about that. It seems to me that … That's a good idea.

Give an opinion

Personally, I think …

1 ________________

In my view, …

Look, all I'm saying is (that) …

Agree

I completely agree!

Exactly!

Yeah, that's true.

That's fair enough.

2 ________________

Neutral

3 ________________

I don't mind.

Disagree

I totally disagree, I think …

Oh please! I mean, what about …

I'm sorry, Gaby, but I think …

4 ________________

I see what you mean, but …

I see what you're saying about … but …

B Highlight the phrases that show *strong* agreement or disagreement.

PRONUNCIATION
Agreeing and disagreeing

12.7 **A** Listen to and read a conversation about agreeing and disagreeing. Then work in groups and practice the conversation copying the word stress and intonation.

Tim: Personally, I think soccer's pretty boring.

Sarah: It seems to me that soccer these days is just all about the money.

Tim: In my view, it's just some guys running around a field kicking a ball.

Beth: I completely agree.

Sarah: Exactly.

Andy: I totally disagree.

Sarah: Oh, please!

B **SPEAK** Work in pairs. Practice agreeing or disagreeing with each other. Talk about other professional sports, for example basketball, golf, rugby, tennis or your own ideas.

A: Personally, I think tennis players earn far too much money.

B: I see what you mean, but it's a very popular sport.

SPEAKING

A Complete the sentences with your own opinions.

1 I think ________________ is the greatest band of all time.

2 In my view, ________________ food is the best food in the world.

3 I think the safest way to travel is ________________.

4 It seems to me that most celebrities are ________________.

5 Personally, I think money makes people ________________.

B Work in pairs. Student A – read one of your sentences in Exercise A. Student B – agree or disagree. Take turns.

Give and respond to opinions

➤ Turn to page 169 to learn how to write a story.

Unit 12 Review

VOCABULARY

A Complete the sentences with the words in the box.

breaking follow headlines report share

1 I generally ______________ the news pretty closely and check it every hour or so.
2 I always check the news ______________ as soon as I get up in the morning.
3 I have an alert on my phone that gives me any ______________ news.
4 I sometimes ______________ news stories on social media.
5 I think different news channels ______________ the news in different ways.

B Complete the crossword.

Across

4 The last episode of a season (6, 5)
5 One show in a TV series (7)
7 For example, BBC, HBO, Cartoon Network, MTV, al Jazeera (7)
8 A program that is broadcast on television or radio (4)

Down

1 A collection of DVDs or Blu-rays of the same series (3, 3)
2 You can watch at any time (2, 6)
3 A set of shows that have the same main characters or the same topic (6)
6 A set of shows as part of a series, traditionally broadcast a year before the next one (6)

C Complete the sentences with the words in the box.

attention brands connect eye logos message slogan

1 In recent years, the world's most powerful ______________ have included Lego, Google and Visa.
2 A recent survey has shown that the world's most recognizable ______________ that don't contain the company name are Nike, Apple and McDonald's.
3 A good ______________ gives a clear ______________ that people can ______________ with. One of the most successful is McDonald's 'I'm lovin' it'.
4 A good advertisement needs to catch your ______________ and grab your ______________.

GRAMMAR

A Dasha was interviewed about her attitude to online news. Read the questions and her answers. Complete what Dasha says when she reports the questions and her answers.

Q Do you have a favorite news website?
1 She asked me if *I had a favorite news website.*
A There are two or three I usually look at.
2 I said ______________
Q What kind of news stories are you interested in?
3 She asked me ______________
A I don't have a preference.
4 I said ______________
Q Are you following a news story right now?
5 She asked me ______________
A I'm following the election.
6 I told her ______________

B Complete the fact file with the verbs in parentheses. Use simple past or past perfect.

THE INVENTION OF THE TELEVISION

Before it [1] ______________ (*become*) a reality, television [2] ______________ (*be*) a dream of inventors for over 100 years. And by the time it was finally invented there [3] ______________ (*be*) many different ideas for television. Despite the many scientists and inventors who [4] ______________ (*each / play*) an important part in the development of the television, it was the British inventor John Logie Baird who on January 26, 1926 [5] ______________ (*give*) the world's first demonstration of true television.

C Choose the correct words to complete the questions.

1 ***Should / Will*** I give you some help?
2 Who do you think ***should / will*** be interested in this?
3 ***Should / Will*** we meet at six?
4 ***Should / Will*** everyone understand this ad's message?
5 Who ***should / will*** I invite to the meeting?

FUNCTIONAL LANGUAGE

Complete the conversation with the words in the box.

disagree see seems strong true view

A: It [1] ______________ to me that things are getting more and more expensive all the time.
B: Yeah, that's [2] ______________. Each time I go to the grocery store, things have gone up in price.
A: In my [3] ______________, soccer players' pay is disgusting!
B: I [4] ______________ what you're saying, but they do give pleasure to millions of people.
A: I'm sorry, but I totally [5] ______________. What do you think, Chris?
C: I don't have a [6] ______________ opinion either way, to be honest. I'm not at all interested in soccer.

Irregular Verbs

Base form	Simple past	Past participle
be	was/were	been
become	became	become
begin	began	begun
break	broke	broken
bring	brought	brought
build	built	built
buy	bought	bought
can	could	(been able to)
catch	caught	caught
choose	chose	chosen
come	came	come
cost	cost	cost
cut	cut	cut
do	did	done
drink	drank	drunk
eat	ate	eaten
fall	fell	fallen
feel	felt	felt
find	found	found
forget	forgot	forgotten
get	got	got
give	gave	given
go	went	gone / been
grow	grew	grown
have	had	had
hear	heard	heard
hit	hit	hit
hold	held	held
hurt	hurt	hurt
keep	kept	kept
know	knew	known
leave	left	left
lend	lent	lent
let	let	let

Base form	Simple past	Past participle
lose	lost	lost
make	made	made
mean	meant	meant
meet	met	met
must	had to	(had to)
pay	paid	paid
put	put	put
read	read	read
ride	rode	ridden
run	ran	run
say	said	said
see	saw	seen
sell	sold	sold
send	sent	sent
set	set	set
shut	shut	shut
sing	sang	sung
sit	sat	sat
sleep	slept	slept
speak	spoke	spoken
spell	spelled	spelled
spend	spent	spent
stand	stood	stood
steal	stole	stolen
take	took	taken
teach	taught	taught
tell	told	told
think	thought	thought
throw	threw	thrown
understand	understood	understood
wear	wore	worn
win	won	won
write	wrote	written

PHONETIC SYMBOLS											
Single vowels			Diphthongs			Consonants					
/ɪ/	fish	/fɪʃ/	/uw/	new	/nuw/	/p/	pen	/pen/	/s/	snake	/sneɪk/
/iː/	bean	/biːn/	/eɪ/	face	/feɪs/	/b/	bag	/bæg/	/z/	zoo	/zuː/
/ʊ/	foot	/fʊt/	/ɔɪ/	boy	/bɔɪ/	/t/	tea	/tiː/	/ʃ/	shop	/ʃɒp/
/uː/	shoe	/ʃuː/	/oʊ/	nose	/noʊz/	/d/	dog	/dɒg/	/ʒ/	television	/'telɪvɪʒən/
/e/	egg	/eg/	/ju/	use	/juz/	/ʧ/	chip	/ʧɪp/	/m/	map	/mæp/
/ə/	mother	/'mʌðər/	/aɪ/	eye	/aɪ/	/ʤ/	jazz	/ʤæz/	/n/	name	/neɪm/
/ɜː/	word	/wɜːrd/	/aʊ/	mouth	/maʊθ/	/k/	cake	/keɪk/	/ŋ/	ring	/rɪŋ/
/ɔː/	talk	/tɔːk/				/g/	girl	/gɜːrl/	/h/	house	/haʊs/
/æ/	back	/bæk/				/f/	film	/fɪlm/	/l/	leg	/leg/
/ʌ/	bus	/bʌs/				/v/	verb	/vɜːrb/	/r/	road	/roʊd/
/ɑː/	arm	/ɑːrm/				/θ/	thing	/θɪŋ/	/w/	wine	/waɪn/
/ɒ/	top	/tɒp/				/ð/	these	/ðiːz/	/j/	yes	/jes/

Grammar Hub

1.1 Question forms

Questions with *do* / *does* / *did*

Do/Does/Did + subject + infinitive
Do you have children?
Does he go to English classes?
Did she write a blog post?
Did they do their homework?

- We use the auxiliary verb (*do, does, did*), without a question word, to ask yes/no questions.

Question words

Question word + *do/does/did* + subject + infinitive
What do you say to a stranger?
Where does he come from?
What did you say to your colleague?
Where did she study psychology?

- We use *What* to ask about things and *Where* to ask about places.

Questions with *be*

Am/Is/Are + subject
Am I in this class?
Are they strangers?

Am/Is/Are + subject + *-ing*
Is she doing her homework now?
Are you having fun?

Was/Were + subject
Was he a sensible person?
Were they good at English?

- We use questions with *be*, without a question word, to ask yes/no questions.
- We can also ask questions with *What*, *Where*, *When*, *Why* and *Who* before the verb *be*.

Questions with the present perfect

Have/Has + subject + past participle
Have you visited that website?
Has he written a bucket list?

- We use present perfect questions, without a question word, to ask yes/no questions.
- We use *ever* to ask about life experiences.

  *Have you **ever** met a famous person?*
- We can also ask question with *What*, *Where*, *When*, *Why* and *Who* before the verb *have*.

1.2 Frequency words and phrases

0% ← → 100%

never rarely occasionally sometimes often normally always

- We use frequency words after *be* and *can*.

  *He **is normally** very sensible.*

  *I **can never** read your handwriting!*
- We use frequency words before other verbs.

  *I **sometimes watch** vlogs online.*

once twice three times	a	day week month year
every so often	now and then	most of the time

- We usually use frequency phrases at the beginning or end of the sentence.

  *I take my dog for a walk **twice a day**.*

  ***Every so often**, I travel to another country.*

1.3 Indefinite pronouns

	-one	*-body*	*-thing*	*-where*
every-	everyone	everybody	everything	everywhere
any-	anyone	anybody	anything	anywhere
some-	someone	somebody	something	somewhere
no-	no one	nobody	nothing	nowhere

- We use the ending *-body* or *-one* with people. They have the same meaning.

  *Every**body** loved the party. OR Every**one** loved the party.*
- We use the ending *-thing* with objects.

  *I always take some**thing** to read on the train.*
- We use the ending *-where* with places.

  *They live some**where** in Italy.*
- We use *any-* in negative sentences.

  *I don't know **any**thing.*
- We also use *any-* in questions.

  *Is there **any**thing unusual about her handwriting?*

Be careful!

- With offers, we can also use *some-* in questions.

  *Do you want **something** to eat?*
- We use indefinite pronouns with singular verbs.

  *Everyone **is** interested. NOT ~~Everyone are interested.~~*
- We use *'s* with indefinite pronouns for possessives.

  Is this anybody's cell phone?

1.1 Question forms

A Put the words in order to make questions.

1 you / do / go / skiing / want / to
Do you want to go skiing?

2 does / what / do / he / weekends / on
____

3 did / you / meet / where / for coffee
____

4 you / tea / are / coffee / or / drinking
____

5 your / new colleagues / were / at the office
____

6 you / been / have / ever / Mexico / to
____

7 tried / that / she / has / new restaurant
____

B Correct the mistakes in each sentence.

1 Why ~~you did~~ *did you* choose that topic?
2 Have you ever meet a graphologist?
3 What you are talking about?
4 Did they went to the movie theater last night?
5 Where you did put the new keyboard?
6 What your best friend's name is?
7 Did you anything nice last weekend?

➤ Go back to page 3.

1.2 Frequency words and phrases

A Write the missing letters.

1 I n *e v e* r get bored writing my blog.
2 She's s________s late for work.
3 They a_______ watch vlogs in their free time.
4 We're n_______y home before 11.
5 He o__________y checks his social media accounts at work.
6 I r______ go online before starting work.
7 He r________ visits his relatives in Italy.

B Put the words and phrases of frequency in the correct place in each sentence. Sometimes more than one answer is possible.

1 We go on vacation. (*once a year*)
We go on vacation once a year.

2 They comment on online articles. (*now and then*)
____

3 I read online tips. (*every so often*)
____

4 She writes for popular magazines. (*most of the time*)
____

5 He takes his dog to the park. (*three times a week*)
____

6 We play computer games on Saturdays. (*always*)
____

7 We meet up for coffee on Sunday. (*usually*)
____

➤ Go back to page 5.

1.3 Indefinite pronouns

A Choose the correct option.

1 I need *something's* / *somebody's* help. (circled: *somebody's*)
2 I want to go *somewhere* / *something* new.
3 There is *nobody* / *nothing* I can do.
4 We don't need *everything* / *anything* else.
5 We go *everywhere* / *anywhere* together.
6 *Someone* / *Anyone* broke the ice.
7 *No one* / *Someone* came to Vant's party.

B Complete the sentences with the correct indefinite pronouns.

1 *Somebody/Someone* left a comment.
2 ________ could get online – there was no internet connection.
3 Do you know ________ at this party?
4 I don't want to speak to you. I have ________ to say to you.
5 Did you write ________ on her Facebook page?
6 There is ________ unusual about this signature. It's strange!
7 They live ________ in Romania.

➤ Go back to page 7.

Grammar Hub

2.1 Adverbs of degree

almost	= *nearly*	She **almost** fell from the balcony.
completely	= 100%	This is a **completely** new idea.
extremely	= stronger than *very*	Life here is **extremely** expensive.
very		The city center is **very** lively at night.
so	= *very*	Living here is **so** convenient.
really	= *very*	This building is a **really** smart design.
fairly	= weaker than *very*	The town is **fairly** crowded on weekends.

- We use adverbs of degree to make something stronger or weaker.
- Adverbs of degree usually come **before** the adjective.
- We can also use *very*, *really*, *extremely* and *completely* before adjective + noun.

Be careful!

- We don't use *so* or *almost* before adjective + noun.
  It's so noisy. NOT ~~*It's a so noisy area.*~~
- We can also use adverbs of degree before adverbs.
  *The pollution problem is improving **very** slowly.*
- We can also use adverbs of degree before verbs.
- When a verb has an auxiliary verb (*have*, *be*, *do*), we usually put the adverb between the auxiliary verb and the main verb.

2.2 Simple present and present progressive

	Positive	Negative
I/you/we/they	**They love** their house.	**I don't live** in a big city.
he/she/it	**She loves** her family.	**He doesn't cook** every evening.

	Positive	Negative
I	**I'm studying** right now.	**I'm not studying** right now.
he/she/it	**She's living** with her parents.	**She isn't living** with her parents.
you/we/they	**We're moving** to the city.	**We aren't moving** to the city.

Question	Positive short answer	Negative short answer
Does he love cooking?	Yes, **he does**.	No, **he doesn't**.
Are they working?	Yes, **they are**.	No, **they aren't**.

- We use the simple present to talk about routines and things which are always or generally true.
- We use the present progressive to talk about temporary actions happening now or around now.
- We also use the present progressive to talk about trends.

2.3 Simple past – regular and irregular verbs

Subject	Positive	Negative
I/you/he/she/it/we/they	**He talked** to Jim yesterday.	**He didn't talk** to Jim yesterday.

Question	Positive short answer	Negative short answer
Did you talk to Jim yesterday?	Yes, **I did**.	No, **I didn't**.

- We use the simple past to talk about finished actions in the past.
- We usually use the time phrases *yesterday*, *an hour ago*, *on Monday*, *in 2015*, etc. with the simple past.

	Infinitive	Simple past positive
Add *-ed*.	ask	asked
Add *-d* after verbs ending *-e*.	decide	decided
Add *-ed* after verbs ending in a vowel + *-y*.	play	played
Change *-y* after a consonant to *-ied*.	study	studied
For verbs ending in a vowel and a consonant, double the consonant before adding *-ed*.	stop	stopped

2.1 Adverbs of degree

A Put the words in order to make sentences.

1 have / they / completely / new / a / designed / building / apartment
They have designed a completely new apartment building.
2 this / extremely / area / expensive / an / is
3 is / park / on / Sundays / crowded / so / the
4 cars / move / slowly / city / the / in / very
5 polluted / is / in / it / places / some / fairly
6 ready / am / move / to / I / almost
7 is / really / there / beautiful / park / a / here / near

B Choose the correct option.

1 I'm *so* / *almost* happy to be living in London!
2 Cleaning up the city is *almost* / *extremely* expensive.
3 Our new apartment is *almost* / *really* nice. I love it!
4 Architects used a *so* / *completely* new design.
5 In the summer, it gets *extremely* / *completely* hot here.
6 It is *almost* / *very* impossible to get to know everyone in your neighborhood.
7 My last house was *fairly a* / *fairly* big, but I didn't have enough space.

➤ Go back to page 13.

2.2 Simple present and present progressive

A Correct the mistakes in each sentence. Use contractions where possible.

1 ~~We be~~ We're living in Rome right now.
2 I stay at my parents' house this week.
3 She's liking doing the laundry very much.
4 They're usually helping with the housework on Sundays.
5 Paul's doing the cooking most of the time.
6 We both look for a permanent job right now.

B Complete the sentences with the correct form of the verb in parentheses. Use contractions where possible.

1 I 'm studying (*study*) French history this year.
2 My mom still ________ (*do*) all my laundry.
3 I ________ (*not / need*) you to help me look for a new place.
4 What ________ (*you / argue*) about now?
5 They ________ (*save*) money to buy a house.
6 She ________ (*not / always / cook*) for herself.
7 He ________ (*talk*) to his cousin right now.

➤ Go back to page 15.

2.3 Simple past – regular and irregular verbs

A Put the verbs into the simple past. Use contractions where possible.

1 They (*go*) to Amsterdam yesterday. went
2 She (*not / visit*) her parents on the weekend. ________
3 I (*buy*) a new laptop. ________
4 (*you / bring*) your bag with you? ________
5 Dan (*take*) the train to work this morning. ________
6 I (*not / leave*) work until 10 last night. ________
7 We (*not / be*) worried when we took our exams. ________

B Complete the conversation with the simple past form of the verbs.

Will: (1) ________ (*you / enjoy*) your childhood?

Rebecca: Yes, my friends and I (2) ________ (*go*) to the movie theater a lot, and we played on our bikes. What sort of things (3) ________ (*you / do*)?

Will: I (4) ________ (*not / have*) a good time. My school (5) ________ (*be*) terrible. I (6) ________ (*take*) my exams three times before I passed.

Rebecca: Oh dear! So you didn't have much free time, I imagine.

Will: Exactly!

➤ Go back to page 17.

Grammar Hub

3.1 *all / some / most / no / none*

- We use *all*, *some*, *most* and *no* before nouns.

  *Give him **all** the money.*

  *There are **no** taxis.*

- We can use *all*, *some*, *most* and *none* with *of* + pronoun or *the/this/that/these/those*.

  *I've stayed in many hotels and I liked **most of** them.*

  *I like **all of** the Greek islands.*

  ***Some of** her trips were by bus.*

  ***None of** the countries were in Africa.*

- With *all*, we don't have to use *of* before a pronoun + noun or *the/this/that/these/those*.

  *Did you spend **all your** money? OR Did you spend **all of your** money?*

- With *all*, we must use *of* before a pronoun without a noun.

  *Did you spend **all of it**? NOT ~~Did you spend all it?~~*

- We cannot use *no* with *of* + pronoun or *the/this/that/these/those*.

  None of us want to leave. NOT ~~No of us want to leave.~~

3.2 Past progressive and simple past

	Positive	Negative
I/you/he/she/it/we/they	**They traveled** by train all night.	We **didn't go** by ferry.

Question	Positive short answer	Negative short answer
Did they enjoy the vacation?	Yes, **they did**.	No, **they didn't**.

- We use the simple past to talk about finished actions or situations, and things that happened one after another.
- See Grammar Reference 2.3 for more information about the simple past.

	Positive	Negative
I/he/she/it	**He was riding** the bus when his phone rang.	**She wasn't biking** to work when the rain started.
you/we/they	**They were sleeping** when I arrived.	**We weren't driving** when the car crashed.

Question	Positive short answer	Negative short answer
Was it snowing outside?	Yes, **it was**.	No, **it wasn't**.

- We use the past progressive for actions or situations that were unfinished at a past time.
- The past progressive describes a longer action and the simple past describes a shorter action.

  *They **were sailing** (=long action) from Portsmouth to Caen when the storm **hit** (=short action).*

- We use *when/while* before the past progressive to describe an action that was in progress when something else happened.

3.3 Verb + *-ing* and *to* + base form

- After some verbs (e.g. *agree*), we use *to* + base form.
- After some verbs (e.g. *enjoy*), we use *-ing*.
- After some verbs (e.g. *hate*), we can use either *to* + base form or *-ing*.

Verb	+ *to* + base form
can't afford	I **can't afford to buy** a new car.
hope	They **hope to meet** again soon.
learn	When did you **learn to drive**?
would like	We **would like to travel** the world.
would prefer	He **would prefer to go** to France.
Other verbs: agree / choose / decide / expect / manage / need / plan / refuse / seem / want	They **decided to go** by plane.

Verb	+ *-ing*
consider	She **considered saying** yes.
enjoy	We **enjoy reading** guide books.
avoid	He **avoided getting** wet on his trip.
spend time	Tina **spent time researching** the Andes.
Other verbs: advise / allow / begin / can't help / continue / finish / keep / mind / regret / stand	I **keep making** mistakes.

Verb	+ *to* + base form or *-ing*
hate	I **hate driving** in bad weather. OR I **hate to drive** in bad weather.
love	We **love visiting** Italy. OR We **love to visit** Italy.
prefer	I **prefer staying** in a hotel. OR I **prefer to stay** in a hotel.
like	They **like going** surfing. OR They **like to go** surfing.
Other verbs: begin / start	It **started to rain**. OR It **started raining**.

3.1 *all / some / most / no / none*

A Put the words in order to make sentences.

1 his / none / journeys / were / by / of / train

None of his journeys were by train.

2 dry / the / of / some / were / seats

______

3 all / the / unhappy / passengers / were

______

4 trip / us / none / wanted / end / of / to / the

______

5 kinds / most / don't / I / like / of / resorts / beach

______

6 have / money / no / left / wallets / our / we / in

______

7 Dilly / problems / airport / some / had / also / the / in

______

B Choose the correct option.

1 *No / None* of the tourists were paying attention.
2 All of *the people / people* were yelling.
3 Most *of taxis / taxis* in London are black.
4 I met *some of / some* nice people on my vacation.
5 How was your vacation? Did you enjoy *all / all of* it?
6 *No / None* visitors can go in this area.

➤ Go back to page 22.

3.2 Past progressive and simple past

A Correct the mistakes in each sentence.

1 We were living in London when the London Eye ~~was opening~~. opened
2 Jan was having an accident while she was sailing in the Pacific.
3 While they asking for directions, I looked at a guide book.
4 She traveled through China when she first met Clive.
5 The pilot was landing the plane when the crash was happening.
6 When the ferry crossed the ocean, we saw some dolphins.
7 She swam in the lake when something was biting her leg.

B Match to make sentences.

1 We were sailing around the island
2 While I was taking photographs,
3 They were not paying attention
4 Someone stole her bag
5 He met Rob
6 Some birds hit the plane

a I dropped my phone.
b while she was lying by the pool.
c while he was biking across Italy.
d while it was taking off.
e when they got on the wrong bus.
f when I started to feel sick.

➤ Go back to page 25.

3.3 Verb + *-ing* and *to* + base form

A Choose the correct option.

1 Avoid *to book / booking* a room at this hotel.
2 Consider *to write / writing* your own travel blog.
3 Refuse *to take / taking* no for an answer.
4 Spend time *to try / trying* different foods.
5 Learn *to enjoy / enjoying* life.
6 Don't agree *to get / getting* in the car with a stranger.

B Complete the text messages with the correct forms of the verbs.

Fay: I would like (**1**) ______ (*stay*) somewhere fun for a weekend trip. Any ideas?

Joy: What about a campsite?

Fay: I can't stand (**2**) ______ (*sleep*) outdoors. Maybe a hostel or a guest house?

Joy: I don't mind (**3**) ______ (*go*) to either. Which would you prefer?

Fay: I'd prefer (**4**) ______ (*stay*) at a hostel. Sound OK?

Joy: Yes, I enjoy (**5**) ______ (*meet*) new people.

Fay: Great! I can't afford (**6**) ______ (*spend*) much money.

Joy: Then a hostel is a good choice – they usually have low prices.

➤ Go back to page 27.

Grammar Hub

4.1 *be going to* + base form and present progressive for the future

	Positive	Negative
I	**I'm going to meet** my friends.	**I'm not going to have** a night out.
he/she/it	**He's going to play** billiards.	**She isn't going to relax** at home.
you/we/they	**They're going to spend** the evening at home.	**We aren't going to see** a play on the weekend.

Question	Positive short answer	Negative short answer
Is he going to hang out with us?	Yes, **he is**.	No, **he isn't**.
Are they going to have a party to celebrate?	Yes, **they are**.	No, **they aren't**.

- We use *be going to* to talk about intentions.

	Positive	Negative
I	**I'm meeting** Steff at 6.	**I'm not having** dinner with Steve tonight.
he/she/it	**She's going** to the movies on Saturday.	**She isn't visiting** her grandparents this weekend.
you/we/they	**We're visiting** Tina tomorrow.	**We aren't playing** in the concert next week.

Question	Positive short answer	Negative short answer
Am I meeting you at 8?	Yes, **you are**.	No, **you aren't**.
Are you watching a movie tonight?	Yes, **we are**.	No, **we aren't**.

- We use the present progressive to talk about arrangements in the future.

Be careful!

- We don't use the present progressive for intentions.

  I'm going to open my own restaurant when I'm older. NOT ~~*I'm opening my own restaurant when I'm older.*~~

4.2 Making predictions

	Positive	Negative
I/you/he/she/it/we/they	**He will go** on a virtual date.	**It won't be** very romantic.
	They may/might fall in love.	**It may/might not be** easy to meet people.

Question	Positive short answer	Negative short answer
Will they go out for dinner?	Yes, **they will**.	No, **they won't**.

- We use *will*, *may* and *might* to make predictions about the future. We use *will* when we are certain. We use *may* or *might* when we are less certain. There is little difference in meaning between *may* and *might*.

- Because *will*, *may* and *might* are modals, they only have one form.

  She might bring her VR headset. NOT ~~*She mights bring her VR headset.*~~
- We use adverbs of probability with *will* to make predictions more or less certain.

  100% *We'll **definitely/certainly** need to bring a warm blanket.*

  75% *She'll **probably** stay at home with her family.*

  50% ***Maybe** they'll go on vacation to Denmark.*

  25% *I **probably** won't cook a meal.*

  0% *You **definitely** won't forget the experience.*

Be careful!

- *Maybe* goes at the beginning of the sentence.

  Maybe you'll play board games. NOT ~~*You'll maybe play board games.*~~

4.3 Subject and object questions

- We ask subject questions when we don't know what/who/which/whose something (or someone) is.

  What is hygge?
- We ask object questions when we want to know more information about something (or someone).

  How do you pronounce hygge?
- Subject questions don't include an auxiliary verb. Object questions do.

  Subject question: Whose blanket is this?

  *Object question: Which restaurant **did** you go to?*

- With subject questions, we don't change the word order in the answer.

  Who is your best friend? Friya is my best friend.
- In object questions, the question word is the object of the sentence.

  ***What** do you do to relax? I play **computer games** to relax.*

4.1 *be going to* + base form and present progressive for the future

A Correct the mistakes in each sentence.

1 I'm going to ~~introducing~~ introduce you to my friends.
2 She going to the theater with Alice tonight.
3 We meet Pamela at 4 pm this afternoon.
4 They going to cook pizza for everyone.
5 She's going buy a cake for his birthday.
6 What time we meeting for lunch?

B Put the words in order to make sentences.

1 to / invite / my colleagues / I'm / to the party / going / all
I'm going to invite all my colleagues to the party.
2 to / I / going / tonight / think / at home / I'm / stay
______
3 are / that new sushi place / to / Karl and Inge / going / try
______
4 sister / seeing / you / again / when / are / your / ?
______
5 on Friday night / having / Tom's / a birthday party
______
6 at five o'clock / meeting / we're / in the central square
______

➤ Go back to page 33.

4.2 Making predictions

A Choose the correct option.

1 I *definitely* / *maybe* won't go to the concert because it's raining.
2 *Maybe you will* / *You maybe will* be home early on Friday.
3 They *will* / *might* definitely go sailing tonight.
4 Robots *might* / *definitely* won't understand human feelings in the future. I don't believe that's possible.
5 I *may* / *will* not have enough money for the tickets. Let's see how much they are.
6 We probably *might not* / *won't* have the party next week.
7 I'll definitely *going* / *go* to college when I leave high school.

B Make sentences with *will* or *might*.

1 Robots ______ (*definitely / do*) all the work in the future.
2 We ______ (*control*) computers with our minds in the future. It's possible.
3 It ______ (*not / be*) a good idea to sell my car. I need to think about it.
4 They ______ (*probably / not / go*) to the party.
5 I don't think robots ______ (*have*) feelings.
6 It ______ (*not / cost*) more than 20 dollars. That's for sure.

➤ Go back to page 35.

4.3 Subject and object questions

A Complete the sentences with the question words in the box. Then select the correct question type: subject (S) or object (O).

how what when where who why

1 ______ is going on the trip to Denmark? *S / O*
2 ______ do you leave for Copenhagen? *S / O*
3 ______ is your favorite board game? *S / O*
4 ______ do you want to meet? *S / O*
5 ______ do you say 'hello' in French? *S / O*
6 ______ is our English class canceled? *S / O*

B Put the words in order to make questions. Then match the answers (a–f).

1 you / have / do / when / classes / English
When do you have English classes? *f*
2 favorite / place / where / your / relaxing / is / for
______ ___
3 does / do / she / free / time / what / her / in
______ ___
4 feeling / Sara / is / how / driving test / about / the
______ ___
5 they / for / when / leaving / are / Bucharest
______ ___
6 best / the / is / who / cook / the / in / family
______ ___

a the bathtub
b worried
c next weekend
d Fred
e She goes to the gym.
f on Thursdays

➤ Go back to page 37.

Grammar Hub

5.1 *can, could, be able to*

- We use *can* to talk about general possibility and ability in the present.

  I can choose when I work.
  They can't come to the meeting.
  Can I speak to you for a minute? Yes, you can. / No, you can't.
- We use *could* to talk about general possibility and ability in the past.

  She could work shifts when she was younger.
  They couldn't come to the meeting last Saturday.
  Could you take long vacations in your last job? Yes, I could. / No, I couldn't.
- We use *be able to* to talk about possibility and ability in the present, usually at a particular time or for a particular reason.

  I'm able to work with different people.
  He isn't able to work late tonight.
  Are they able to work nights? Yes, they are. / No, they aren't.
- We use *be able to* directly after another verb because *can* has no *-ing* or *to* + base form.

  I like being able to work nights. NOT ~~*I like can work nights.*~~
- We use *was/were able to* to talk about possibility and ability in the past, usually at a particular time or for a particular reason.

  She was able to find a new job.
  They weren't able to get the bus to work.
  Was he able to find the office? Yes, he was. / No, he wasn't.

5.2 Obligation, necessity and permission: *must, have to* and *can*

	Positive	Negative
I/you/he/she/it/we/they	**You can wear** casual clothes in the office. **You must get** to work before 9 am.	**You can't wear** jewelry. **You must not be** late.
I/you/we/they	**You have to get** to work before 9 am.	**They don't have to use** English at work.
he/she/it	**He has to get** to work before 9 am.	**She doesn't have to work** on Sundays.

Question	Positive short answer	Negative short answer
Can she wear earrings?	Yes, **she can**.	No, **she can't**.
Do we have to wear a tie?	Yes, **you do**.	No, **you don't**.
Does he have to have special training?	Yes, **he does**.	No, **he doesn't**.

- We use *can* for something that is allowed.
- We use *can't* for something that is not allowed.
- We use *must* and *have to* for something that is necessary or a rule.

Be careful!

- *Must not* has a different meaning to *don't have to*.

  must not = not allowed

  *You **must not** wear sportswear in the office.*

  must not = modal of deduction (in American English but NOT in British English)

  *They **must not** be at home. The car is gone.*

  don't have to = not necessary (but possible)

  *You **don't have to** wear dress clothes to work, but you can if you want.*
- In questions, we usually use *have to* and not *must*.

  Do you have to wear boots? NOT ~~*Must you wear boots?*~~

5.3 Present perfect with *for* and *since*

	Positive	Negative
I/you/we/they	**I've worked** here for 12 years.	**They haven't called** since last week.
he/she/it	**She's worked** in telemarketing since 2017.	**She hasn't checked** her messages for two days.

Question	Positive short answer	Negative short answer
Have you worked in a restaurant before?	Yes, **I have**.	No, **I haven't**.
Has he finished the project?	Yes, **he has**.	No, **he hasn't**.

- We use the present perfect to talk about actions and situations that started in the past but are unfinished and so continue until the present time.

  *I **have worked** here **for** three weeks. (= and I am still working here now)*
- We use *for* to show the amount of time, and *since* to show when the action or situation started.

  *She has been at this company **since** January.*
  *She has been at this company **for** six months.*
- We use *How long* plus the present perfect to ask about the length of time until the present.

  ***How long has** Maria **worked** there?*
- We also use the present perfect to talk about things that happened in the past at an unspecified time and our experiences up to now.

  I've done a lot of different jobs.

Be careful!

- The verb *go* has two past participles: *been* and *gone*.
- We use *been* when someone has gone somewhere and come back.

  Bill has been to a lot of job interviews.
- We use *gone* when someone has gone somewhere and not come back yet.

  Jeff has gone for an interview and he'll be back later.

5.1 *can, could, be able to*

A Complete the sentences with the words in the box.

able can (x2) can't could to were

1 As a manager, you ___can___ have a company car!
2 I ___________ do this. Can you help me?
3 She's not ___________ to work on Saturday.
4 ___________ you work the night shift tomorrow?
5 We ___________ able to get a lot of work done yesterday.
6 At my last job, I ___________ start late on Fridays.
7 Brenda's self-employed so she's able ___________ choose when she works.

B Put the words in order to make sentences.

1 hate / not / make / decisions / I / being / to / able
I hate not being able to make decisions.
2 wants / able / she / buy / to / house / be / to / a
____
3 last / in / finish / job / my / could / at / four / I
____
4 wants / able / to / she / take / be / long / vacation / a / to
____
5 training / he / do / the / can't / because / involves / special / job / it
____
6 they / being / like / from / work / able / home / to
____

➤ Go back to page 43.

5.2 Obligation, necessity and permission: *must, have to* and *can*

A Choose the correct option.

1 You *can't* / *can* do this job unless you have training.
2 You *must not* / *don't have to* do this work today. Next week's fine.
3 We *can* / *must* wear casual clothes on a Monday. It's our choice.
4 You *can* / *have to* believe in your idea for it to be a success.
5 Simon *must not* / *doesn't have to* be rude to the manager. He'll lose his job!
6 I *can* / *don't have to* take the bus. It's easy to walk there.
7 Everyone *can* / *must* start work at 9. It's a rule.

B Complete the text messages with the words in the box.

can can't don't have to has to have to

Hannah: (1) ___________ you meet me and Lily for coffee after work – at five thirty?

Fatima: No, I **(2)** ___________ . We **(3)** ___________ work late today, remember?

Hannah: Oh, yeah. Well, I **(4)** ___________ work late because I did all my work this morning. Have you asked Lily?

Fatima: She **(5)** ___________ stay too. She told me this morning.

Hannah: OK. Another time then.

➤ Go back to page 45.

5.3 Present perfect with *for* and *since*

A Choose the correct option.

1 I have wanted to work there *for* / *since* a long time.
2 I have worked here *for* / *since* 2014.
3 We haven't had a day off *for* / *since* a long time.
4 They've worked in recruitment *for* / *since* the last 10 years.
5 She hasn't spoken to the manager *for* / *since* months.
6 Giles hasn't worked *for* / *since* he lost his job in accounts.
7 Things have changed *for* / *since* we did our research.

B Make sentences with the present perfect.

1 she / do / a lot of charity work
She's done a lot of charity work.
2 they / be / in your office / for an hour
____
3 you / change / your appointment / three times
____
4 we / not have / a pay raise / for a while
____
5 How long / she / be / the owner of the company / ?
____

➤ Go back to page 47.

Grammar Hub

6.1 Quantifiers *too* and *enough*

- We use *too* + adjective or adverb, *too much* and *too many* to mean more than the right amount.

  I am ***too tired****.*

  You drink ***too much*** *cola and you eat* ***too many*** *candies.*

Be careful!

- We use *too many* with countable nouns.

  They buy ***too many*** *snacks.*
- We use *too much* with uncountable nouns.

  We eat ***too much*** *sugar.*
- We use *enough* + noun to mean the right amount.

  We have ***enough*** *drinks for everyone.*
- We use *not enough* + noun to mean less than the right amount.

  She ***doesn't have enough*** *time to cook.*

Be careful!

- When we use *too* and *enough* with adjectives or adverbs, we put *too* **before** the adjective or adverb and *enough* **after** the adjective or adverb.

  I feel ***too sick*** *to have dinner.*

  I don't feel ***well enough*** *to have dinner.*

  You exercise ***too hard****.*

  You don't exercise ***hard enough****.*

6.2 *-ing* forms

- We use the present participle *-ing* form to talk about things that are happening now or around now and that are not finished. This is the present progressive.

  You're ***doing*** *really well at yoga.*
- We use the *-ing* form as an adjective to describe a noun.

  He has developed a ***growing*** *interest in Nordic walking.*
- We use the *-ing* form as a gerund to make a noun.

  They like ***working out*** *at the gym twice a week.*

6.3 Present perfect with *just*, *already* and *yet*

	Positive	Negative
I/you/we/they	**I've** just **seen** the doctor.	**I haven't seen** the doctor yet.
he/she/it	**She's left** the hospital already.	**He hasn't gone** to the gym yet.

Question	Positive short answer	Negative short answer
Have you taken your painkillers yet?	Yes, **I have**.	No, **I haven't**.
Has the nurse just **given** you some medicine?	Yes, **he has**.	No, **he hasn't**.

- We use the present perfect with *just* in positive statements to say that something happened very recently.

  I have ***just*** *passed my fitness test.*
- We use the present perfect with *already* in positive statements to say that something happened before now, or earlier than expected.

  We have been to the grocery store twice today ***already****.*
- We use the present perfect with *yet* in negative statements to say that something hasn't happened, but it still might.

  You haven't finished your vegetables ***yet****.*
- We use the present perfect with *yet* in questions to ask if something has happened.

  Have you cleared the dinner table ***yet****?*

Be careful!

- *Just* goes before the past participle.

  I've ***just*** *eaten some fruit.* NOT ~~*I've eaten some fruit just.*~~
- *Yet* goes at the end of the sentence.

  Have you gone vegetarian ***yet****?* NOT ~~*Have you yet gone vegetarian?*~~
- In American English, *already* usually goes at the end of the sentence. In British English, *already* goes before the past participle.

  I've stopped eating meat ***already****.* OR *I've* ***already*** *stopped eating meat.*
- See Grammar Reference 5.3 for more information about the present perfect.

6.1 Quantifiers *too* and *enough*

A Choose the correct option.

1 Don't eat too *much* / *many* eggs.
2 I am *enough* / *too* tired to jog.
3 Make sure you are getting *enough* / *too much* sleep.
4 You don't drink *enough* / *too much* water.
5 I have eaten too *many* / *much* candy.
6 The gym closes *too* / *enough* early.
7 We don't have *enough* / *too much* food in the fridge.

B Match to make sentences.

1 We have too ___
2 You don't do ___
3 We don't have ___
4 There are too many ___
5 She has too much ___
6 He's too ___

a enough exercise.
b sick for soccer practice.
c people in this yoga class.
d enough milk.
e many cups on the table.
f energy to sit still.

➤ Go back to page 53.

6.2 *-ing* forms

A Correct the mistakes in each sentence.

1 We both enjoy ~~go~~ going for walks.
2 To jog is my favorite form of exercise.
3 I'm watch a good TV show about superfoods.
4 She doesn't like swim in the ocean.
5 Recently, there has been an increase number of accidents in the home.
6 My nextdoor neighbor isn't to do very well right now.
7 A rise number of people can't afford to buy medicine.

B Put the words in order to make sentences. Then choose gerund (*G*), adjective (*A*) or present participle (*PP*) for the words in **bold**.

1 doesn't / **being** / her / on / like / she / own — *G* / *A* / *PP*
She doesn't like being on her own.
2 love / doctor / **visiting** / we / family / our — *G* / *A* / *PP*
___
3 now / **growing** / in / there / is / interest / a / pilates — *G* / *A* / *PP*
___
4 **studying** / food / we're / health / in / class / groups — *G* / *A* / *PP*
___
5 my / **cooking** / free time / activity / favorite / is — *G* / *A* / *PP*
___
6 now / people / vitamins / of / taking / **increasing** / are / numbers — *G* / *A* / *PP*
___

➤ Go back to page 55.

6.3 Present perfect with *just*, *already* and *yet*

A Write *just*, *already* or *yet*.

1 Have you had anything to eat ___?
2 He hasn't asked her to work out with him ___.
3 I've run two marathons this year ___.
4 She's ___ finished her workout – she's showering now.
5 It's only 11 a.m., but Jack's eaten his lunch ___.
6 **A:** Who was on the phone?
B: Frida. She's ___ returned home from the hospital.

B Make sentences with the present perfect and *just*, *already* and *yet*.

1 you / see / your exam results / ?
Have you seen your exam results yet?
2 they / lose / 5 pounds / from their diet
___
3 I / have / a phone call / from the nurse
___
4 we / not use / our new oven
___
5 she / take / her medicine / today
___
6 you / buy / the food / for tonight / ?
___
7 I / see / Pamela / in the grocery store
___

➤ Go back to page 57.

Grammar Hub

7.1 Articles

- We use *a/an* to refer to something indefinite when it is one example of many. We usually use it when we refer to something for the first time.

  *Petros told me **a** funny joke.*
- We use *the* to refer to something definite, which we know. This is usually because it has already been mentioned.

  *Petros told me a funny joke. **The** joke was about …*
- We use *the* when there is only one of something.

  *Do you usually use **the** internet?*
- We use – (no article) to refer to a plural or uncountable noun or something in a general sense.

  *I love finding **bargains** when I go shopping.*

Be careful!

- We don't use *the* before meals, days, streets, and singular place names.

  I eat dinner at 6 every evening. NOT ~~*I eat the dinner at 6 every evening.*~~
- We use *the* before the names of oceans and rivers and countries whose names are plural.

  ***the** Atlantic Ocean / **the** Nile River / **the** United States / **the** Philippines*
- We use *an* before a vowel sound. We use *a* before a consonant sound, even if the word begins with *a, e, i, o* or *u*.

  an article, an old friend

  a university, a European citizen

7.2 *used to*

	Positive	Negative
I/you/he/she/it/we/they	**I used to be** able to speak French.	**They didn't use to have** the internet in the 80s.

Question	Positive short answer	Negative short answer
Did you use to work hard at school?	Yes, **I did**.	No, **I didn't**.

- We use *used to* to talk about past situations that do not exist now. These include past habits and past states.

  Past habit: *We **used to watch** more TV before we had the internet.*

  Past state: *He **used to be** very anxious but he's more relaxed these days.*

Be careful!

- We use *use to* with the auxiliary verb *did*.

  *I didn't **use** to chat online for hours.* NOT ~~*I didn't used to chat online for hours.*~~

  *Did you **use** to be addicted to video games?* NOT ~~*Did you used to be addicted to video games?*~~
- In the negative, we can also say *never used to*.

  *I **didn't use** to chat online for hours.* OR *I **never used** to chat online for hours.*

7.3 No article (*school, the school*)

- When we are referring to a place in terms of the **activity** associated with a place, we use **no** article.

  He studied Math in college. NOT ~~*He studied Math in the college.*~~

  My grandfather never went to high school. NOT ~~*My grandfather never went to the high school.*~~
- When we are referring to the **physical place**, we use an article.

  ***The** college I go to is called Cambridge University.* NOT ~~*college I go to is called Cambridge University.*~~ *This is **a** good school.* NOT ~~*This is good school.*~~

7.1 Articles

A Choose the correct option.

1 (*The*) / *A* / – way you feel about life can affect your health.
2 I heard a great saying. *The* / *A* / – saying goes: 'Smile and the world smiles with you.'
3 George wasn't in *the* / *a* / – very good mood this morning.
4 What did you have for *the* / *a* / – lunch today?
5 *The* / *A* / – research they did into the effects of laughter was very interesting.
6 Sarah put *the* / *an* / – angry face at the end of her text message.
7 We usually have a lot of *the* / *a* / – fun at parties.

B Complete the text messages with *the*, *a*, *an* or –.

Emma: Do you want to see (**1**) ______ movie on the weekend?

Ian: Great! (**2**) ______ movie theater on Orwell Street has four screens. I'll see what's playing.

Emma: Maybe try to find (**3**) ______ comedy because (**4**) ______ horror movies and thrillers make me too scared!

Ian: Sure! I need (**5**) ______ good laugh! I'll find out and let you know.

Emma: OK.

➤ Go back to page 63.

7.2 *used to*

A Correct the mistakes in each sentence.

1 I used ~~working~~ *to work* in a restaurant.
2 Did you used to live here?
3 They didn't used to be friends.
4 She use to study all the time.
5 We used live in Germany.
6 He used surfing the internet for hours every day.
7 You used to being good at remembering names.

B Make sentences with *used to*.

1 your school / give you / all your books / ?
Did your school use to give you all your books?
2 in the past, / people / not have / things like the internet
______
3 in the 1990s, / cell phones / be / much bigger
______
4 in the early days, / the internet / be / very unreliable
______
5 you / find / it hard / to study at school / ?
______

➤ Go back to page 65.

7.3 No article (*school, the school*)

A Complete the sentences with the words in the box. Use the definite article *the* if necessary.

college ~~college~~ prison school school

1 I started studying math in *college* but I soon dropped out.
2 They brought the child up badly and he ended up in ______ for robbery.
3 The ______ next to my house is called Gregory's. It's for talented children.
4 It's easy to make friends at ______. I had lots as a kid.
5 Anna also went to ______ where I studied Law.

B Complete the text with *the* or – (no article).

(1) *The* college I work at is called St. Anne's. I'm a professor there. When I was a kid, I used to hate (2) ______ school. (3) ______ school I went to was very bad and it didn't have good amenities. I loved it when I went to (4) ______ college, though, because (5) ______ college I studied at was very modern, and it's also where I met my best friend, Jillian.

➤ Go back to page 67.

Grammar Hub

8.1 Reflexive pronouns

Subject pronoun	Reflexive pronoun	
I	myself	I see **myself** performing in this band for two more years.
you (singular)	yourself	You know **yourself** better than anyone else does.
him	himself	He works for **himself** as a photographer.
her	herself	She's the only actress I know who likes watching **herself** on TV.
it	itself	This problem won't fix **itself**. We need to do something.
we	ourselves	We are going to treat **ourselves** to front row seats at the theater.
you (plural)	yourselves	I hope you all enjoyed **yourselves** at the show.
they	themselves	They bought **themselves** an expensive sculpture.

- We use a reflexive pronoun as the object of a verb when the subject and the object are the same person or thing.

  *I taught **myself** how to play the guitar.*
- We can use a reflexive pronoun after the object of a verb. This is to emphasise the person or thing that does the action.

  *She chose the costumes for the play **herself**.*
- We use *by* + reflexive pronoun to say we do something alone or with no help.

  *He worked out what had happened **by himself**.*
- For emphasis, we can also use *all by* + reflexive pronoun.

  *I can't believe you did it **all by** yourself!*
- We use *each other* when two or more people or things perform the same action to the other person/people.

  *Eric and Patricia sang **each other** a song.* NOT ~~*Eric and Patricia sang **themselves** a song.*~~

Be careful!

- We don't use reflexive pronouns after prepositions of place. We use object pronouns.

  *I took my camera with **me**.* NOT ~~*I took my camera with **myself**.*~~

8.2 Infinitive of purpose

- We can use *to* + base form when we express the purpose or reason for doing something.

  *I went to the art store **to get** some paint.*
  *We went to the ticket office early **to avoid** the lines.*

Be careful!

*Trine went to the concert **to see** her favorite band perform.* NOT ~~*Trine went to the concert **seeing** her favorite band perform.*~~

8.3 First conditional

Condition *If + simple present,*	Result *will/won't*
If **you go** to the festival,	**you'll have** a great time.
If **it doesn't rain**,	**we'll go** to the street fair.
If **it's** busy,	**we won't go** to the theater.
If **you don't ask** for help,	**you won't get** any.

Result *will/won't*	Condition *if + simple present*
You'll meet the artist	**if you visit** the gallery tonight.
She won't go to the concert	if **it's** expensive.

Question	Positive short answer	Negative short answer
If Star Wars **is** playing at the movie theater, **will you go**?	Yes, **I will**.	No, **I won't**.
Will you go if Star Wars **is** playing at the movie theater?		

- We use the first conditional to talk about possible situations in the future.
- The *if*-clause describes the action or condition.

  ***If he sells all his art**, he'll get a bigger studio.*

  The result clause says what will happen.

  *If he sells all his art, **he'll get a bigger studio**.*
- We can use other modal verbs (e.g. *can*, *could*, *might*, *should*) instead of *will*.

  *If you sing really well, you **can** become famous.*
  *If it's open, we **might** go to the museum.*
  *If you win an award, we **should** celebrate.*
- We can use *should* to ask questions and make suggestions.

  ***Should** we work on our paintings if you're not too tired?*

Be careful!

- We use a comma (,) when the *if*-clause comes first.

  If you go, I'll come too. NOT ~~*If you go I'll come too.*~~
  I'll buy your ticket if you get the popcorn. NOT ~~*I'll buy your ticket, if you get the popcorn.*~~

8.1 Reflexive pronouns

A Correct the mistakes in each sentence.

1 I bought ~~me~~ *myself* a membership to a book club.
2 We didn't give ourself enough time to set up the exhibit.
3 Paul, be careful! Please don't hurt himself climbing over those seats.
4 He wrote the songs for his album all by itself.
5 You look tired, Eleni. You should look after yourselves and get more sleep.
6 I wish our friends Pete and Lynne could be ourselves around strangers.
7 The show I organized ran myself – it didn't take a lot of work.

B Write the missing reflexive pronoun.

1 We bought *ourselves* a new piano.
2 Jane, please don't compare ______ to other people.
3 Rachel hurt ______ singing on stage.
4 The problem with my music player fixed ______.
5 They bought ______ tickets to see Adele in concert.
6 He asked ______ if he was happy as a writer.
7 We must learn to love ______ before we can love others.

➤ Go back to page 73.

8.2 Infinitive of purpose

A Make sentences with *to* + base form.

1 I / play / the violin / relax
I play the violin to relax.
2 she / attend / drawing classes / spend / time / with other artists
______
3 we / go / to the movie theater / early / get / good seats
______
4 some people / visit / Paris / just / see / the Louvre
______
5 they / sell / their art / on the street / last weekend / make / money
______
6 she / go / to voice lessons / every evening / improve / her singing
______
7 we / travel / to Florence / next year / do / some photography
______

➤ Go back to page 75.

8.3 First conditional

A Check (✓) the sentences that are correct. Correct the mistakes in the others.

1 She will give you an autograph if you ~~will~~ ask her.
2 If I have time, I will paint your portrait tomorrow. ✓
3 He stars in the movie if they pay him well.
4 I go with you to the movie theater if we can watch a comedy.
5 The audience will love us, if we play our best songs.
6 If we all join the book club, it will be a lot of fun.

B Complete the sentences with the correct form of the verbs in the box.

ask buy ~~call~~ go have like

1 I *'ll call* Claire if you call Simon.
2 If you get the movie tickets, I ______ the snacks.
3 If it rains tomorrow, we ______ a concert in the park.
4 I ______ to the audition if you come with me.
5 You'll love *Wicked* if you ______ musicals.
6 If she ______ for my help, I'll give it to her.

C Complete the conversation with the correct form of the verbs in parentheses.

Wes: (1) What about next week's gallery opening? If you *organize* (*organize*) the food, I *'ll take care of* (*take care of*) the drinks.
Trisha: (2) OK. What about setting up the artwork? If I ______ (*do*) that, ______ (*you / send*) out the invitations?
Wes: (3) Sure. Should I invite students from the university? If they ______ (*come*), we ______ (*not have*) enough food and drinks.
Trisha: (4) I know … It's a problem. If we ______ (*invite*) all of them, the gallery ______ (*get*) too full!
Wes: (5) If everyone ______ (*show*) up, there ______ (*probably / not be*) enough space.
Trisha: (6) If that ______ (*happen*), people ______ (*might damage*) the art.
Wes: You're right. Let's not invite them, then.

➤ Go back to page 77.

Grammar Hub

9.1 Second conditional

Condition *If* + simple past,	Result *would/wouldn't*
If **you spent** less money,	**you would be** happier.
If **I didn't work** all the time,	**I'd make** more friends.
If **it were** expensive,	**I wouldn't buy** it.
If **they didn't travel** a lot,	**they wouldn't gain** new experiences.

Result *would/wouldn't*	Condition *if* + simple past
You'd discover your interests	if **you traveled** more.
She wouldn't do it	if **she didn't want** to.

Question	Positive short answer	Negative short answer
If **you had** a lot of money, **would you give** it to charity?	Yes, **I would**.	No, **I wouldn't**.
Would you give money to charity if **you had** a lot?		

- We use the second conditional to talk about hypothetical situations in the present or future. The *if*-clauses can be an unlikely or impossible situation.

  Unlikely: *If I **won** the London marathon, I **would be** so happy!*

  Impossible: *If I **were** you, I **wouldn't lend** him the money.*
- We only use a comma (,) when the *if*-clause comes first.
- We can use other modal verbs (e.g. *could*, *might*) as an alternative to *would* in the main clause.

  *If she tried something new, it **could open** her mind.*

  *If you had more free time, you **might feel** happier.*
- When the *if*-clause is clear or is implied, we usually only state the result clause.

  What would you do if you won a million dollars?

  I'd leave my job! And I might buy a new house.

Be careful!

- With *I*, *he*, *she* and *it*, we usually use *were* in the *if*-clause, not *was*.

  *If I **were** rich, I would give money to my favorite charity.*
- We only use *would* in the result clause.

  If we had children, we'd buy a bigger house. NOT ~~*If we would have a family, we'd buy a bigger house.*~~

9.2 Essential adjective clauses

	Relative pronoun	
Person	who	The friend **who** lent me the money is named Jack.
	that	The person **that** gave away the money is a billionaire.
Thing	which	The salary **which** I earn is too small.
	that	The donation **that** he made is very large.
Possession	whose	The man **whose** wallet I found thanked me.
Place	where	The company **where** I work supports many charities.
Time	when	The year **when** Rockefeller died was 1937.

- We use an essential adjective clause to give information about and identify a noun (person or thing).
- We can use *who* or *that* for people, and *which* or *that* for things.

  *The person **who** lent me the money is named Jack.* OR *The person **that** lent me the money is named Jack.*

  *The donation **that** he made is very large.* OR *The donation **which** he made is very large.*
- We can leave out the relative pronoun when it is followed by a subject and verb, rather than just a verb.

  Relative pronoun + subject and verb: *The charity **that** she supports helps animals.* OR *The charity she supports helps animals.*

  Relative pronoun + verb: *The person **that lent** me the money is named Jack.* NOT ~~*The person **lent** me the money is named Jack.*~~

9.3 Gerunds

- Gerunds are a type of noun.

  Noun: *He likes **clothes**.*

  Gerund: *He likes **shopping**.*

  Noun: ***Money** doesn't bring happiness.*

  Gerund: ***Owning** things doesn't bring happiness.*
- We use gerunds after prepositions.

  *I dream **about setting up** my own business.*

  *He's good **at trading** things online.*
- We can use gerunds directly after some verbs. See Grammar Reference 3.3 for more information.

  *They **like** making a profit.*

  *We **love** doing online research.*
- We can use gerunds as either subjects or objects.

  *Subject: **Cleaning** the house is boring.*

  *Object: She hates **cleaning** the house.*
- Gerunds can act like verbs and take an object.

  *She hates doing **the ironing**.*

Be careful!

- If the verb ends in *-e*, remove the final *-e* before adding *-ing*.

  make → making — *He enjoys **making** money.*

  give → giving — *She likes **giving** money to charity.*

9.1 Second conditional

A Correct the mistakes in each sentence. Make second conditionals.

1 If I could travel, I *would* discover more about myself.
2 If people aren't obsessed with money, the world would be a better place.
3 If I had the choice, I will buy experiences, not possessions.
4 Carol would travel more if she have not children.
5 You would inspire other people if you would do something amazing.
6 Did you throw away your all possessions if I asked you?
7 If I could take two months off work, I traveled around India.

B Complete the conversation with the correct form of the verbs in parentheses.

Molly: I just played the lotto. It's $10 million tonight. Imagine what (1) *would happen* (*happen*) if I (2) ______ (*win*)!
Nelly: Well, you (3) ______ (*be*) rich – that's for sure! What (4) ______ (*you / do*) with the money?
Molly: If I (5) ______ (*have*) $10 million, I (6) ______ (*give*) most of it to my family, or to charity, you know?
Nelly: Really? I (7) ______ (*not / do*) that. I'd buy a big house, and some expensive artwork.

➤ Go back to page 83.

9.2 Essential adjective clauses

A Choose the correct option.

1 I know many people *which* / (*who*) would love to travel.
2 The student *who* / *whose* father is a well-known philanthropist has plenty of money.
3 The charity *who* / *that* I usually donate to is *Help the Children.*
4 This is the city *where* / *which* I went to college.
5 Wealthy people *that* / *which* join the Giving Pledge can inspire others.
6 That was the time *when* / *where* Rockefeller gave away most of his fortune.
7 He started his own charity *which* / *whose* helps protect the environment.

B Match to make sentences.

1 My cell phone is the possession *b*
2 The London Marathon is an event ___
3 Andrew Carnegie was another person who ___
4 The money ___
5 She's the woman ___
6 South America is where ___
7 She gained a lot of experience ___

a gave away most of his wealth.
b that I could never give away!
c she traveled as a student.
d that raises millions of dollars for charity.
e that he left will be given to charity.
f when she was traveling in India.
g who set up the charity.

➤ Go back to page 85.

9.3 Gerunds

A Complete the sentences with the gerund form of the verbs in the box.

do give have make ~~save~~ set up spend

1 He isn't very good at *saving* money.
2 She usually dreams of ______ a family of her own.
3 Gareth is looking forward to ______ his own business.
4 Andrew Carnegie was famous for ______ away almost all his money.
5 ______ research is one of the most enjoyable things about my course.
6 We really need to stop ______ so much money on entertainment.
7 We hope that our business will start ______ a profit.

B Complete the sentences with the gerund form of the verb in parentheses. Then choose subject gerund (*S*) or object gerund (*O*).

1 They aren't good at *making* (*make*) a living. S / (O)
2 ______ (*dream*) of new places to visit is my favorite way to pass the time. S / O
3 ______ (*spend*) money on designer clothing is a total waste. S / O
4 The most important thing to practice and be good at is ______ (*be*) yourself. S / O
5 Saving money may involve ______ (*do*) without certain luxuries. S / O
6 ______ (*be*) a successful trader is harder than it sounds. S / O
7 You cannot enjoy life unless you spend it ______ (*live*) for today. S / O

➤ Go back to page 87.

Grammar Hub

10.1 Comparatives and superlatives

	Comparative	Superlative
One syllable adjective	adj + *-er* (+ *than*) slow → slow**er**	*the* + adj + *-est* cheap → **the** cheap**est**
Short adjectives ending in *-e*	adj + *-r* (+ *than*) late → late**r**	*the* + adj + *-st* late → **the** late**st**
Short adjectives ending in one vowel + one consonant	double the consonant + *-er* (+ *than*) big → bi**gger**	*the* + double the consonant + *-est* big → **the** bi**ggest**
Adjectives ending in *-y*	adj without *-y* + *-ier* (+ *than*) easy → eas**ier**	*the* + adj without *-y* + *-iest* heavy → **the** heav**iest**
Longer adjectives (two + syllables)	*more* + adj (+ *than*) expensive → **more** expensive	the most + adj useful → **the most** useful
Irregular adjectives	good → **better**	good → **the best**
Regular adverbs	*more* + adv (+ *than*) quickly → **more** quickly	the most + adv efficiently→ **the most** efficiently
Irregular adverbs	badly → worse far → farther/further fast → faster hard → harder well → better	badly → the worst far → the farthest/furthest fast → the fastest hard → the hardest well → the best

- We use comparatives to say how two or more things are different.
- We use superlatives to say that something is top or bottom of a group.
- To make a negative comparative, we use *less* instead of *more*.

  *My e-reader was **less** expensive than yours.*
- To make a negative superlative, we use *the least* instead of *the most*.

  *This phone works **the least** efficiently of them all.*
- We use the pattern *get/become* + comparative adjective + *and* + the same comparative adjective to talk about change over time.

  *Computers are **getting smaller and smaller**.*
- For longer adjectives, we use *get/become* + *more and more* + comparative adjective.

  *Computer games are **becoming more and more realistic**.*

Be careful!

- We only use *than* when it is followed by the thing we are comparing.

  This phone is better than this phone.
  NOT ~~This phone is good but this one is better than.~~
- We don't put *the* before a superlative when we use a possessive adjective.

  What was your biggest mistake when buying gadgets? NOT ~~What was your the biggest mistake when buying gadgets?~~

10.2 More comparative structures

- We use *as* + adjective/adverb + *as* to say that two things are the same in some way.

  *Your phone is **as good as** mine.*
  *My drone flies **as quickly as** yours.*
- For emphasis, we use *just as … as*.

  *You are **just as** good **as** I am at this video game.*
- We use *not as* + adjective/adverb + *as* to say that two things are different in some way.

  *Your computer **isn't as fast as** mine.*
  *I **don't** use technology **as regularly as** you do.*

10.3 *need to*

	Positive	Negative
I/you/we/they	**You need to prove** what you're saying.	**We don't need to do** any more research.
he/she/it	**He needs to make** preparations.	**She doesn't need to wear** a spacesuit.

Question	Positive short answer	Negative short answer
Do you need to prepare for the test?	Yes, **I do**.	No, **I don't**.
Does she need to report her findings?	Yes, **she does**.	No, **she doesn't**.

- We use *need to* like *have to* to say that something is or isn't necessary.

  *Astronauts **need to** be fit. OR Astronauts **have to** be fit.*
  *Astronauts **don't need** to be young. OR Astronauts **don't have to** be young.*
- The verb *need* is followed by *to* + infinitive.

  *Astronauts need **to be** fit. NOT ~~Astronauts need **being** fit.~~*

10.1 Comparatives and superlatives

A Correct the mistakes in each sentence.

1 Exercising is a lot more ~~interested~~ interesting with a fitness tracker.
2 This is the better device I've ever owned.
3 You bought the more expensive phone in the store.
4 This laptop is worst than my old one.
5 Your tablet is more light than mine.
6 This tablet starts the more quickly than my other devices.
7 Technology is getting more the more advanced.

B Complete the sentences with the correct form of the adjectives and adverbs in parentheses.

1 This new cell phone is ___lighter___ (*light*) than my old one.
2 My computer is ________ (*expensive*) thing I own.
3 An e-reader is ________ (*good*) for reading books than a laptop.
4 Computers are getting ________ and ________ (*cheap*) every year.
5 You can check spelling ________ (*quick*) online than you can by using a dictionary.
6 Although my phone was ________ (*heavy*) one in the store, I bought it for all its features.

➤ Go back to page 93.

10.2 More comparative structures

A Choose the correct option.

1 When my computer crashes, I get ***just*** / ***as*** annoyed as everyone else does. (as circled)
2 My tablet is ***as not*** / ***not as*** useful as I thought it would be.
3 Is your drone ***as much fun*** / ***fun as much*** as you expected it to be?
4 Getting more computer memory is ***just as simple as*** / ***simple as just*** connecting a USB.
5 Video calls are as cheap ***than*** / ***as*** normal calls on a computer.
6 This GPS is not ***as reliable as*** / ***reliable as*** it should be.
7 Your internet connection is just ***as fast as*** / ***fast as*** mine.

B Make sentences. Use contractions where possible.

1 tablets … = useful … laptops
Tablets are just as useful as laptops.
2 tablets … > useful … laptops
Laptops aren't as useful as tablets.
3 TV advertising … > effective … advertising on the radio
____
4 the GPS on my phone … = good … the GPS in the car
____
5 4G … > fast … 3G internet
____
6 new models … > reliable … old models
____

➤ Go back to page 95.

10.3 *need to*

A Make questions with *need to*. Then write short answers.

1 you / need / find / a solution ✓
Do you need to find a solution? Yes, I/we do.
2 astronauts / need / wear / spacesuits all the time ✗
____
3 she / need / follow / a schedule ✗
____
4 the food / need / be / canned ✓
____
5 astronauts / need / be / fit ✓
____
6 I / need / repair / this computer ✗
____

B Make sentences with *need to*.

1 You / not / use a telescope to see the ISS
You don't need to use a telescope to see the ISS.
2 the scientists / do / more research on the subject
____
3 people / think / about the future
____
4 you / find / a solution
____
5 he / confirm / what he believes
____
6 they / not / install / an app
____

➤ Go back to page 97.

Grammar Hub

11.1 The passive voice (simple present and simple past)

	Positive	Negative
I	**I am told** the desert is beautiful.	**I'm not expected** to be an expert on the environment.
he/she/it	It **is visited** by lots of people.	**It is not understood** by many people. **It isn't understood** by many people.
you/we/they	**You are advised** to stay away from the volcano.	**They aren't studied** by scientists.

Question	Positive short answer	Negative short answer
Am I allowed to take photographs?	Yes, **you are**.	No, **you aren't**.
Are we permitted to get close to the waterfall?	Yes, **we/you are**.	No, **we/you aren't**.

	Positive	Negative
I/he/she/it	**I was told** to read the article.	**She wasn't asked** to help.
you/we/they	They **were invited** to the island.	The clothes **weren't needed** on the journey.

Question	Positive short answer	Negative short answer
Was she joined by her friends?	Yes, **she was**.	No, **she wasn't**.
Were they told what to do?	Yes, **they were**.	No, **they weren't**.

- We use the passive voice when we don't say who or what causes the action (usually because the person or thing is not known, not important or obvious).

  *The new road to the site **was opened** last year.*
- We also use the passive voice with *by* when we know who does/did an action and we want to emphasize it.

  *This report was produced **by** scientists from Cambridge University.*
- We can sometimes say the same thing in the active or passive voice. The choice usually depends on the topic we are talking about.

  Active: *Many tourists **visit** the site.* (The topic is tourists.)

  Passive: *The site **is visited** by many tourists.* (The topic is the site.)

Be careful!

- We don't use *by* + the agent unless it is important, useful information.

  The research is paid for by the World Wildlife Fund. NOT ~~*The research is paid for by someone.*~~

11.2 Adjective + infinitive

- When we want to use an adjective to describe an action, we can use adjective + infinitive.

  *It's **interesting to study** the life cycle of a mammal.*

  *It was **nice to watch** animals in their natural habitat.*
- When we want to say that an adjective doesn't describe an action, we use the negative form of the verb.

  *It **wasn't** easy to make a living as a scientist.*
- When we want to say that an adjective describes the opposite of an action, we use *not* + infinitive.

  *It's important **not to do** any damage to the environment.*

11.3 *even*

- We use *even* as an adverb to suggest that something is surprising.

  *Recycling is not difficult – there is **even** a recycling bin at the office.*

  *You don't **even** have to leave your room to find things made of plastic.*

  *She doesn't **even** know where the Pacific Ocean is!*
- We use *even* before main verbs and after auxiliary verbs and modals.

  *We **even found** plastic waste on Mount Everest.*

  NOT ~~*We found even plastic waste on Mount Everest.*~~

  *Plastic **can even** be found on Mars* NOT ~~*Plastic even can be found on Mars.*~~
- We can also use *even* before nouns.

  ***Even** experts make mistakes sometimes.*

11.1 The passive voice (simple present and simple past)

A Correct the mistakes in each sentence.

1 The volcano ^is located in the middle of a jungle.
2 The cliffs were form 200 million years ago.
3 The museum opened by the President last night.
4 The mountain is make of a strong type of rock.
5 The city doesn't known for its art.
6 The new park wasn't open by anyone famous.
7 She attracted to Africa because of the wildlife.

B Complete the text messages with the correct passive form of the verbs in parentheses.

Gloria: How was your trip to Uluru?

Toby: Great! I learned a lot. I (**1**) *was helped* (*help*) by all the tourist information there.

Gloria: Like what?

Toby: Well, it (**2**) ________ (*make*) of sandstone and it's nearly 350m high.

Gloria: Cool. What else did you learn?

Toby: It (**3**) ________ (*create*) over 600 million years ago.

Gloria: Wow, that's really old!

Toby: I know! Also, it (**4**) ________ (*own*) by the native Australian people.

Gloria: I thought the government owned it.

Toby: It's (**5**) ________ (*not own*) by them. They just manage it.

➤ Go back to page 103.

11.2 Adjective + infinitive

A Put the words in order to make sentences.

1 easy / understand / a person's / it's / to / body language
It's easy to understand a person's body language.
2 necessary / be / it's / quiet / to / near / wild animals
____
3 fascinating / take / was / photos of insects / to / it
____
4 good / live / green / a / it's / to / lifestyle
____
5 to / is / educational / it / wildlife shows / watch / ?
____

B Choose the correct option.

1 It's *good not* / *not good* to feed the animals in the zoo.
2 It's *important not* / *not important* to make wild animals angry or upset.
3 It's *not easy* / *easy not* to take the perfect photo.
4 It's *necessary not* / *not necessary* to be an expert to enjoy studying animals.
5 It's *not essential* / *essential not* to go near crocodiles.
6 It's *not safe* / *safe not* to go traveling in the wild on your own.
7 It's *essential not* / *not essential* to have top quality equipment in order to take great photos.

➤ Go back to page 105.

11.3 *even*

A Choose the correct place to put *even*, A or B.

1 Most (A) people haven't (B) thought about it before.
2 (A) some experts are surprised (B) that the problem is so serious.
3 A lot of people (A) don't (B) realize that plastic lasts so long.
4 There (A) is (B) a place to recycle glass on my street.
5 You (A) can't (B) walk 100 meters without seeing some plastic that has been thrown away.

B Put *even* in the correct place in each sentence.

1 A lot of people don't ^even notice the pollution.
2 The base camp for Mount Aconcagua is very high.
3 There are many solutions – we can stop using plastic.
4 There are a lot of organizations in my town – there's a bird-watchers' club.
5 I love all animals, and I like spiders.
6 I know some adults who don't know the difference between a lion and a tiger.

➤ Go back to page 107.

Grammar Hub

12.1 Reported speech

Direct speech	Reported speech
simple present '**We like** Channel 4 News best.' '**Do you like** Channel 4 News best?'	simple past Most people said (that) **they liked** Channel 4 News best. She asked them if **they liked** Channel 4 News best.
present progressive '**We are watching** the news.'	past progressive They said (that) **they were watching** the news.
will '**I will** watch TV later.'	*would* She said (that) **she would** watch TV later.
may '**Elle may** buy the box set.'	*might* He said (that) **Elle might** buy the box set.
can '**We can** record the episode.'	*could* They said (that) **they could** record the episode.

- We use reported speech to report what people say or report their thoughts or ideas.
- We use a reporting verb in the simple past.

  *He **said** … They **told** me … She **asked** him if …*
- We usually go back one tense from the tense the speaker used, but we usually don't go back one tense with the simple past.

  *'I'**m watching** TV.' → He said he **was watching** TV.*
  *'We usually **went** to the movie theater.' → He said they usually **went** to the movie theater.*

- We also need to change some pronouns (*I* to *he/she*, *my* to *his/her*, *your* to *my*, etc).

  *'I like **your** radio show,' said Lola. →*
  *Lola told me that **she** liked **my** radio show.*
- We sometimes also need to change other words.

Direct speech	Reported speech
now 'We're going to watch the news **now**.'	*then / right now* They said they were going to watch the news **then / right now**.
tonight 'I will be on social media **tonight**.'	*that night* He said he would be on social media **that night**.
tomorrow 'We'll set the budget **tomorrow**.'	*the next day / the following day* She said they would set the budget **the next day**.
today 'That new show is on TV **today**.'	*that day* He said that new show was on TV **that day**.
here 'There are some reporters **here**.'	*there* She said there were some reporters **there**.

12.2 Past perfect

	Positive	Negative
I/you/he/she/it/we/they	**I'd heard** the story before you read it.	**She hadn't seen** the ad before yesterday.

Question	Positive short answer	Negative short answer
Had you visited the news website before?	Yes, **I had**.	No, **I hadn't**.

- When we are talking about two events in the past, we use the past perfect to show that one event happened before the other.

past ————————————→ present
↑ I saw you on the news. ↑ You told me about it.

*I **had seen** you on the news before you told me about it.*

- We usually use *just* and *already* with the past perfect.

  *The movie had **just** started when we arrived at the movie theater.*
  *Had they seen the show **already**?*

Be careful!

- If we use the simple past with *when*, the meaning is different to when we use the past perfect.

  *I **checked the news** when I left. (= I checked the news **after** I left.)*
  *I **had checked the news** when I left. (= I checked the news **before** I left.)*

12.3 *should*

Subject	Question
I/we	**Should I buy** tickets for the movie?

- We use *should* to make offers and suggestions.

  offer: *Should **I turn** the TV on?*
  suggestion: ***Should we** go to the movie theater tonight?*
- We also use *should* to ask for suggestions.

  *Which episode **should we watch** this evening?*

Be careful!

- We only use *should* with *I* and *we*.

  *Which episode **should we watch** this evening? NOT ~~Which episode should you watch this evening?~~*

- We use *will* to ask questions about the future.

  ***Will you binge-watch** the show this weekend?*

12.1 Reported speech

A Report the statements.

1 Paul and James: 'We're going shopping tonight.'
They said _(that) they were going shopping that night._
2 Tina: 'I'll post it online later.'
She said ______
3 Roy: 'I can't help with the budget.'
He said ______
4 James: 'Don't watch the show without me!'
He told me ______
5 Helen: 'Can I borrow your box set?'
She asked me if ______
6 Alan: 'Are they going to show the ad tonight?'
He asked me if ______
7 Nora: 'You may need to speak to a journalist today.'
She told me that ______

B Complete the text messages with the correct form of the verbs in parentheses.

Pat: Fred said you (**1**) _went_ (*go*) to the movie theater with him the other night.

Nuala: Yeah. He told me he (**2**) ______ (*want*) to watch a new sci-fi movie, but I asked him if we (**3**) ______ (*can*) see a comedy instead. I said I (**4**) ______ (*not feel*) like seeing a serious movie.

Pat: He said you (**5**) ______ (*see*) *Ride Away* in the end. Was it good?

Nuala: That's right. We (**6**) ______ (*be going to*) choose *Hideout*, but it was on too late. *Ride Away* was the best option.

➤ Go back to page 113.

12.2 Past perfect

A Correct the mistakes in each sentence.

1 Someone had ~~drop~~ _dropped_ a newspaper on the ground.
2 I was late, but the movie wasn't starting, so it was OK.
3 The show have just begun when we arrived.
4 They had saw the movie twice already.
5 The journalist has already left when she got to the meeting.
6 Had you just seen the show before last night?
7 **A:** Had she posted it before?
B: Yes, she did.

B Complete each sentence with the correct form of the verb in parentheses.

1 The movie _had already begun_ (*already begin*) when I arrived.
2 I didn't watch the movie because I ______ (*already see*) it.
3 They didn't want to watch the news because they ______ (*already read*) the newspaper.
4 We ______ (*just start*) the trip home when the accident happened.
5 I ______ (*find*) the DVD that my girlfriend had dropped behind the couch.

➤ Go back to page 115.

12.3 *should*

A Choose the correct option.

1 *Should* (circled) / *Will* we see what's on TV?
2 *Should* / *Will* I invite Amy over to watch the show?
3 *Should* / *Will* they release the show on DVD soon?
4 *Should* / *Will* we binge-watch the show this weekend?
5 *Should* / *Will* this catch people's attention?
6 What movie ***should*** / ***will*** we see at the movie theater?
7 What ***should*** / ***will*** you say to the journalist?

B Write questions using *should* or *will*.

1 we / share / our photos online tonight
Should we share our photos online tonight?
2 they / release / the new movie / this weekend
______
3 I / pay / for the movie tickets
______
4 she / finish / her journalism course this year
______
5 we / watch / something exciting this weekend
______

➤ Go back to page 117.

Vocabulary Hub

1.1 People

A SPEAK Work in pairs. Look at the pictures. Describe the people and their relationships. Use the words in the box to help you.

children colleagues couple friends grandparents
parents relatives strangers students teacher

B Choose the correct words to complete the sentences.

1 Sally and Nicole are good ***friends*** / ***strangers*** and they go to the same college.
2 Jamal is a photography ***colleague*** / ***teacher***. He knows a lot about cameras.
3 Every weekend, I go to stay at my ***grandparents'*** / ***couple's*** house.
4 I never know what to say to ***strangers*** / ***parents*** when I meet them for the first time.
5 Janelle and Carla are ***colleagues*** / ***students***, and they work together in the office very well.
6 All of my ***relatives*** / ***teachers*** live in the same town – we're a very close family.

➤ Go back to page 3.

1.2 Types of people

A Match the descriptions (1–10) with the types of people in bold in *Three of the best*.

1 a person who likes animals *animal lover*
2 a woman who has three children ________
3 a person who is very interested in food ________
4 a person who enjoys seeing other places ________
5 a person who watches or takes part in sports ________
6 a person who plays computer games ________
7 a person who enjoys spending time with others ________
8 a person who loves reading ________
9 a person who writes online regularly ________
10 a person who listens to music regularly ________

B Complete the sentences with the words in the box.

coffee dog father positive soccer

1 I'm a ________ owner. I take it for a walk twice a day.
2 I'm a big ________ drinker. Cappuccino is my favorite, but I also like espresso.
3 I'm a ________ of two. My wife and I have two daughters.
4 I'm a ________ person. I try not to worry or complain.
5 I'm a ________ fan. My favorite team is Manchester United.

➤ Go back to page 4.

2.3 Life events

Match the life events (1–10) with the pictures (a–j).

1 have a baby / children
2 go to college
3 get a job
4 get married
5 leave home
6 fall in love
7 get your own place
8 retire
9 learn to swim
10 leave school

➤ Go back to page 17.

3.3 Accommodations and amenities

A Label the pictures with the words in the box. Which types of accommodations have you stayed in?

apartment	beach resort	campsite	chalet
cruise ship	five-star hotel	guest house	hostel

B SPEAK Work in pairs. What do the words in **bold** mean? Explain them. Then decide who would say each sentence. Write guest (*G*) or receptionist (*R*).

1 The **front desk** is open 24 hours. Just dial nine on the phone in your room.
2 We don't have any **double** or **twin rooms** for tonight, I'm afraid, but there are two **single rooms** available.
3 I understand the **dorms** in the hostel are non-smoking, but can I smoke on the **balcony**?
4 All our rooms have **safes** for your valuables, quiet **air conditioners** and beautiful **ocean views**.
5 Hello, is that **room service**? I'd like to order some food, please. It's room 442.
6 If you'd like to exercise or have a massage, our **gym**, pool and **spa** are on the fourth floor.
7 We're **checking out** tomorrow and we'd like to book an **airport transfer** for 10 am, please.
8 You have booked a **self-service apartment**, but there is a restaurant by the pool if you'd like to eat there.

➤ Go back to page 27.

4.2 Suffixes

A Complete the diagrams with the verbs in the box. Check your answers in the *Macmillan English Dictionary*.

agree ~~develop~~ ~~discuss~~ improve invent predict

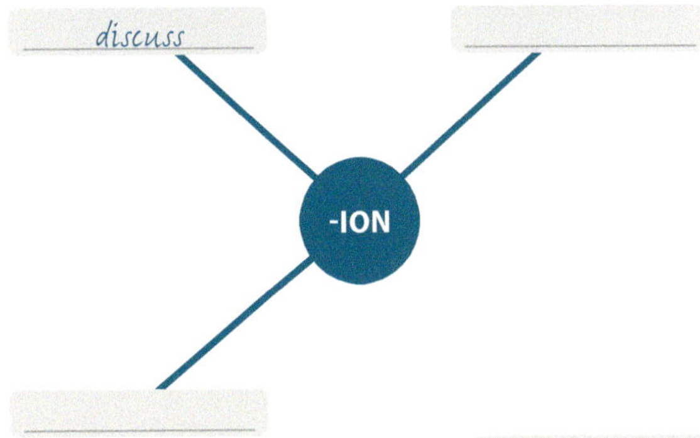

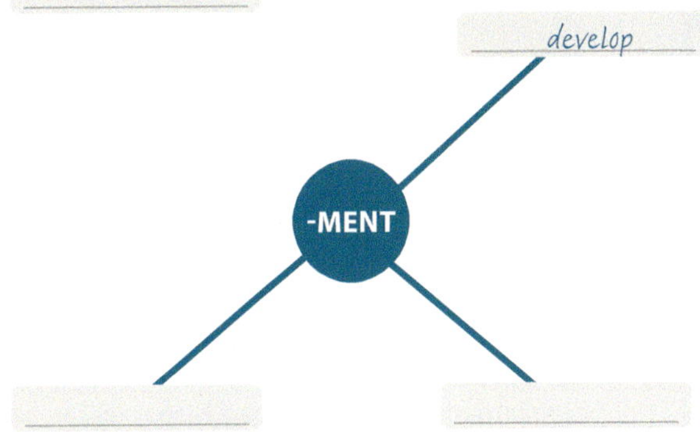

B Complete the diagrams with the adjectives in the box. You need to change the spelling in some of the words when you add a suffix. Which ones? Check your answers in the *Macmillan English Dictionary*.

~~able~~ active ~~happy~~ kind possible sad

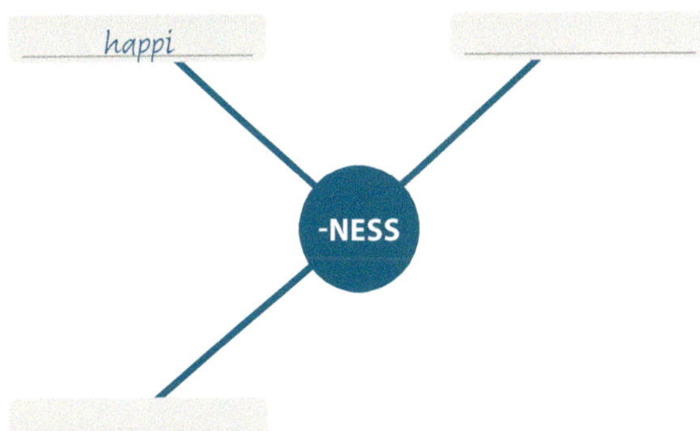

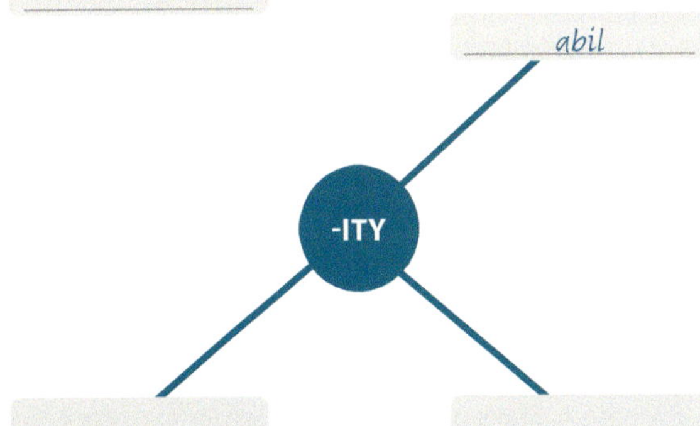

➤ Go back to page 35.

4.3 Relaxing

A Complete the blanks in blue in the survey with the words in the box. Read *Make yourself at home* on page 36 again to help you.

a good book | board games | by the fire | friends or family | get together | homemade food | hot bath | quiet night | relaxed atmosphere | simple things | some candles | some time out

How *hygge* is your lifestyle?

1 It's a rainy Sunday afternoon. Do you prefer to …

- **a** go to a shopping center and spend some money?
- **b** order delivery food and switch on the game console?
- **c** sit down with [1] ______ and read all afternoon under a cozy blanket?

2 How would you rather celebrate your birthday?

- **a** Go out with friends and stay out until late.
- **b** Meet friends in the [2] ______ of a café or restaurant and have a nice meal.
- **c** Have [3] ______ over to eat [4] ______ and play [5] ______.

3 What makes you happiest?

- **a** Money, shopping, vacations, etc.
- **b** A chance to [6] ______ with family and friends.
- **c** The [7] ______ in life, like a [8] ______ in or a long walk in the country.

4 It's Friday night and your workweek is over. Would you rather …

- **a** go out with your colleagues?
- **b** go home, watch TV and have an early night?
- **c** go home, have a nice, [9] ______ and then sit [10] ______ and dry off?

5 How do you create the perfect atmosphere at home?

- **a** Turn on the lights, turn up the music and dance around the living room.
- **b** Close the curtains, turn on the TV and lie on the couch.
- **c** Light [11] ______, play some soft music and take [12] ______ to relax.

Finished? Work out your score: a = 0, b = 1, c = 2

B SPEAK Work in pairs. Ask and answer the questions in Exercise A. Make a note of your partner's answers. Go to the **Communication Hub** on **page 155** and check your scores. Who has more *hygge* in their lives?

➤ Go back to page 37.

5.3 *work* + preposition

A Complete the diagram with the words in the box.

a design firm | a hospital | accounts | Volkswagen

work

- \+ *at/for* + a named company, for example, [1] ______
- \+ *for* + type of company, for example, [2] ______
- \+ *in* + area of business or department, for example, [3] ______
- \+ *at/in* + place, for example, [4] ______

B Write the correct prepositions to complete the sentences.

1. He works ______ Base One IT Services.
2. We work ______ a law firm.
3. They work ______ a restaurant.
4. She works ______ a telemarketing company.
5. He works ______ the IT department.
6. They work ______ Human Resources.

➤ Go back to page 47.

6.2 Exercise

A Label the pictures of sports and activities with the words in the box.

biking | field hockey | jogging | marathon running | Nordic walking | racquetball | working out at the gym | yoga

1 ______

2 ______

3 ______

4 ______

5 ______

6 ______

7 ______

8 ______

B Complete the instructions with the correct form of the verbs in the box. You will need to use some of the verbs more than once.

burn do go lose play run stay ~~work out~~

Find someone who …

1 hates *working out* at the gym.
2 can give a tip on how to ________ weight in a healthy way.
3 ________ jogging or running regularly.
4 knows someone who has ________ a marathon, a half-marathon or a 10 km race.
5 knows how to ________ racquetball.
6 ________ in shape by walking or biking to school or work.
7 knows how many calories an average person ________ in a day.
8 ________ yoga or goes to an exercise class.
9 has a parent or grandparent who ________ Nordic walking.
10 regularly ________ a team sport such as field hockey or soccer when they were in school.

➤ Go back to page 54.

6.3 Food groups

A Write the food words in the box in the correct place.

avocado banana cod lettuce lobster oats rice shrimp tomato tuna wheat

Fruits and vegetables	Grains	Seafood

B Complete the lists with words from Exercise A.

1 Foods that are mostly used in salads: cucumber, ________, ________.
2 Foods that are used in breakfast cereals: nuts, ________, ________, ________.
3 Examples of shellfish: crab, ________, ________.

C Complete the sentences with words from Exercise A.

1 I think I'll have a ________ sandwich.
2 The ________ is ground into flour, and this is the main ingredient of bread.
3 A prawn looks just like a ________, but is smaller.
4 Sushi is made with raw fish, rice and sometimes ________ and ________.
5 I prefer white fish, like haddock and ________.

➤ Go back to page 57.

7.1 Feelings

A Match the adjectives (1–6) with their meanings (a–f).

1 pleased
2 cheerful
3 confused
4 anxious
5 relaxed
6 scared

a frightened or worried
b calm and not worried
c worried because you think something bad might happen
d happy and satisfied
e behaving in a happy, friendly way
f unable to understand something or think clearly about it

B Which words in Exercise A have similar meanings to these words? Are the words positive or negative?

glad: ________, ________

nervous: ________, ________

C Complete the sentences with adjectives from Exercise A. More than one answer may be possible.

1 I'm feeling ________ because I have an exam tomorrow.
2 Olaf's finished all of his work, so he's in a ________ mood.
3 That was a hard day, but now it's over I can feel ________.
4 I'm not going anywhere near that spider – I'm too ________.
5 I don't understand these questions – they just make me feel ________.
6 Jordi's really ________ now that he has passed his driving test.

➤ Go back to page 63.

7.2 Shortened words

A Work in pairs. How do you shorten these words? Circle the parts of the words that can be shortened.

internet introduction information website newspaper laboratory airplane suitcase cell phone microphone

B Complete the sentences with shortened words from Exercise A.

1 We need more ________ before we can make a final decision.

2 The singer dropped the ________ halfway through the song.

3 So many of the ________ on the ________ are basically just full of pictures of people's cats.

4 I asked the staff to let me take my ________ on to the ________ as carry-on luggage.

5 Read the ________ to this article in the ________ and see if you can understand it.

6 My parents are going to buy me a new ________ when I start working in the ________ at college.

➤ Go back to page 65.

8.1 Music

Label the pictures (1–2) with the words in the box. You will need to use some words more than once.

audience drummer drums guitar guitarist keyboard player keyboards light show microphone singer stage

1

2

➤ Go back to page 73.

8.2 Types of art

Look at the pictures (1–8). Label them with the words in the box.

abstract art exhibit gallery landscape photograph portrait sculpture still life

The Hay Wain by John Constable

1 ________

Sunflowers by Vincent van Gogh

2 ________

Mona Lisa by Leonardo da Vinci

3 ________

Guitar on chair by Juan Gris

4 ________

David by Michelangelo

5 ________

Lunch atop a Skyscraper by Charles C. Ebbets

6 ________

A collection of landscapes

7 ________

The Louvre, Paris

8 ________

➤ Go back to page 74.

9.3 *make* and *do* expressions

Match the expressions (1–6) with the pictures (a–f).

1 make a mess
2 make a mistake
3 do some damage
4 make a decision
5 do your homework
6 make a complaint

➤ Go back to page 87.

10.1 Electronic devices

A Label the pictures of electronic devices (1–6) with the words in the box.

drone e-reader fitness tracker power bank tablet USB drive

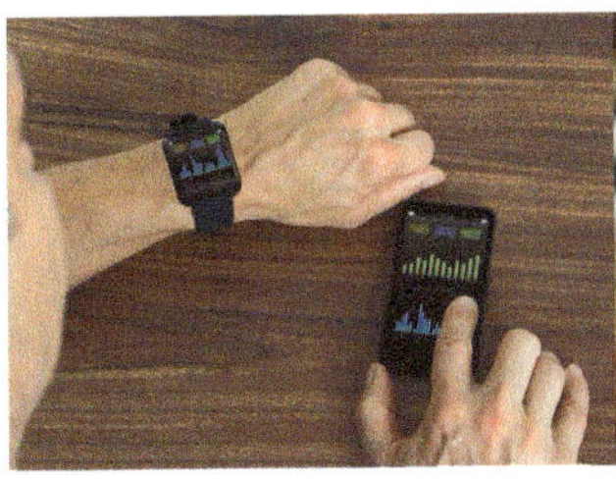

1 ______________

2 ______________

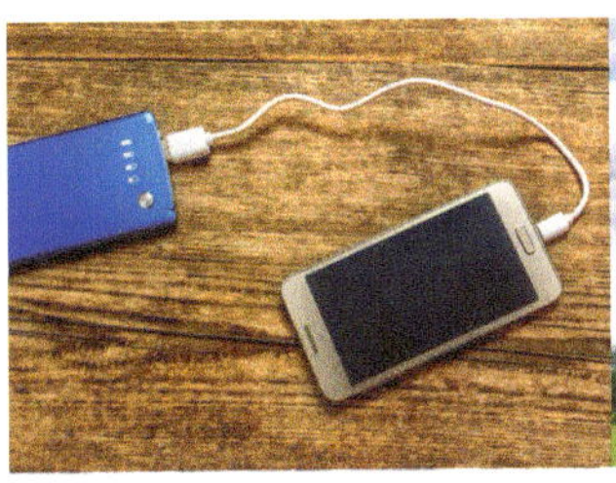

3 ______________

4 ______________

5 ______________

6 ______________

B Complete the sentences with the devices in Exercise A. There is one word you do not need.

1 A ______________ is great when you are not at home and your phone battery runs out.
2 He always uses his ______________ to transfer large files.
3 I wear my ______________ 24 hours a day. I love it because it tells me how many steps I take.
4 Tina got a ______________ for her birthday, but she was flying it in the backyard and it got stuck up in a tree!
5 My husband won't buy an ______________ because he says he loves the feel and smell of paper books.

➤ Go back to page 92.

11.1 Natural features

Label the pictures (1–8) with the words in the box.

bay canal cave cliff desert ocean rainforest valley

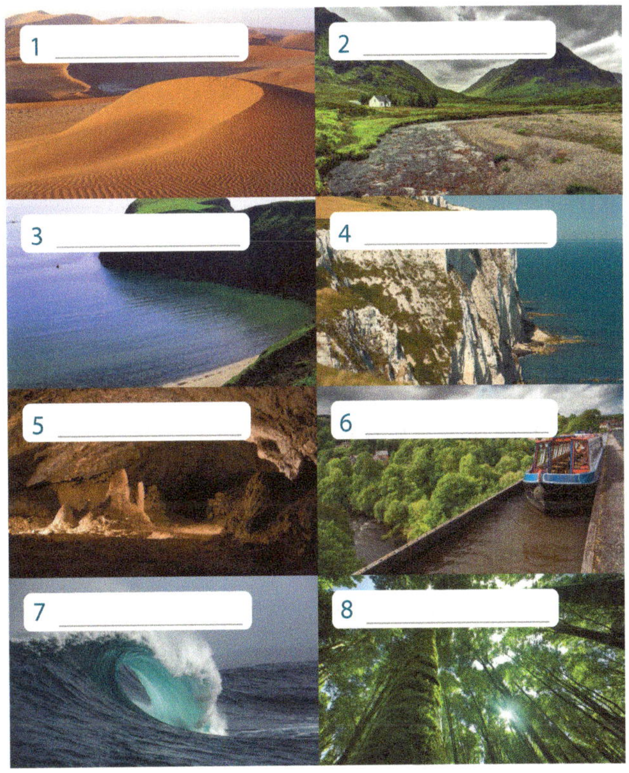

➤ Go back to page 102.

11.2 Animals

Write the animal words in the box in the correct place.

alligator ant ~~bear~~ bee butterfly crocodile duck eagle elephant fly frog gorilla lion lizard monkey mosquito moth owl panda parrot penguin shark snake tiger toad tuna

Mammals	Birds	Insects
bear		

Reptiles	Amphibians	Fish

➤ Go back to page 104.

Communication Hub

7.3 Student A

MICHAEL KEARNEY: the world's youngest college graduate

1984: born and grew up in Honolulu, Hawaii

4 months: spoke his first words

6 months: told his doctor, 'I have a left ear infection'

10 months: learned to read

School: didn't go to school; his parents taught him at home; went to high school for one year; graduated and received his high school diploma when he was six

College: went to college to study anthropology; graduated from the college at age ten; *The Guinness Book of Records* lists him as the world's youngest college graduate; appeared on TV chat shows; received a master's degree in biochemistry when he was 14, a master's degree in computer science when he was 18 and a doctorate in chemistry at age 22

Career: started teaching at a college at age seventeen

Other information

2006 and 2008: competed in several TV quiz shows and won over $1,000,000

➤ Go back to page 67.

9.2 Student A

A Write a definition for each word. Start your sentences with *'This is …'* and use an adjective clause.

1. a philanthropist
   This is someone who gives money to help people.
2. a course book
   ______
3. a vegetarian
   ______
4. a hashtag
   ______
5. a cell phone
   ______
6. money
   ______

B Read your definitions to Student B. Can he/she guess what you are describing?

➤ Go back to page 85.

4.2 Student C

ROBOT RELATIONSHIPS

Meet Pepper, the world's friendliest robot. Pepper's Japanese makers say the cute little robot can understand 70–80 percent of conversations with a human. They even say Pepper can understand when someone is happy or sad. And this is just the beginning. Experts predict that in the future, humans will probably develop close relationships with robots.

Right now, most of the robots in Japan look like Pepper, but it definitely won't be long until robots look, sound and move like humans. Erica, a robot developed by Professor Hiroshi Ishiguro of Osaka University, can show basic feelings on her face and gives us a better idea of what is already possible.

Experts such as Ishiguro think that developments in technology might help scientists to make machines that really understand human feelings. This means your robot might be able to figure out if you are happy or sad and use this information to talk and behave like a friend. That could make it possible for robots to take care of people. Some experts even believe that one day it may be possible for robots to feel love.

Glossary

expert (n) someone who knows a lot about a particular subject

➤ Go back to page 34.

3.2 Students C and D

Work in pairs. Look at the pictures to tell a story. Think about:

1. What happened during the journey?
2. What decisions did people make?
3. How did the people feel at the end of the journey?

➤ Go back to page 25.

11.2 Students A and B

Work in pairs. Choose one of the hobbies or activities and give suggestions and advice to improve. Use the phrases in the box.

It's better (not) It's easy It's essential It's good
It's important It's (not) necessary It's useful It's sensible

learn a musical instrument	live a 'green' lifestyle
play a sport	keep an animal as a pet
learn a language	have a job interview
keep fit and healthy	host a party

➤ Go back to page 105.

7.1 Student B

A Listen to Student A and write down the sentences he/she says.

B Read these sentences to Student A, who will write them down. Be careful to pronounce *a* and *an* using the weak sound /ə/ (schwa). Check Student A's sentences are correct.

1 It's **a** great idea.
2 We had **a** fun day.
3 It was **an** amazing time.
4 It was **a** total surprise.
5 He told **a** funny story.

C Tell your partner about events or situations that the sentences in Exercise B describe.

➤ Go back to page 63.

9.1 Group B

A SPEAK Look at questions 1–3 in Exercise B. What would you do in each situation? Why?

B Think of two more questions. Write them down. Use the second conditional.

1 If you had to choose between a luxury break for two in your country's capital and the very latest smart television with theater sound, which would you choose?
2 If you had to choose between a well-paid job in a city you don't like and a slightly lower-paid job in a city you like, what would you do?
3 If you won \$500, what would you spend it on? What about if you won \$5000 or \$50,000?
4 ______________________________
5 ______________________________

➤ Go back to page 83.

4.2 Student B

Social media

Social media is everywhere and is a normal part of many people's lives. However, experts agree that the way we use social media will change in the future.

Ten years ago, people used social media to share messages. Then everyone got cameras on their phones and began sharing pictures and video. But if Mark Zuckerberg of Facebook is right, you and your friends will soon put on your VR (Virtual Reality) headsets and meet in amazing 3D virtual worlds. Zuckerberg and Facebook are spending a lot of money on developing VR social media.

With VR social media, it will be possible to meet your friends 'inside' pictures and videos. This means, for example, that you will be able to spend time together at the top of mountains or the bottom of oceans! It will also be possible to hang out in virtual versions of real clubs or museums, or just about anywhere in the world (or the universe) you can imagine.

There is still a lot of work to do on the technology, so you might have to wait a while before you can share your selfies from the far side of the moon! However, experts agree that VR is the future of social media.

Glossary

expert (n) someone who knows a lot about a particular subject
virtual (adj) almost the same as the real thing

➤ Go back to page 34.

12.2 Group A

Box sets and on-demand viewing are better.

Here are some ideas for your argument. Add some ideas of your own.

- You can watch episodes when you want to and when is convenient for you.
- You will never miss an episode.
- It is easier to find a time to watch an episode or several episodes with other people, which can …

  be a fun social event.

  bring people closer together because of shared interest.

  help people to get to know each other.

➤ Go back to page 115.

12.2 Group B

Traditional weekly TV shows are better.

Here are some ideas for your argument. Add some ideas of your own.

- You look forward to the show more.
- You don't become too obsessed with the show.
- There is no danger of binge-watching, which can …
  be bad for your health or eyesight.
  make your brain too active and cause sleeplessness.
  waste time.

➤ Go back to page 115.

10.2 Student A

A Look at the pictures. Think about how you will answer the questions. Write notes.

1. Can you describe the two pictures on page 155?
2. Which of these two ways of managing your money do you prefer and why?
3. What computer skills and knowledge about the internet does someone need to manage an online bank account?

B DISCUSS Your partner will ask you the questions in Exercise A.

C CHANGE Now ask your partner the following questions.

1. Can you describe the two pictures on page 155?
2. Which of these ways of communicating with other people do you prefer and why?
3. What computer skills and knowledge about the internet does someone need to make video calls?

D Can you think of one more question to ask?

➤ Go back to page 95.

9.2 Student B

A Write a definition for each word. Start your sentences with *'This is …'* and use an adjective clause.

1. a businessman or businesswoman
   This is someone who works in business, especially in a top position.
2. a magazine
3. a professor
4. an emoji
5. the internet
6. food

B Read your definitions to Student A. Can he or she guess what you are describing?

➤ Go back to page 85.

12.2 Students A and B

Are you a binge-watcher? Are you addicted to TV? Take the quiz! Check (✓) the sentences that are true for you. Then read what it means below.

You know you're a binge-watcher and addicted to TV if …

- you have ever said or thought 'Just one more episode'. ☐
- you dream, or daydream, about the show you're currently watching. ☐
- you feel that you know the show's characters as well as your actual friends. ☐
- when the series ends, you feel depressed (for around ten seconds until you start the next one). ☐
- you've stayed up all night, or at least until 3 am, watching episodes of a show. ☐
- the show is your favorite topic of conversation. ☐
- you want other people to watch the show and love it as much as you do. ☐
- watching the show, or even thinking about watching the show, is the best part of your day. ☐

What it means:

1–3 checks: You enjoy watching TV shows. You are not addicted to TV, yet, but you are perhaps an occasional binge-watcher.

4–6 checks: You are addicted to TV and probably a frequent binge-watcher. Be careful this doesn't take over your life.

7–8 checks: You need to get a life!

➤ Go back to page 115.

3.3 Student A

The central three-star Hotel Rambla Park is 50 m from Barcelona's famous Las Ramblas walking street and close to some of its best stores, markets and restaurants. This attractive hotel has a good restaurant with room service and a small pool. All rooms are non-smoking and have air conditioners, free wi-fi and a TV. One-way airport transfers are available for 15 dollars per person. The front desk is open 24 hours.

Room type: Double or twin room (extra bed available) – 40 dollars per person, per night including breakfast.
Single room: 60 dollars per night including breakfast.

Share Like Comment

➤ Go back to page 27.

10.2 Student B

A Look at the pictures. Think about how you will answer the questions. Write notes.

1 Can you describe the two pictures?
2 Which of these ways of communicating with other people do you prefer and why?
3 What computer skills and knowledge about the internet does someone need to make video calls?

B DISCUSS Your partner will ask you the questions in Exercise A.

C CHANGE Now ask your partner the questions below.

1 Can you describe the two pictures on page 154?
2 Which of these two ways of managing your money do you prefer and why?
3 What computer skills and knowledge about the internet does someone need to manage an online bank account?

D Can you think of one more question to ask?

➤ Go back to page 95.

12.3 Groups

Choose one of the products for your advertising campaign.

a

b
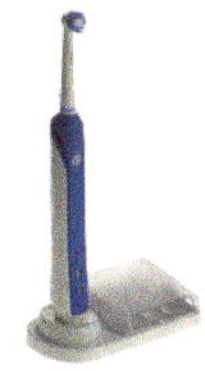
c
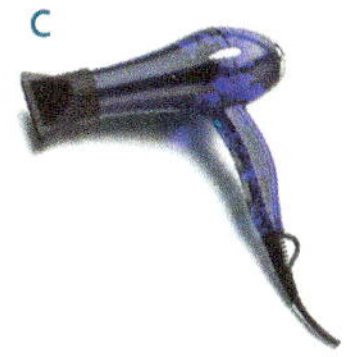

➤ Go back to page 117.

4.3 *Hygge* scores

What does your score mean?

7–10 points: Your lifestyle is already very *hygge*. Have you thought about moving to Denmark?!

4–6 points: Your lifestyle is fairly *hygge*, but you could still learn a thing or two from the Danes.

0–3 points: Your lifestyle is not *hygge* at all. Be kind to yourself and let some more *hygge* into your life!

➤ Go back to page 148.

10.3 Students A and B

Do you have what it takes to work in space? Complete our survey to find out.

Check (✓) the things you do or would like to do in your job.

- Follow a detailed schedule ○
- Do research and collect data ○
- Do experiments and make discoveries ○
- Test or work with new technologies ○
- Solve problems ○
- Repair equipment ○
- Work away from home ○
- Study the mind or body ○
- Do dangerous work ○
- Work alone ○
- Work in a team ○

Results

1–4 checks: Space is probably not your place.
5–8 checks: You could try a job in the sky.
9+ checks: You'd be great for work on Mars or in the stars.

➤ Go back to page 97.

3.3 Student B

Gaudí House Hostel is a half-hour walk or ten-minute bus trip from the center of Barcelona and is perfect for travelers on a budget. The eight-person dorms (choose between male only, female only or mixed) are comfortable, the bathrooms are clean and the kitchen area has everything you need to cook for yourself. Guests can leave their valuables in the safe at the front desk. Wi-fi is available in the front desk area. (Note: air conditioning is not available in dorm rooms.)

Room type: Dorm bed 25 dollars per person, per night. (Add breakfast for only 5 dollars per person, per day!)

Share Like Comment

➤ Go back to page 27.

10.3 Groups

SPEAK Work in groups. Read the fact file and discuss the questions.

Mission to Mars

Distance: When Earth and Mars are closest, the distance between them is 57.6 million kilometers.
Journey time: 6–8 months one-way. Crew will be away from Earth for around two years.
Communication: As the ship moves farther away from Earth, it will take up to 40 minutes to send and receive messages to and from Earth.
Mission: To visit and land on Mars and look for life. Crew will do research and experiments and collect data about the red planet.

1 What will be the biggest challenges for the crew on the mission to Mars?
2 What are the five most important skills and personal qualities crew members will need?
3 What kind of problems might they have to solve on the journey?
4 What will an average day be like on the space ship?

➤ Go back to page 97.

7.1 Student A

A Read the sentences to Student B who will write them down. Be careful to pronounce *a* and *an* using the weak sound /ə/ (schwa). Check Student B's sentences are correct.

1 It was **a** great party.
2 It's **a** really funny movie.
3 It was **an** amazing view.
4 We had **a** lot of fun.
5 It put **a** smile on my face.

B Listen to Student B and write down the sentences he/she says.

C Tell your partner about events or situations that the sentences in Exercise B describe.

A: My sister's 18th birthday was a great party. It was an amazing time and we had a lot of fun. We …
B: It was an amazing view from the top of the Eiffel Tower. I went there last year with …

➤ Go back to page 63.

4.2 Student A

Work–life balance

Everybody loves long weekends, so why do they happen so rarely? When we have three full days off work, there is more time to relax and spend time with friends and family. The good news is that some people think it might not be long until *every* weekend is a long weekend.

Experts and business leaders predict that better technology will do more of our work for us. This will allow us to have shorter workweeks in the future. In fact, it is already beginning to happen. Carlos Slim, the famous Mexican telecoms billionaire, has introduced a shorter week for some of his older, more experienced employees. In Japan, companies such as car maker Toyota have found that working shorter hours leads to happier employees, and higher profits.

A better work–life balance won't be the only good thing about shorter workweeks. Offices will use less energy for lighting, computers and air conditioning. Also, there will be fewer car trips to work, which is better for the environment.

Glossary

expert (n) someone who knows a lot about a particular subject
profit (n) money you make by selling something or from your business

➤ Go back to page 34.

9.1 Group A

A **SPEAK** Look at questions 1–3 in Exercise B. What would you do in each situation? Why?

B Think of two more questions. Write them down. Use the second conditional.

1 If you had to choose between having a new cell phone and seeing your favorite band, which would you choose?

2 If you had to choose between a meal for two and an item of clothing, which would you choose?

3 If you could have a weekend break anywhere in the world, where would you go?

4 ______________________________

5 ______________________________

➤ Go back to page 83.

3.3 Student C

The Olympic Apartments are close to Barcelona's beaches and have beautiful ocean views. The famous Las Ramblas walking street is a 20-minute walk away. The two- and three-bedroom with room service apartments are simple and clean. Guests can pay to use the gym and spa on the first floor. Stores, public transportation and restaurants are all very close. All apartments have a balcony and air conditioners. Wi-fi is available for an extra 5 dollars per day.

Room type: Two-bedroom with room service apartment – 100 dollars per night for up to four people.

➤ Go back to page 27.

5.1 Groups

Group A jobs: banker, nanny, professional soccer player, politician

Group B jobs: doctor, pilot, social worker, actor

Group C jobs: lawyer, nurse, soldier, teacher

➤ Go back to page 43.

11.2 Students A and B

According to psychologists, the first animal you chose is how you like to see yourself. The second animal is how other people see you. And your third choice is what you are really like.

➤ Go back to page 104.

7.3 Student B

Judit Polgár:
chess Grandmaster

1976: born in Hungary

Education: did not go to school; her parents brought her and her two sisters up as part of an 'educational experiment'; chess was the subject her parents chose

6 years: started playing in international tournaments

9 years: won her first international tournament

15 years: became the youngest person ever to become a chess Grandmaster

Career: was the world's number one female chess player for 20 years; has beaten 11 current or former male world champions

Other information

2012: started the Judit Polgár Chess Foundation; the aim is to introduce children around the world to chess

2014: retired from competitive chess; became head coach of the Hungarian National Men's Chess Team

➤ Go back to page 67.

3.2 Students A and B

Work in pairs. Look at the pictures and tell a story. Think about:

- what happened during the journey.
- what decisions the people made.
- how the people felt at the end of the journey.

➤ Go back to page 25.

W checking your writing

Use it or *lose it*

Welcome. This is a blog for language learners written by … a language learner!
My favorite tip for people interested in learning languages is 'use it or lose it'. It means 'practice the language and you won't forget it'. I started this blog to practice my English. Would you like to practice your English? Send me a message in English and I'll reply. Twice a week, I'll post the most interesting messages on the blog.

About me

I'm Karolina. Tea drinker, [1]bloger and hard-working [2]langage learner. [3]I've 20 years old and I'm Polish. I study law in college, and English in my free time. I go to English classes [4]three times week and I practice for half an hour every day. I have to be [5]wel organized to get everything done! Of course, I'm [6]serious with learning, but I also really enjoy it.
My blog [7]aren't my only hobby. I'm a book lover and I'm also [8]interest in old black and white movies. I read and watch in Polish and English.
I'm a curious, sociable person and [9]I like talk to people who ask questions. I'm interested in creative types and I love meeting new people – especially other language learners (in the real world and online). I think that makes me a [10]person people. I hope you enjoy the blog. Remember … use it or lose it!

A Read the home page of Karolina's blog and answer the questions.

1 What is her blog about and who is it for?
2 How can you help Karolina?

B Work in pairs. Read the *About me* section of Karolina's blog. Then cover the blog and discuss what you remember about:

1 her work or studies
2 her likes and dislikes
3 the type of person she is

C Work in pairs. In Karolina's *About me* section there are ten mistakes with grammar, vocabulary and spelling. Correct them. Use the information in the box to help you.

Checking your writing

Follow these tips to help make your writing better.

- Always read your writing slowly and carefully before you finish.
- Try and find and correct any mistakes.
- Check your grammar.
- Check the vocabulary and spelling and be careful with any new language.

D Which colors are the different types of mistakes in Karolina's writing?

1 grammar mistakes ______
2 vocabulary mistakes ______
3 spelling mistakes ______

E Find and correct one mistake in each sentence. Then decide what type of mistake it is. Write grammar (*G*), vocabulary (*V*) or spelling (*S*).

1 I love to travell and I study tourism. ______ __
2 Why you did start this blog? ______ __
3 I try to learn a new word ever day. ______ __
4 I usually am online during the evenings. ______ __
5 I guess I'm an independant type. ______ __
6 I'm responsible with updating the website. ______ __
7 Are you want to know more about our group? ______ __
8 I've never write a blog before. ______ __

WRITING

A PLAN You are going to write an *About me* section for your own blog, website or social media page. Take notes about your work or studies, your likes and dislikes and the type of person you are.

B WRITE Use your notes and Writing Exercise A to help you write your blog. Then check your writing using the list below and the strategies in the Writing skills box.

- [ ] I have mentioned my work or studies.
- [ ] I have mentioned some of my likes and dislikes.
- [ ] I have described my personality and the type of person I am.
- [ ] I have checked my work for mistakes with grammar, vocabulary and spelling.

C REVIEW Work in groups. Read the group's profiles. Can you recommend any blogs, websites, magazines, books, TV shows or movies the people in your group might be interested in?

2 Writing ● Write an email of complaint

W– linking words

A Read Emma's email about a problem in her neighborhood. What is she complaining about?

To: Mr. Black
Re: Road safety complaint

Dear Mr. Black,

I'm writing to complain about the dangerous roads outside my apartment building.

My main complaint is that the roads are dangerous **because** there are no crosswalks **or** traffic lights outside my apartment building. This is a problem for a number of reasons.

First of all, the traffic is very fast on the main road **and** this makes crossing difficult for older people and mothers with young children. The second problem is that there is a popular children's play area across from the main road, **but** the children have no way to cross the road to use the play area. The last problem is that the grocery store parking lot entrance is on the corner of two busy roads, **so** it makes it more difficult to cross the road.

I would like to offer you two solutions for this problem.

First of all, I think you should make a crosswalk on the busy road between the grocery store and the children's play area. I also think you need to make a second crosswalk across the main road from the apartment building to the play area. You could put traffic lights on this intersection to make it safe for children to use.

I hope you will make this dangerous road safer for the older people and children in our neighborhood.

I'm looking forward to hearing from you.

Sincerely yours,

Emma Lopez

B Read again and answer the questions.

1 How many problems and solutions does Emma mention?
2 Do you think Mr. Black will do what Emma wants him to do?
3 What tense does she use to begin and end her email?

C Look at the words in **bold** in Emma's email. Then complete the rules in the box with *and*, *but*, *or*, *so*, or *because*.

Linking words

We can join sentences and link ideas with *and*, *but*, *or*, *so* and *because*. This helps you to write longer and more interesting sentences.

We use [1]__________ to add more information.
We use [2]__________ to give contrasting information.
We use [3]__________ to give a negative alternative.
We use [4]__________ to give a result.
We use [5]__________ to explain why.

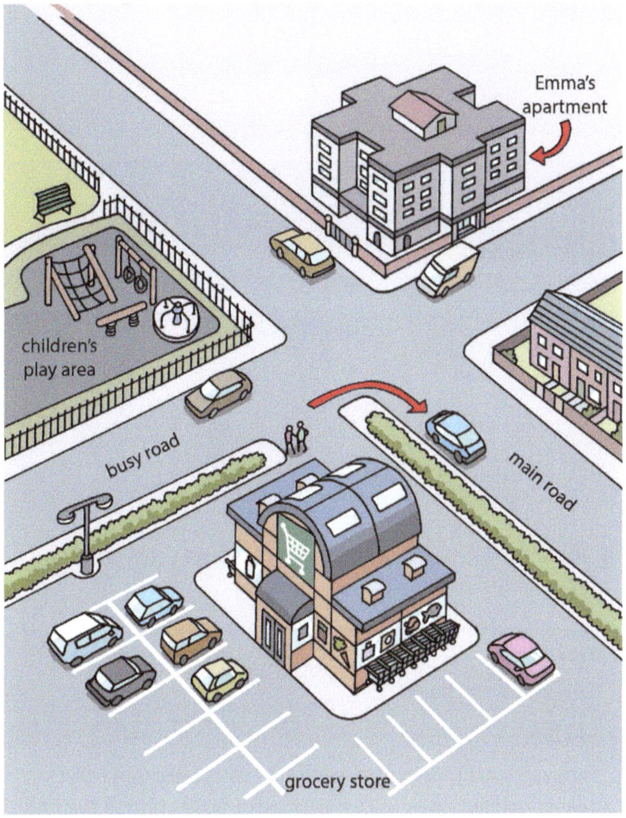

D Complete the sentences with *and*, *but*, *or*, *so* or *because*.

1 The air is dirty __________ there are too many cars.
2 There should be more parks for children __________ teenagers.
3 We shouldn't litter __________ play loud music.
4 We like the play area, __________ it's too small.
5 More children are living here, __________ the neighborhood should be safer.

WRITING

A PLAN You are going to write an email of complaint. Think of a problem in your neighborhood and two or more solutions to your problem.

B WRITE Write your email of complaint.

- Use Emma's email and the Writing skills box to help you.
- Check your writing for mistakes with grammar, vocabulary and spelling.

C REVIEW Work in groups. Read your emails and decide which one will be the most successful.

3 Writing

Write an email about a travel experience

W – ordering events

A Work in pairs. Discuss the questions.

1 Why do some people feel it is important to have a vacation?

2 What kind of problems do people have on vacation?

B Read Amal's email. Underline any of the problems you thought of in Exercise A.

To: Cleo
Subject: We're back!

Hi Cleo,

How are you? Thanks for feeding the cat. We're home, but there's no electricity, so I'm writing this on my phone. We had a terrible vacation. Scott broke his leg!

First, bad weather delayed our flight. We arrived at the chalet in the middle of the night, so the next morning we were really tired. After breakfast, we went to the ski lifts, but they were closed because it was too windy.

The following day, it wasn't so windy and we had a great time on the slopes in the morning. Then, we stopped for some lunch, but when I wanted to pay I couldn't find my wallet!

Two days later, the real disaster happened. We were skiing down a busy slope when Scott fell over and broke his leg. We had to fly to the local hospital in a helicopter. His leg is in a cast for the next six weeks.

I'll call you tomorrow.

Amal

C Read again and number the events in the order they happened (1–6).

___ Scott had an accident.
___ There was a problem at Amal's home.
_1_ The flight left the airport late.
___ It wasn't possible to go up the mountain.
___ Amal lost something.
___ The weather was better.

D Find and underline the words that helped you order the events. There are six words or phrases.

E Complete the sentences with the words in the box. Use the information in the box to help you.

Ordering events

When you write about an experience, use sequencing words and phrases like the ones you underlined in Amal's email to help readers follow the order of events.

after ~~first~~ hours morning next then

1 _First_, we missed the bus, so we had to take a taxi.

2 The following ________, I got the correct visa and crossed the border on foot.

3 The ________ day, we woke up to the sound of the ocean.

4 We drove for four hours, and ________ stopped for some lunch.

5 Two ________ later, my friend found her cell phone behind the couch.

6 ________ a quick lunch, we began walking again in the rain.

F Work in pairs. Cover Amal's email and retell the story using sequencing words and the events in Exercise C.

WRITING

A PLAN You are going to write an email to a friend about a good or bad travel experience. Think about the following:

1 Was it a good or bad experience?
2 Where were you and who were you with?
3 What happened?
4 How did the experience end?

B WRITE Write an email to a friend. Use the checklist to help you.

- [ ] I have written to a friend.
- [ ] I have started with an informal greeting and finished with an informal sign-off.
- [ ] I have used sequencing words and phrases to order the events.
- [ ] I have checked my spelling, vocabulary and grammar.

C REVIEW Work in pairs. Read your partner's email and ask questions about his/her experience.

4 Writing — Write an invitation and reply

W– informal emails

A Read Marta's message and answer the questions.

1 Why is Marta messaging her friends?
2 What kind of evening is she planning on Saturday?
3 What should her guests bring?

To: elviraandjan, ravi.gupta, stuart.jackson
Subject: Hygge Evening
Hi guys,
[1]How are things? Hope you're OK. [2]Life's good, but as usual, I'm looking forward to the weekend.
Actually, that is why I'm writing. [3]Are you doing anything on Saturday night? I'm planning a *hygge* evening around 7 pm at my place. [4]Can you make it?
I'm going to bake some cookies, light lots of candles and we could play a board game or watch a movie – or both! 😃
Anyway, [5]let me know whether you can come. All you need to bring is yourself, some warm socks and a wool sweater 😉
[6]It would be nice to see you.
Marta

B Look at Marta's message again. Match the underlined phrases (1–6) with the phrases with a similar meaning (a–f).

a Let me know if you're coming.
b Would you like to come?
c Everything is fine.
d Do you have any plans for …?
e How's life?
f I hope you can make it.

C Read two replies to Marta's message. Who is and is not coming to her *hygge* evening?

Dear Marta,
Nice to hear from you!
Thanks for inviting us on Saturday. We'd love to come, but we're going to Jan's parents' house for dinner, so I'm afraid we can't make it. I'm meeting them for the first time! I'm sure it will be fine, but I am a little nervous. Your *hygge* evening sounds much more relaxing!
Anyway, I'll let you know how it goes. Let's get together soon. I have so much to tell you.
See you soon,
Elvira

Hi Marta,
Long time no see. I hope you're well!
Thanks for the invitation for Saturday. A *hygge* evening sounds like just what I need, and I'd love to come. Who else will be there? Are Elvira and Jan coming?
Are you sure I can't bring any food? I could make some homemade snacks or something.
Let me know. It'll be gr8 to see you.
Love,
Ravi

D Read again and underline the phrases Marta's friends use to:

1 say thank you
2 say yes to the invitation
3 say no to the invitation
4 give a reason for saying no
5 mention the next time they'll meet

E Complete the box with words from the emails in Exercises A and C.

Informal emails

Start informal emails with a friendly greeting.
- *Dear Marta,*
- *Hi/Hello Marta,*
- *Hi* [1] ______ (to a group; men, women or mixed)

Mention your last contact with other person.
- *Nice to hear from you.*
- *Long time no* [2] ______ (when you haven't seen the person for a long time)

Use emoticons and abbreviations, but don't overuse them.
- *It'll be* [3] ______ *to see you.*

Don't use full forms. Use contractions.
- *I hope ~~you are~~ you're well.*
- *We ~~would~~* [4] ______ *love to come.*

Finish with a friendly goodbye.
- *Bye for now,*
- [5] ______ *soon,*
- *Love,*

WRITING

A WRITE Work in pairs. You are organizing a party at your place. Write a message inviting another pair of students. Use Exercise E above to help you. Write 100–150 words.

B WRITE Swap messages with another pair of students and reply to their invitation. Use the Writing skills box to help you. Write 50–100 words. Include the following information:

- say thank you for the invitation
- say yes or no to the invitation (if no, give a reason)
- mention the next time you'll meet

5 Writing — Write a cover email

W – beginning and ending emails and letters

English-speaking vacation nannies and mannies (job s632)

Vacation Hands agency is looking for English-speaking nannies and mannies (male nannies) to travel with families on their summer and winter vacations. You will take care of the children during the day and babysit in the evenings. Experience is an advantage. Good pay, plus all travel, accommodations and food included. Reply with a résumé and a copy of your passport to Olga Zatorska at ol.zator@vacationhands.nett

A Work in pairs. Read the advertisement. Would you or anyone you know be interested in this job? Why/Why not?

B Read Maurice's cover email. Do you think Maurice will be offered an interview? Why?

To: Ms. Zatorska
Subject: Vacation manny job

[1]<u>Dear Ms. Zatorska,</u>

[2]<u>I am writing to apply for</u> the job of vacation manny with the Vacation Hands agency. [3]<u>I attached</u> a copy of my résumé. [4]Right now, I am studying at the University of Edinburgh and am available to work from July 1st to September 30th.

[5]<u>I speak fluent</u> English and Spanish and enjoy working with children. Last summer, I was an activities supervisor at a summer camp for 6–12-year-olds. My energy and creativity made me popular with the children. I believe <u>this experience</u> will be very useful. [6]<u>A job with</u> the Vacation Hands agency would be an exciting opportunity to learn new skills and work in an international environment.

[7]<u>I look forward to hearing from you.</u>

[8]<u>Sincerely yours,</u>

Maurice Garcia

C Read again. Put the different parts of a cover email in the correct order (1–7).

___ why you want this job
___ what you are doing now and when you are available
___ polite ending
___ reason for writing
_1_ a formal greeting
___ details about your experience and character
___ attachments, for example, your résumé

D Look at the box. Which beginnings and endings are formal (F)? Which are informal (I)?

Beginning and ending emails and letters

Beginning		Ending	
1 Hello,	_I_	7 See you soon,	___
2 Dear Sir/Madam,	___	8 Bye for now,	___
3 Dear all,	___	9 Lots of love,	___
4 Hi everyone,	___	10 Sincerely yours,	___
5 Dear Mr. Cox,	___	11 Yours truly,	___
6 Dear Diane,	___	12 Kind regards,	___
		13 Best wishes,	___

E Replace the <u>underlined</u> phrases in the email with similar phrases in the box.

Dear Sir/Madam, I am fluent in
I hope to hear from you soon.
I would like to apply for Please find attached
the knowledge and skills I developed there
Working for Yours truly,

F Work in pairs. What kind of skills, experience and personality would be helpful for this summer job?

Waiters and waitresses wanted (job h384)

Are you looking for part-time work? We need friendly, hard-working people to join our evening table service team at Blue Moon Asian Food Center. Experience is an advantage, but we will give full training. Attractive wages and free meals. Write with a résumé to noi.warumdee@mail.nett.

WRITING

A PLAN You are going to write a cover email to apply for the job in Writing Exercise F. Take notes for a cover email. Use Exercise C to help you.

B WRITE Write your cover email. Use the strategies in the box and Maurice's email to help you.

W ordering information

A Read the product reviews from an online shopping website and match each review (1–3) with a picture (a–c).

a

b

c

1 **Really useful** ★★★★★
I bought this cool little device to help me get in shape, and **I'm very** [1] ___happy___ **with it**. It's comfortable and **I like the color**. It tells me how many steps I've taken, and how many calories I've burned each day. It also gives me information about how I slept. **It's very** [2] ________ and I find it motivates me to do more exercise than before. **It's made of** rubber, so it's waterproof and also very light. **It was definitely** [3] ________ **the money** and it arrived the day after I ordered it. [4] ________ **recommended** for anyone who is interested in health and fitness.

2 **Ouch!** ★★★★★
I bought this a few weeks ago to help me exercise. **It was a** [5] ________ **price** and it seems to be **well made**. **It was easy to put together** and **came with** a book full of different exercises to try. **The only** [6] ________ **is** it is really difficult to use! My stomach muscles aren't very strong and I find most of the exercises in the book impossible. I'm sure with enough practice it will get easier, but for now I have to say I don't look forward to using it. [7] ________ **for** those who don't mind the pain!

3 **Save your money** ★★★★★
My girlfriend bought me these as a birthday present, but **I was very** [8] ________ **with them**. Yes, **they look nice** and are comfortable to wear, but there's one big problem. **They are really** [9] ________ **quality.** I wore them in the gym once, and after about half an hour, I noticed there was a hole in the side. Obviously these were very **badly** [10] ________. I sent them back to the website and got a new pair, but after a few more trips to the gym … it happened again! **I don't recommend these** at all. They were **a real** [11] ________ **of money.**

B Read again. Complete the phrases in **bold** with the words in the box.

disappointed	highly	made	happy	poor	problem
reasonable	recommended	useful	waste	worth	

C Read again. Which phrases in **bold** describe positive things about the products, which describe negative and which are neutral?

I'm very happy with it. = positive

I was very disappointed with them. = negative

It's made of … = neutral

D Read the information in the box. Then read the reviews again and number the parts of a review in the correct order (1–4).

Ordering information

Think carefully about the order in which you present information in reviews and other types of factual writing. Organize your ideas into clear and logical paragraphs to make your writing easy for readers to follow.

negative points ___
recommendation (or not) ___
positive points ___
why you bought the product ___

E Work in pairs. Describe one product you have bought recently that you recommend and one that you do not.

WRITING

A PLAN Imagine you have bought one of the products below. Take notes on the following questions.

a pair of running sneakers

a fitness game for a game console

a winter sports jacket

a mountain bike

1 What positive points does the product have?
2 What negative points does the product have?

B WRITE Write a 100-word review of the product for a shopping website. Explain why you bought it and what positive and negative points it has. Then make a recommendation.

C REVIEW Work in groups. Read you classmates' reviews. Which are the best and worst products?

W – using survey report language

A Look at the chart. What does it show? Do any of the findings surprise you?

Percentage of population aged 25–34 with a college degree in English-speaking countries in 2015

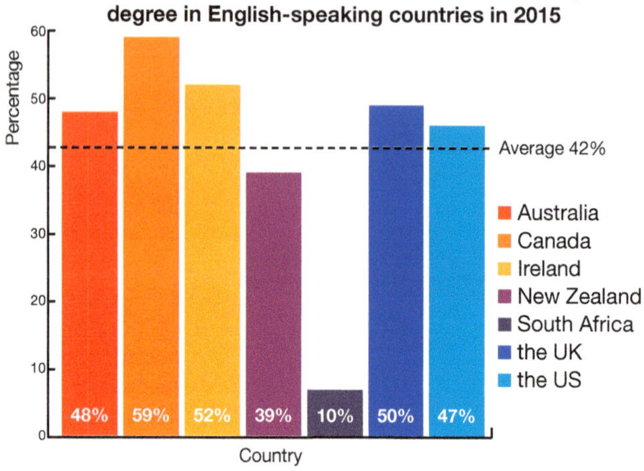

(c) OECD (2018), Population with tertiary education (indicator).

B Complete the survey report with the correct country.

The survey compares the percentage of people aged 25 to 34 with a college degree in English-speaking countries. According to the survey, an average of 42 percent of the population of these countries are graduates. [1] ________________ has the highest percentage of graduates at 59 percent. In contrast, [2] ________________ has the lowest with just ten percent of the population having a college degree. The number of graduates in [3] ________________ is just over 50 percent, while in [4] ________________ the figure is just under 50 percent. Similarly, the figure for [5] ________________ is 47 percent, while in [6] ________________, 39 percent of people aged 25 to 34 are graduates.

C Look at the survey report again and complete the words and phrases in the box.

Using survey report language

We can say what the survey is about with:

- *The survey shows …*
- *The survey* [1] ________________ *…*
- *According* [2] ________________ *the survey, …*

We can express differences with:

- *By/In comparison, …*
- *By/In* [3] ________________*, …*

We can express similarities with:

- [4] ________________*, …*
- *Both …*

We can give data and statistics by using:

- *… has the highest percentage of graduates at 59 percent.*
- *… an average of 42 percent of the population …*
- *… has the lowest with just 7 percent …*
- *… the figure for the US is 47 percent …*

Note the different uses of prepositions (*at, of*).

D Complete the sentences with the best words or phrases. Use the strategies in the box to help you.

1 As of 2015 the birth rate in the US is just under two children per family. ________________, in Europe it is around 1.5.

2 ________________ the survey, 41 percent of ________________ men and women play sports to keep fit. Thirty percent say they play sports for social reasons.[1]

3 The survey ________________ IQs of brothers and sisters. It ________________ that the oldest generally has the highest IQ.

WRITING

A PREPARE You are going to write a survey report about World Happiness. Read about the report. What areas of life do you think the survey asks questions about?

The World Happiness report is an annual survey. It collects data from over 150 countries to find out which country has the happiest population. The survey asks people to decide how happy they are with different areas of their life.

B PLAN Look at the survey results.

- Decide which of the data you will include.
- Decide how you can compare and contrast the data.
- Use the report in Writing Exercise B to help you.
- Use the information in the *World Happiness* report.
- Use phrases from the Writing skills box.

C WRITE Write about 100–120 words. Check your writing for grammar, vocabulary and spelling.

World Happiness report

Top four countries	score (out of 10)
Norway	7.54
Denmark	7.52
Iceland	7.50
Switzerland	7.50
Bottom four countries	**score**
Syria	3.46
Tanzania	3.35
Burundi	2.91
Central African Republic	2.69

Helliwell, J., Layard, R., & Sachs, J. (2017). World Happiness Report 2017, New York: Sustainable Development Solutions Network.

D DISCUSS Work in groups. Why do you think the countries in the survey are the happiest in the world?

1 Special Eurobarometer 412 "Sport and physical activity". © European Union, 1995-2017

Write a review

W– describing and recommending

A Read the movie review. Is it positive or negative? Underline the words and phrases that tell you this.

La La Land is set in modern-day Los Angeles. It stars Emma Stone and Ryan Gosling. It tells the story of a romance between Mia (played by Emma Stone) and Seb (played by Ryan Gosling). She is an actress and he is a jazz pianist. The movie is a musical, but it is also a classic love story with some wonderful music and singing and some old-fashioned dancing. At the same time, it is exciting, beautiful and heart-breaking. I found myself completely engaged with the story and with the lives of Mia and Seb. The acting was excellent. Emma Stone and Ryan Gosling were perfect as Mia and Seb. If you like musicals, you'll love this movie.

Share Like Comment

Comments:

Stacey99: I agree. Great movie. I wasn't expecting that ending, but it's definitely worth seeing.

BillyTom: I liked the ending. I didn't imagine the story would finish that way. It was a nice twist!

DashaV: This movie is a work of art, full of color and life. A modern-day classic.

Rob78: Not my favorite movie. But to be fair, I don't like musicals!

B Number the topics in the order they are written about in the review.

The movie

- ___ the plot or story
- 1 where the movie is set (location)
- ___ writer's opinion of the movie
- ___ writer's opinion of the actors
- ___ writer's recommendation
- ___ movie genre

C Read the comments again. Does each person like or dislike the movie? Underline the words and phrases in the comments that tell you this.

D Cover Exercises A, B and C. Complete the missing words in the phrases from the review and comments.

Describing and recommending

1. *La La Land* is s___ in …
2. It s_______ Emma Stone and Ryan Gosling.
3. It tells the s_______ of …
4. The m_______ is a musical.
5. The a_______ was …
6. It's (definitely) w_______ seeing.

E Write the missing words to complete the review.

The movie is _______ in Los Angeles in 1961. It _______ the true _______ of the author P.L. Travers and moviemaker Walt Disney. Disney wants to make a movie using one of Traver's books. It _______ Tom Hanks. The _______ is excellent. This movie is definitely _______ seeing.

WRITING

A PREPARE You are going to write review of a movie that you have seen.

B PLAN Take notes for each topic in Writing Exercise B.

C WRITE Use the review in Exercise A and the strategies in the Writing skills box to help you write your review. Write about 100 words.

D REVIEW Work in pairs. Can you find someone in the class who has seen the same movie? Read your partner's review and write a comment. Then work with another pair and add comments to their reviews.

9 Writing

Write a 'for sale' advertisement

W– describing a product

A Read the advice for writing a 'for sale' advertisement. Complete the advice with the words in the box.

accessories buyer condition details specifications

The key to a great ad

Attention: The title of the advertisement needs to get the [1] _____________'s attention. Keep it short and simple. Start with the best or key feature of your item. This could be the price, its [2] _____________ or simply that it is a very popular item. If it has a fixed price, use words like 'only' and 'bargain'.

Description: Your advertisement needs a detailed description of the item. If needed, include the [3] _____________, such as size, height and width. Include any [4] _____________ that it comes with, such as a battery charger. Include pictures to show what condition the item is in.

Action: Encourage the buyer to take action. For example, invite them to contact you with questions or for more [5] _____________. Say how you will post the item and offer free postage if possible.

B Look at the advertisements. Do they follow the advice? Find and underline examples of:

- best or key features
- how good the price is
- specification (size or dimensions)
- accessories
- condition
- contacting the seller

digital camera – only $150

The camera is almost new and hardly used. It comes in the original box and with a case, strap and spare battery. See picture. Please contact me if you have any questions.

Pen and ink drawing – auction

This is an original and signed pen and ink drawing by British illustrator William Miller. It shows a mountain scene in Scotland. The dimensions are 35 cm x 18 cm. The work is in good condition with a few minor marks. Please contact me for further information.

Men's sneakers (size 40) – $40

I am selling a pair of sneakers. They are size 40 and are yellow with gray stripes. They are in excellent condition with just a few light marks. I am selling them for the bargain price of $40. Free delivery. If you have any questions, just ask.

C Complete the box with words from the advertisements.

Describing a product

Introducing the item

- *This is …*
- *I am* [1] _____selling_____ …

Describing its condition, specification and accessories

- *in excellent/good* [2] _____________, *almost* [3] _____________, *hardly* [4] _____________
- *It comes in the original* [5] _____________
- *… with (just) a few (light/minor)* [6] _____________
- *It comes with …*
- *The dimensions are …*

Contacting the seller

- *Please contact me if you have any (further)* [7] _____________.
- *Please contact me for further* [8] _____________ */details.*
- *If you have any questions, just* [9] _____________.

D Correct the mistakes and rewrite the sentences from online 'for sale' advertisements.

1 The phone comes in the origin box.

____

2 I sell a Sony Bravia 65XE9005 TV.

____

3 The camera is near new and is excellent condition.

____

4 The item in good condition with a few lightly marks.

____

5 Please contact for further informations and details.

____

WRITING

A PLAN You are going to write a 'for sale' advertisement. Choose one of the items in the pictures or choose an item of your own. Invent some details about the condition of the item.

B WRITE Write your advertisement. Use the Writing skills box, the ads and the advice to help you. Write 50–75 words.

C DISCUSS Work in groups. Show your advertisement to your group. Is anyone interested in buying your item?

W making recommendations

A Work in groups. Answer the questions.

1 How many school subjects can you think of in one minute?

2 Which were your favorite and least favorite subjects at school, and why?

3 Were/Are you more interested in science, art, language or humanities (history, geography, etc)?

B Work in pairs. Read Bee's question on an online message board. What recommendation would you make for Bee and why?

Woohaa Answers

Bee, Thailand: Should I buy a laptop or a tablet?
I'm not sure whether to buy a laptop or a tablet. I need a computer for work, but also for entertainment at home and while I'm traveling. What do you think?

C Now read Dylan's answer and underline any ideas you or your partner said in Exercise B. What other advantages and disadvantages of laptops and tablets does Dylan mention?

Best answer
Dylan, US
This is not an easy decision, Bee. If you choose the wrong computer, you might regret it. Before you decide, think about size and weight, performance and price.
Most laptops are bigger and heavier than the average tablet. This is partly because they have a normal keyboard. Size and weight may be a problem if you travel a lot or need to carry your computer to work each day.
When it comes to performance, laptops are usually faster and have a bigger memory than tablets. They are also better for people who need to have several apps or programs open at the same time. On the other hand, the battery in a tablet computer will probably last longer between charges than the one in a laptop.
Of course, your budget is also important. Generally speaking, laptops are more expensive than tablets. If you travel regularly and want to spend less money, I'd recommend a tablet. If you want better performance and a normal keyboard, I'd suggest buying a laptop.
I think you should do some more research online. You could also talk to someone in a computer store and ask for their opinion. Good luck!

D Read the information in the box. Then find and underline four examples of the structures in the box in Dylan's answer.

Making recommendations

You can tell people what you think they should do using the following language:

- *I think you should* + base form
- *You could* + base form
- *I'd suggest* + noun **or** verb + *-ing* **or** *you* + base form
- *I'd recommend* + noun **or** verb-*ing* **or** *you* + base form

E There is one mistake in each recommendation. Correct the mistakes.

1 I think you should getting a new phone rather than a used one.

______

2 I'd recommend you checking a used phone carefully before you buy it.

______

3 You could reading more about different brands online.

______

4 I'd suggest to buy a used phone because you'll get better performance for your money.

______

F Work in pairs. Imagine a friend has asked you the following questions. What would you recommend and why? Compare your ideas.

1 Should I travel for six months or get a job right away when I finish college?

2 What brand of computer do you think I should I buy?

3 Should I study science or language?

WRITING

A WRITE Read Corey's question on the *Woohaa Answers* website. Write a reply of at least 100 words comparing the two options and making recommendations.

Woohaa Answers

Corey, Germany: Should I buy a new or used phone?
Should I buy a new cell phone or a used one? I don't have a lot of money to spend on it, but I'd like the best one I can afford. What do you think?

B REVIEW Work in groups. Read your group's recommendations. In what ways are they similar or different to yours?

11 Writing

Write an email giving suggestions and advice

W – making suggestions and giving advice

A Look at the places in the pictures. Where do you think they are? Read the emails quickly and match them with the pictures. Were your ideas correct?

1

2

3

a
To: Sam
Subject: RE: Any advice?

You really must visit the Joshua Tree National Park when you're in California. It isn't far from Los Angeles and it's really easy to get to by car. It's named after the famous Joshua trees that are found there. It's an amazing desert landscape with huge rocks and boulders everywhere. If I were you, I'd spend at least two days there. You can camp there, but it's a good idea to book in advance.

b
To: Carlos
Subject: RE: Vietnam tips

In Vietnam, Halong Bay is a must. There are thousands of different-sized islands and rock formations coming out of the ocean. It really is an incredible place. According to legend, the bay was formed when an angry dragon destroyed a mountain with its tail. It isn't too far from Hanoi. I'd recommend taking an organized tour from there.

c
To: Teresa
Subject: RE: Where to go

If you're in northern England, you really should visit the island of Lindisfarne. It's about a mile from the mainland and you can drive across to it when the tide is out. But when the tide comes in, it becomes a true island. It's a magical place with some beautiful beaches. I suggest you head to the north part of the island to get away from the crowds of people. Make sure you check the times of the tides so you know when it's safe to cross.

B Read again and complete the table.

	a	b	c
Name of place			
Location			
Key features			
How to travel there			

C Complete the box with words from the emails.

Making suggestions and giving advice

When/If you're in …
I suggest you …
I'd [1] ______________ + verb + -*ing* …
You (really) [2] ______________ */ ought to / must* …
If I [3] ______________ *you, I* [4] ______________ …
… is a must.
Make [5] ______________ *you …*
It's a good [6] ______________ *to …*

D Write the words in the correct order to make sentences.

1 It's / to / a / book the train in advance / idea / good
2 I / in April or May / suggest / go / you
3 I'd / at least two or three days / staying / recommend
4 If / in Krakow, / you're / the Wieliczka Salt Mine / visit / really / you / should
5 When / in Oxford, / you're / make / you / sure / the Natural History Museum / visit
6 If / I'd / you, / were / I / for a few days / rent a car

WRITING

A PLAN Imagine a friend is visiting your country or a country you know. You are going to write a short email (50–100 words) to make some suggestions and to give some advice about a place to visit.

B WRITE Use the Writing skills box and include information about:

- where it is
- how to get there
- the main features of the place

C REVIEW Work in groups. Read each other's emails. Which place would you most like to visit?

12 Writing

Write a story

W writing a story

A Work in pairs. Read the news story then close your books and retell the story to your partner. What do you think of Brett Sanders's actions?

Texan driver paid speeding ticket with over 22,000 pennies.

Brett Sanders was driving at 39 mph in a 30 mph zone when he was stopped by police and was given a $212 fine.

Sanders said the fine was too much and that he wanted to make some kind of complaint. So, he ordered over $212 in pennies from the bank and put them into two large buckets. He then went to the payment office and poured the 22,000 coins onto the counter. When he had finished this, he immediately walked out of the building. A friend filmed him while he was doing this. He told reporters that after he had done it, he 'felt great'.

According to the payment office, Sanders had actually overpaid by $7.81. They called him to offer a refund, but Sanders was happy to let them keep the change.

Many people have said Sanders's actions were wrong. At the same time, other people think it was a good way to make a point. What do you think?

B Look at the box. Find and underline more examples of the three tenses in the news story.

Writing a story

Tenses

When we tell a story, we usually use three main tenses.

We use the simple past for the main events in the story.

- *So, he ordered over $212 in pennies from the bank and put them into two large buckets.*

We use the past progressive for background activities or situations that were in progress when the main events happened.

- *Brett Sanders was driving at 39 mph in a 30 mph zone when he was stopped by police and was given a $212 fine.*

We use the past perfect for events that happened before one of the main events or that happened before the time of the story.

- *When he had finished this, he immediately walked out of the building.*

Sequence words

We use sequence words to connect the events and make the sequence clear.

- *Brett Sanders was driving at 39 mph in a 30 mph zone when he was stopped by police …*
- *So, he ordered over $212 in pennies from the bank …*
- *He then went to the payment office and poured the 22,000 coins onto the counter. When he had finished this, he immediately walked out of the building.*
- *A friend filmed him while he was doing this. He told reporters that after he had done it, he 'felt great'.*

C Choose the correct words to complete the news story.

A surfer 1***was rescued / had been rescued*** yesterday 2***while / after*** he 3***was spending / had spent*** 32 hours at sea. It 4***got / was getting*** dark 5***when / then*** the helicopter rescue team 6***spotted / were spotting*** him 13 miles off the coast of Scotland. He 7***was / had been*** exhausted and thirsty, but he survived as he 8***wore / was wearing*** a wetsuit and 9***was / had been*** still on his surfboard.

WRITING

A PREPARE Look at the pictures and imagine what the story is. You are going to write a short story using all the pictures. Use this as you first sentence:

A man was arrested yesterday for driving a children's electric car.

B PLAN Takes notes and think about the tenses and the sequence words you need to use.

C WRITE Write the story (130–150 words). Check what you have written and make any necessary changes.

D REVIEW Work in groups. Read some of your classmates' stories. How similar are your stories?

Audio scripts

UNIT 1

Lesson 1.1, Listening, Exercise C

1.1 **P = Paul I = Isabelle**

P: Hello, and welcome to *Everyday Psychology*. I'm Paul Ross, and with me today is psychologist and expert on relationships, Isabelle Ackerman.

I: Hello, Paul. Hello, listeners.

P: Isabelle, today's topic is meeting new people. Now, we regularly meet new people at work or in our social lives, but it can be difficult to talk to someone we don't know. I mean, what do you say to a stranger at a party or a new colleague at the office? Is it OK to talk about some topics, but not others? Have you ever met someone new and had no idea what to talk about? Today, you have some advice to help us 'break the ice' and start conversations with new people.

I: Yes, I do. Let's begin with a very simple tip. When you meet someone new, start with a smile. A smile can help us feel more relaxed, but that's easy to forget when you feel nervous.

P: And of course a friendly face is easier to talk to.

I: Yes. A nice way to continue a conversation is to say something positive. You could talk about the place or situation you are in and then ask a question. For example, at a party, try 'Are you having fun?' or 'I love this music! What is your favorite band?' To a new person at work, you can say 'Oh, I'm glad it's lunchtime. How's your first day going?'

P: So no complaining about the boss!

I: Not at first, no. But it is good to ask about other people. For example, in a new group of students, ask 'Do you know our teacher?' or, at a wedding ceremony, 'Did you enjoy the ceremony?' or 'How do you know the happy couple? Were you at school together?' Don't be negative about other people because you don't know who they know.

P: Yes, that could be dangerous.

I: Interests and studies are always good, safe topics to talk about. Questions like 'What kind of music do you like?' or 'Where did you study?' are usually easy to answer. Remember, ask lots of questions and give lots of answers. A successful conversation is like a game of tennis!

P: It takes hours and makes you tired?

I: Very funny. When you feel more relaxed, ask some personal questions. 'Where are you from?', 'Are you married?' and 'Do you have children?' are good examples. But be careful. Don't discuss topics like religion or politics with someone you don't know.

P: Some great tips. Isabelle, thank you very much. That's all for this week. Remember, many great friends meet after a smile and a simple 'hello'. Good luck breaking the ice and meeting new people. Please join us for the next episode of *Everyday Psychology* – we'll be discussing the hot topic …

UNIT 2

Lesson 2.2, Listening, Exercise B

2.2 **P = Presenter R = Richard**

P: More and more of the world's young people are going home to live with their parents after college. Why? And what is it like living at home again as an adult? How do parents feel about the situation? Today, we talk to members of 'the boomerang generation' and their parents about the advantages and disadvantages of living together again. Let's start with Richard …

R: I'm Richard Woodman, from the US. I'm 25 years old and at the moment, I'm living at home with my mom and dad. I … uh … graduated two years ago, but I'm still looking for a permanent job. I love my parents, but we … um … well, they are difficult to live with. We argue about the rules all the time. I'm sleeping in my old room and living with the people who took me to the park when I was little! I know I'm lucky to be here, but it's … you know … it isn't easy.

Lesson 2.2, Listening, Exercise C

2.3 **P = Presenter R = Richard G = Gordon A = Alice C = Carla**

P: More and more of the world's young people are going home to live with their parents after college. Why? And what is it like living at home again as an adult? How do parents feel about the situation? Today, we talk to members of 'The boomerang generation' and their parents about the advantages and disadvantages of living together again. Let's start with Richard …

R: I'm Richard Woodman, from the US. I'm 25 years old and at the moment, I'm living at home with my mom and dad. I … uh … graduated two years ago, but I'm still looking for a permanent job. I love my parents, but we … um … well, they are difficult to live with. We argue about the rules all the time. I'm sleeping in my old room and living with the people who took me to the park when I was little! I know I'm lucky to be here, but it's … you know … it isn't easy.

G: My name is Gordon Woodman. I'm Richard's dad. Of course, Richard's mom and I are, well, we're happy he is staying with us … most of the time. We're his parents and he can always rely on us, but we uh … we hope he finds the right job and, well, moves out as soon as possible. I want to make his bedroom into my home office. And his music, it's … well you know, thump, thump, thump all day and night. It drives me crazy! Anyway, we think he needs to be more independent. We love him, but he's unhappy, and he isn't learning about adult life living here with us.

A: Hi, I'm Alice Melo from Philadelphia, in the US. I'm 28 years old and I graduated last year. I work as a dentist and, at the moment, I'm living with my parents to save money for my own place. Well, I'm trying to save money anyway, ha ha! I studied in Colorado, but I … uh … couldn't find a job there, so, you know, I came back home. More and more of my friends are moving back home. It's great! Mom cooks and does all my laundry. She won't take any money from me … I tried, but … uh … so I'm not paying any bills. Of course, I help … sometimes … I help with the housework and the yard, I mean, now and again, you know. One day, I will do something special to thank them.

C: I'm Carla Melo, Alice's mom. We're very happy our daughter is home again. She's working hard and she wants to get her own place, but I always tell her she can live here with us forever! She's an adult now, I know, but she's still my baby! This year, my husband is traveling a lot for work, for his job, you know, so I'm very happy Alice is here with me. I don't like being on my own. I can talk to her, and she can save money and enjoy her mom's cooking.

UNIT 3

Lesson 3.2, Listening, Exercise C

3.4 **C = Chloe M = Matt**

C: Welcome to this week's *Amazing Adventures* podcast. I'm Chloe Cole, and with me is sailor and survival expert Matt Cabral. This week, the amazing story of the Robertson family and how they survived a month lost at sea in the Pacific Ocean.

In 1970, Dougal and Lyn Robertson and their four children were living on a farm in northern England. One ordinary day, Neil, one of their ten-year-old twins, said he wanted to leave the farm and sail around the world. Most families would probably laugh and say 'don't be silly', but the Robertsons saw the chance for an adventure. They sold their business, bought a boat, and on January 27th, 1971, started their journey across the Atlantic. Matt, what do you think of their decision?

M: Incredible. I mean, Dougal was an experienced sailor, but it was still a brave decision. Maybe not very sensible, but definitely brave!

C: Ha ha, yes. Well, sensible or not, the Robertsons made it across the Atlantic safely in their 13-meter boat, *The Lucette*. But on June 15th, 1972, while they were sailing out into the Pacific Ocean, things started to go very wrong.

Their boat was passing the Galapagos Islands when they noticed something large in the water behind them. It was a group of killer whales swimming toward the boat. Douglas, the eldest son, has said that when he saw the whales, he thought they were going to kill and eat the family. Well, the whales hit and sank their boat, but amazingly, the Robertsons all made it onto their small life raft, scared, but alive. I mean, they were very unlucky, weren't they, Matt?

M: Yes, they were. On average, there are only two to three accidents with boats and whales per year. But believe it or not, it wasn't all bad. I mean, first, the whales didn't eat them.

C: Ha! That's true.

M: And the life raft and another very small wooden boat survived the accident. And luckily they were carrying some water, some dry bread, cookies, a bag of onions and some fruit in the life raft.

C: Yes, but after six days, all the food was gone, so they collected rainwater to drink, and killed turtles and ate the meat and drank the blood. Then, 17 days after the accident, their life raft failed and they had to move to their wooden boat. It was called *The Ednamair* and was only three meters long. Can you imagine the whole family in that small boat?

M: It sounds like an impossible situation. You have to be strong and stay positive to survive something like this. There was only one dry seat in the boat, so most of the time they were sitting in water. But they didn't give up hope.

C: And finally, 38 days after the accident, a Japanese fishing boat found them and took them to dry land and safety.

M: It's an incredible story of survival.

C: Yes, it is. And now, Douglas Robertson works as an accountant in London, and amazingly, he has said that he actually enjoyed the family's adventure!

UNIT 4

Lesson 4.1, Listening, Exercise B

4.1 **S = Sylvia G = Greg**

S: Greggy! Ohhhhhh! It's so nice to see you!

G: Hi, Syl. Give me a hug. It's nice to see you, too … Do you have to call me Greggy?

S: Ha ha. Yes, and I'm going to introduce you to all my new friends as 'Greggy'. Was the trip OK?

G: Sure, sure. Mom gave me a ride to the station. She sends her love. She misses her darling daughter et cetera, et cetera. She's gonna call later.

S: Oh, good. How's Claire? Are you two OK? Still madly in love?

G: Oh, yeah, you know. Lucky girl.

S: Stop it.

G: She wanted to come this weekend, but tomorrow evening she's having dinner with some old friends. They arranged it a long time ago.

S: Of course. Never mind. Hopefully she'll make it next time. I have so many plans for us this weekend! It's such a great city. I can't wait to show you around. Are you hungry?

G: Always.

S: Yep, silly question. Let's go for lunch.

G: Wow, this place is cool.

S: Nice, right? I hang out with my friends here a lot. I think I'm going to bring Mom and Dad here, too … if they ever come and visit!

G: Ha! They will. And then they'll never leave!

S: Ha!

G: So, what are all these plans you have for us then?

S: Well, when we've finished lunch, I'm gonna text Angie and Mark and tell them to come and meet us, and we're going to go for a walk and show you the city center. Then we're meeting Duncan and Alicia at three o'clock, and I think we're going for coffee somewhere, but I'm not sure where.

G: Duncan and Alicia?

S: Oh, they're great. You'll like Duncan. He's a little like you.

G: What, handsome and intelligent?

S: Uhh … more like he's always thinking about his next meal.

G: I like him already.

S: After that, we're going to the market to look around; it's a beautiful old building, and we're going to do some food shopping because Duncan is making a curry dish for us all tonight. He's a great cook. Alicia says she and Duncan are going to open a restaurant one day. Anyway, …

G: Sounds great.

S: OK, so then tonight, we're going to the theater.

G: The theater?

S: Yes, I have tickets for a Shakespeare play.

G: What?

S: Ha ha! Only joking. We're seeing a comedy show. One of my friends is filming the show and he got us some free tickets.

G: Phew. That's more like it. What a great day you have planned, Syl! I can't wait.

S: And that's just today. Wait until you hear about tomorrow … In the morning, we're …

G: Uh, Syl, hang on. Did you hear that?

S: What?

G: Listen!

S: What? Is it the music?

G: No … no … it's … I think … yes, it's the sound of my empty stomach. Are we getting something to eat, or what?

S: Pfffft. You and your stomach. Pass me a menu …

UNIT 5

Lesson 5.3, Listening, Exercise B

5.6 **G = Gemma B = Barry**

G: Good morning. You must be Barry. I'm Gemma.

B: Oh mmmm hmmfff … sorry. I'm just finishing my sandwich!

G: That's OK … Egg sandwich, is it?

B: Uh … Yes, egg. Sorry. My favorite. Nice to meet you, Emma.

G: It's Gemma.

B: Excuse me?

G: It's Gemma, not Emma.

B: Sorry! What a terrible start.

G: Please don't worry, Barry. Gemma Lockwood. Base One IT Services. I work in Human Resources. Sorry we're a little delayed today. Have you been here long?

B: Actually, I've been here since 9 am.

G: You've been here for … three hours?

B: Yes, well, I didn't want to be late. That's why I was hungry.

G: OK … well … uh … good! Come in and have a seat.

B: Thanks.

G: So, Barry, we are looking for people to work at our head office on the customer service team. First, could you tell me a little about yourself?

B: Ha ha. OK. Well, I'm Barry. I'm uh … 23 years old. Single, male, blond hair. Rather nervous in interviews … ha. I uh … I'm one meter tall, I have a cat named Yoda and I love … uh … egg sandwiches, ha ha, and … um … computers and … wait, did I just say one meter tall? Ha ha sorry. Uh … I'm one meter and seventy centimeters tall, and I …

G: Uh … Barry, maybe we could focus on your work experience. You work for a telemarketing company at the moment, is that right? How long have you worked there?

B: Uh, well, I left my old job in June … and now it's … well, I … I've worked at the call center for six weeks. Have you read my résumé? I did send one. I mean, I wrote everything there, so …

G: Uh … yes, but … tell me more. For example, why do you want to change jobs and work for Base One?

B: Oh, well, that's easy; I hate my job at the call center! I sit on the phone all day long asking people questions and nobody wants to talk to me. People get really angry and sometimes, well, they hang up the phone.

G: I … see. Uh … So, what do you know about Base One?

B: About what? OH! Yes … well … I'm … I think it's … could you repeat the question, please?

G: Uh … well … OK. What do you know about Base One IT Services?

B: Um, well Base One is a … great IT company, with … great services … and the office here is … um … really cool. And, you seem very nice, and I …

G: Barry, ahem! Teamwork is very important for us here at Base One. Can you tell me about a time when you worked as part of a team?

B: Um, you mean a real example?

G: Uh, yes.

B: Let me think … uhh, I … um, actually … uhh …

G: Um … OK. It says on your résumé that you enjoy skydiving. Wow! How long have you been interested in that?

B: Oh, well. I've liked skydiving since I was a teenager. It just looks so exciting! I've always wanted to try it.

G: So you haven't actually tried skydiving?

B: Well, I really want to.

G: And French poetry?

B: What?

G: Your résumé says you enjoy French poetry.

B: Does it? Oh yes! That's right. Of course, French poetry – love it.

G: Uh, Barry, I, uh, I think we've finished for today.

B: Oh, great – that was quick.

G: Yes, uh … do you uh … do you have any questions?

B: Um … No! No, I don't!

G: OK, so thanks again and … please don't call us … we … uh, we'll contact you. Thank you, Barry.

B: No, thank YOU, Emma.

UNIT 6

Lesson 6.1, Listening, Exercise C

6.1 **P = Pippa DS = Doctor Singh M = Michael DT = Doctor Tremblay L = Lia**

P: G'day, Australia! Pippa Chan on chatfmmelbourne.nett. Today, we are talking about health myths.

Half an hour on the internet leaves most people pretty confused about what's good for their health and what isn't. You know, one article says 'you drink too much coffee, but you don't drink enough water', then the next says coffee is good for you, but too much water is dangerous! Confusing? Very!

I mean, let's say you are one of the many people who goes through life feeling tired a lot of the time. If you look online, you'll find one expert that says 'you don't sleep enough' and another that says 'you sleep too much'. Ha! And if you can't sleep? Oh, it's because you go to bed too early. No, no, no it's because you don't go to bed early enough! And of course EVERYthing makes you fat.

So how do we know what to believe? Well, we've been down to Melbourne City Hospital to ask some medical professionals about the reality behind some common health myths. Let's hear from the experts …

DS: Hi. I'm Dr. Singh and I work at Melbourne City Hospital. My myth concerns how much water we need to drink. Most people have probably heard that not drinking enough water can cause headaches. And they are right – that isn't a myth. But many of us have probably also heard that we need to drink eight glasses of water per day to stay healthy – well, that isn't exactly true. The eight glasses, or around two liters, includes all liquids: tea, coffee, juice, et cetera – plus the water you get from food, which is around one fifth of your daily total. So how much water should we drink? Well, my advice is drink when you are thirsty and you'll be OK.

M: Hi, my name is Michael. I'm a nurse here in Melbourne. Many people believe that eating fatty food makes them fat, but in fact, that isn't the whole truth. Eating more calories than you need makes you fat. Yes, it's true that fat has lots of calories, but so do carbohydrates and sugars. It isn't actually too much fat that makes you fat, it's too many calories. Some fat is necessary, so you can still enjoy your burger as part of a balanced diet. And to burn those extra calories? Get up off that couch and get moving!

DT: Hi, I'm Dr. Tremblay from Canada. The Australian winter is here and so are colds and flu. You remember Grandma's advice … 'Hat! Scarf! Keep warm, or you'll catch a cold.' Well, Australia isn't as cold as Canada, but it is sensible to make sure you're warm enough. However, the truth is that cold weather doesn't cause colds and flu. They are caused by viruses. You are more likely to catch a cold inside, where there are lots of people. And remember, if you have a cold and are suffering with a headache, a cough or a sore throat, get plenty of rest, drink warm drinks – unless you have a temperature – and make sure you are getting enough vitamins. Don't take antibiotics! They don't kill viruses and they won't help a cold.

L: Hi, I'm Lia. I'm a medical student from London and I want to talk about eggs! Some people believe that you shouldn't eat more than one or two eggs a week. This is probably because of old advice. In the past, the warning was always 'too many eggs are bad for your heart', but we now know that an egg or two per day doesn't increase the risk of heart disease in healthy people. Egg-cellent news for egg lovers – Egg-xactly what they wanted to hear! Ha ha – sorry!

P: Wow! Thank you to all our egg-sperts. Interesting stuff! We'll be back with music from Enrique Egg-lesias after the break.

UNIT 7

Lesson 7.3, Listening, Exercise C

7.4 **S = Shauna**

S: Welcome to *Great Minds*. I'm Shauna Andrews, and today we're talking about William James Sidis. You have possibly never heard of him. But he is perhaps one of the most intelligent people who ever lived. He had an IQ of between 250 and 300.

He was born in the United States in 1898, and grew up in New York. His parents, who were originally from Ukraine, were doctors and were both highly intelligent.

They wanted to give their son the best possible chance in life. So, his mother gave up her job and taught him at home. He didn't go to school. And they brought him up to have a 'love of knowledge'.

As a result, Sidis was reading and writing at 18 months, and enjoyed reading the *New York Times* newspaper. He wrote several books and newspaper articles before he was four and, by the time he was eight, he spoke seven languages. He also made up his own language, which he called 'Vendergood'. At 11, he went to college to study math – to Harvard University, actually. And in fact, he had previously given a math lecture there when he was nine. Sidis became front page news and news reporters followed him everywhere at the college. He became known as a child prodigy all over the country.

Sidis graduated from Harvard University with a degree in mathematics at age 16. He then joined Rice University as a teacher of math. However, he found teaching difficult, especially because of his age. After only eight months, he left Rice University and went back to Harvard, this time to study law.

While studying law, he became more and more interested in the political and social issues of the day. And as a result, he dropped out of the university before he finished his degree. This was a big turning point in his life. Soon after, in 1918, he was arrested while he was taking part in an anti-war demonstration. He received an 18-month prison sentence. However, he didn't go to prison and instead he spent a year in a hospital. It was actually the hospital where his parents worked.

After this, Sidis tried to stay out of the public eye. He moved from city to city around America and he had a number of simple low-paid jobs. He became more and more lonely and finally, he had a falling out with his parents and lost contact with them. The newspapers printed stories about how the child prodigy had failed as an adult.

After his death in 1944, many people questioned his high IQ and many of his other childhood achievements. Despite this, Sidis has been the subject of a number of books and academic studies and he is still one of the world's greatest child prodigies.

UNIT 8

Lesson 8.1, Listening, Exercise C

8.2 **L = Lizzie S = Suzy**

L: Welcome to *Music matters* with me, Lizzie Reid. Our taste in music says a lot about who we are. But why do we have different tastes in music? To answer this question, we are joined by Professor Suzy Harrison, an expert in the psychology of music. Welcome, Suzy.

S: Hello, thank you.

L: So, why do some people, say, prefer rock music or blues or jazz, while other people prefer pop or rap music?

S: Well, there are three main points which might explain our taste in music. The first is the music we grew up with. We don't choose this music ourselves, of course. But as a child, the music that we hear at home is familiar and comforting. Later in life, these same sounds bring back these feelings and this gives us pleasure. So, when we start to discover music by ourselves, it is influenced by what we listened to when we were growing up.

L: So, you're saying our first musical influence is our parents and our brothers and sisters?

S: Yes, that's right – particularly, our older brothers and sisters. Secondly, music brings people together. It creates an atmosphere and mood that people can share. So the second point is that we listen to certain types of music to help us form or join social groups. We want to be with people similar to ourselves. In contrast, for other people, musical taste is a way to make themselves different from other people. It's a way to be an individual. If you listen to music that others don't like, people will see you differently.

L: Yes, and I suppose it's true that we are generally attracted to people with similar music tastes to our own.

S: Yes, that's generally the case. And the third point is about how we feel when we listen to the music. Music can help to create a mood! For example, when you want to study, you might listen to something in the background, something without words – classical music, for example. And when you're preparing for a night out, you might want to energize yourself and play something loud and full of energy – maybe some rock or pop or reggae music. At other times, you might play the same sad song over and over again. Because of the internet, finding music is very quick and easy for our different moods. Interestingly, studies have shown that because of this easy access to different kinds of music, people today like a much wider range of music styles compared to previous generations.

L: I see. So, our individual taste in music is a combination of three things: the music we grew up with, the need to fit in with other people and finally, to match our different moods?

S: Yes, that's right. Of course, one thing may be stronger than the others. But, yes, over time it is most likely a combination of these things which influence our music choices.

L: Very interesting, Professor Harrison. Thank you for speaking to us today.

S: You're welcome.

Lesson 8.3, Listening, Exercise C

8.7

A: … Well, I'd say the main difference between movies and books is how they tell the story and how we connect with it.

B: Yes, I agree. Books allow the reader to use their imagination. We can visualize the story and the people and the places in our own way. With movies, on the other hand, we see what the director and the actors want us to see. There's much less possibility for us to use our own imagination.

A: I agree. And another important difference is that with books, the story generally moves more slowly and goes into more detail. With a movie, though, the whole story needs to start and finish in 90 minutes. So, in a book, we have more time to get to know the characters and to understand them. I think this makes the experience more personal and engaging.

B: Well, yes, I see what you mean – a book can be more engaging, but at the same time, a movie can be much more exciting and gripping than a book. It can use sounds and images and dialogue all at the same time. We use our different senses. And for many people, this is more entertaining than reading a book. Music can also make the movie more interesting and memorable.

A: That's true. I think another important difference is that with a book, the chapters provide natural breaks in the story. This gives us time to think about what we have read. A movie doesn't give us this opportunity.

B: Yeah, and also, of course, watching a movie is usually a social experience. We generally watch a movie with other people and then talk about it and share our opinions. But reading a book is more individual and personal. I think that's a really important difference.

A: Yes, I agree that reading is a less sociable activity. Although, book clubs are very popular these days. I guess that's a similar social experience.

B: And one more thing is that people usually say that the book is better than the movie. Compared to the book, people usually say they are disappointed by the movie – especially if they have read the book first. However, I think in many cases people actually prefer the movie.

A: Interesting. That's something that we can …

Lesson 8.3, Listening, Exercise E

.8
1 Books allow the reader to use their imagination. With movies, on the other hand, we see what the director and the actors want us to see.
2 With books, the story generally moves more slowly. With a movie, though, the whole story needs to start and finish in 90 minutes.
3 We generally watch a movie with other people … But reading a book is more individual and personal.
4 Reading is a less sociable activity. Although, book clubs are very popular these days.
5 People usually say they are disappointed by the movie. However, in many cases people actually prefer the movie.

Lesson 8.3, Vocabulary, Exercise B

.9
1 It was totally engaging and the acting was amazing.
2 I was, well, a little bored by the end. It isn't very memorable, I'm afraid.
3 You won't be disappointed. The singing was incredible.
4 It's really gripping. And it's very moving and sad, too.

UNIT 9

Lesson 9.2, Listening, Exercise B

.3 Today's lecture is about philanthropy. Philanthropy, as you know, is the act of giving away a large amount of money which is used to benefit society.

There are many famous and not so famous people who have given away large amounts of money. Two of the 20th century's most famous philanthropists are John D. Rockefeller and Andrew Carnegie. Rockefeller of course made his money from oil and Carnegie from the steel industry. Rockefeller gave away about $540 million before his death in 1937, and Carnegie gave away about $350 million. This was about 90 percent of his wealth. And today there are many celebrities who have given money to charity. For example, the TV personality Oprah Winfrey has so far given away around half a billion dollars.

But perhaps today's most well-known philanthropists are Bill Gates and his wife Melinda, and Warren Buffett. Their main aim is to improve global health and to end poverty. And between them, they have already given away tens of billions of dollars. In 2010, they also created the Giving Pledge. The Giving Pledge asks …

Lesson 9.2, Listening, Exercise D

.4 But perhaps today's most well-known philanthropists are Bill Gates and his wife Melinda, and Warren Buffett. Their main aim is to improve global health and to end poverty. And between them, they have already given away tens of billions of dollars. In 2010, they also created the Giving Pledge. The Giving Pledge asks the world's richest people to give away at least half of their wealth in their lifetime. In its first ten years, many people agreed to this, including Facebook's Mark Zuckerberg, Virgin boss Richard Branson and Ann Gloag, who started the international transportation group Stagecoach.

However, not everyone agrees that the Giving Pledge is a good thing, and some people have decided not to join. So, let's now look at five modern-day philanthropists that you may or may not have heard of.

First, Carlos Slim. Slim is a Mexican businessman and is one of the world's richest men. He made his money in telecommunications and is worth around $80 billion. He has so far given away about $8 billion. However, he has not joined the Giving Pledge because he disagrees with the approach of Bill Gates and Warren Buffet. Instead, he believes that education and jobs are the best way to end poverty.

Next, we have Sara Blakely, an American businesswoman. She recently became the world's youngest self-made female billionaire, and she was also the first woman to join the Giving Pledge. Her philanthropy focuses mainly on women's and girls' education and career possibilities. She believes that if there are more women in powerful positions, this will make the world a better place.

Li Ka-shing is a Hong Kong businessman and has promised to give away one third of his $30 billion fortune. His aim is to promote education and health, but mainly in China. He has not joined the Giving Pledge. This is because he wishes to keep control of how and when he gives his money away.

Billionaire Meg Whitman was the president of eBay for ten years. She has said that she would refuse if she was invited to join the Giving Pledge. Instead, she has her own charity that focuses on the environment and education.

And finally, Azim Premji. Premji is one of India's richest people. He has joined the Giving Pledge and has already given away one quarter of his wealth. Premji's aim is to improve Indian school education and he has also set up a university which promotes educational thinking.

So, what do you think? Is the Giving Pledge a good thing? And what about philanthropy in general? What are the pros and the cons of this …

UNIT 10

Lesson 10.1, Listening, Exercise A

10.1 **1:** I travel and fly a lot for work, and this device means my bag is a lot lighter than it used to be. I can honestly say it's the best gadget I've ever bought. Before I got it, I always used to carry three or four heavy novels with me, but now I can fit hundreds into my coat pocket. I bought the cheapest one, but the battery lasts for a long time and it has a dictionary. You can check words so much more quickly than in a paper dictionary. You just touch the word you don't know and it shows you the meaning.

2: This is definitely the most useful piece of technology I own. I don't enjoy driving in new cities or foreign countries, but I can find my way so much more easily than in the past thanks to this smart device. Obviously, it was more expensive than an old-fashioned paper map, but I don't regret buying it. My wife and I don't argue about which way to go anymore! It's very reliable – it never makes mistakes and even tells you when there is traffic or a speed camera.

3: This has to be the greatest invention of the 21st century! I take it everywhere with me and it is just the right size to fit in my bag. They are getting cheaper and cheaper – mine cost less than a lot of phones do these days. I don't have many apps on it, and most of the time, I just use it to go online or watch videos – the screen is so much bigger than on my phone. The best thing about it is that it starts so quickly. It's much faster and more convenient than my old laptop. The worst thing about it is that I now spend even more time online!

4: Every Saturday morning, I go to the city park and meet other … uh … fans. We spend a lot of time talking about our favorite 'toys', as my girlfriend calls them, and arguing about which is the best, or which turns the most quickly, or a thousand other things! And of course we fly and race them. Mine is a little heavier than some of them because it has a camera, but I can take pictures and videos from the air. And of course, they are not just for fun – they have many possible uses. You know, delivering packages, helping the police, taking pictures for scientific research and so on.

UNIT 11

Lesson 11.1, Listening, Exercise B

11.3 **P = Presenter M = Mike**

P: Welcome to this week's edition of the *Travel Show*. Today, we are joined by travel writer Mike Harold. A year ago, Mike decided to visit the Seven Natural Wonders of the World. Last week, he finally achieved his goal. Mike, tell us a little about the seven natural wonders.

M: Well, the Seven Natural Wonders of the World was the idea of the Seven Natural Wonders organization. The organization was created to promote and to protect the natural wonders of the world. Not just these seven, but many others as well.

P: So, how did they choose the seven places?

M: The decision was based on three main things. The places were chosen according to how unique the place is, how important it is and, finally, its pure natural beauty.

P: And why did you decide to visit them?

M: Well, I've always loved traveling and I like a challenge! As a travel writer, I thought this was an interesting thing to do professionally.

P: OK, so, what are the seven natural wonders?

M: First, I visited the Great Barrier Reef. The reef is 2600 km long and is located off the northeastern coast of Australia. It's made of over 400 different kinds of coral and is the largest and most colorful coral reef in the world. It really was amazing.

After that, I went to the Grand Canyon, in the US. It was chosen as a natural wonder because of its enormous size and incredible scenery. The canyon was created by the Colorado River, which you can see at the very bottom. It's the most popular of the seven natural wonders and is visited by over five million people a year.

The next place was the most difficult to get to, as it's located in the Himalayan mountain range.

P: Ohh, this has to be Mount Everest!

M: Yes, the highest place on Earth. I didn't go to the top, but I went to the base camp, which is at about 5000 meters. The views were unbelievable.

P: I can imagine. And where did you go next?

M: My fourth natural wonder was Victoria Falls. This, of course, is the famous waterfall on the Zambezi River in southern Africa. It is actually on the border of two countries, Zambia and Zimbabwe. The waterfall is almost two kilometers wide and over 100 meters high. It really was an incredible sight.

For numbers five and six, I traveled to Central and South America. The first is perhaps the least well known. It's the Paricutin volcano in Mexico.

P: Yes, I must admit, I've never heard of this.

M: Well, it was only formed in 1943, so it's fairly new! It was also the first time modern science saw the creation of a volcano – and that's why it's a natural wonder. I was able to climb the volcano and walk around the crater and look inside. I then went to South America to see a more familiar 'wonder' – the bay and natural harbor of Rio de Janeiro in Brazil. The bay includes several islands and is surrounded by beautiful beaches and spectacular mountains with some great views.

P: And I understand for the final natural wonder, you had some good luck.

M: Yes, I did. The final natural wonder I saw was the northern lights, or aurora borealis. I went to Iceland to see them. You can only see them at certain times of the year. And yes, I was very lucky. It really was amazing. And the perfect way to finish my challenge.

P: That sounds amazing! Thanks for sharing your journey with us.

UNIT 12

Lesson 12.3, Listening, Exercise C

12.4 **K = Kerry A = Alex**

K: Hi, Alex, over here!

A: Hey, Kerry, long time no see! Isn't this amazing?!

K: What's going on? It's so busy!

A: YES! She did it.

K: Did what? What is this?

A: Well, it's an ad campaign for sneakers. If you run past the ad, past the billboard, … if you run fast enough, you win a pair of sneakers. It's smart, isn't it?

K: Oh, yeah. That's really cool. And yes, a really smart idea. What brand is it for? I can't see a logo or anything.

A: It's for Reebok, I think. Yes, look, there's the Reebok logo.

K: And what's 'fast enough'? Does it say how fast you have to run?

A: I'm not sure, but everyone seems to be going pretty

quickly. Look, watch this guy ... Go! Go! ... Oh, no. He didn't do it.

K: You should try it, Alex. Go on. Win yourself some new sneakers. You're a fast runner, aren't you?

A: Actually, I'm not so sure I am, to be honest. I think I'll just watch.

K: We were talking about advertising in a class at the university last week. Have you seen that one for vacuum cleaners? That's another smart one.

A: I'm not sure. What is it?

K: Well, they made a video of cars going through a tunnel. They then added a billboard to the background which showed a huge vacuum cleaner so that it looked like the cars were sucked into the vacuum cleaner.

A: Oh, I think I have seen that, actually.

K: And when they put the video online, people didn't know if it was real or just a video. It created a lot of interest and discussion. It was a very successful ad.

A: Oh, I see. I thought it was a real billboard.

K: No, it's just a video. They did it because they didn't have enough money for an actual billboard campaign.

A: Oh, that's really smart. Really original. And simple.

K: Yes, that's what we were talking about in the class last week – what makes a good ad. And it's exactly that in my opinion – something simple and original.

A: Yeah, and something with a clear message, something you can connect with. And a catchy slogan you can easily remember, you know, like McDonald's 'I'm lovin' it'.

K: Yeah, but I think the most important thing is that it catches your eye and gets your attention in the first place. Like this Reebok one.

A: Yeah, I agree. You know what, I think I might try it. Should I?

K: Yes, go for it. You can do it. Alex, Alex, Alex ...

Macmillan Education Limited
4 Crinan Street
London N1 9XW

Companies and representatives throughout the world

American Language Hub Level 2 Student's Book ISBN 978-0-230-49697-2
American Language Hub Level 2 Student's Book with Student's App
ISBN 978-0-230-49701-6

Written by Daniel Brayshaw and Jon Hird
With thanks to Edward Price and Carol Goodwright for additional authoring and to Signature Manuscripts for the Grammar Hub pages.

First published 2020

Designed by emc design ltd
Illustrated by Peter Lubach, Rasmus Juul, Rose Frith represented by Lemonade Illustration
Cover design by Restless
Cover image by Getty Images/Linghe Zhao
Picture research by Emily Taylor and Victoria Gaunt
Café Hub videos produced by Creative Listening
Café Hub video scripts written by James and Luke Vyner

Authors' acknowledgements

Daniel Brayshaw would like to thank the whole team for their invaluable support. Also, a special thanks to Sue Kay and Vaughan Jones for all their advice and guidance, and to my wife, Lucyna Brayshaw, for everything. Last but not least to Flash, our dog, for insisting I take regular breaks from the desk. Good boy.

Jon Hird would like to thank the Macmillan Education Editorial team for their input, ideas and hard work in shaping the content of the book.

The authors and publishers would like to thank the following for permission to reproduce their photographs:

Alamy p150(2-band), Action Plus Sports Images p148(4), AF archive p76(5), Ian Allenden p161, Alvey & Towers Picture Library p29(tr), Claudio Baldini p70(c), Axel Bueckert p69(3), the box studio p155(c), Roger Cracknell 01/classic p160, Cultura p42(ken), 158, Cultura Creative (RF) p82, John Davidson Photos p151(6), Deymos Photo p163(c), Stephen Dorey/Bygone Images p166(bcl), Gioia Emidi p151(10.1–6), Jürgen Fälchle p96, GeoPic p22, Photo Stock/National Geographic Creative p71, Givaga p69(7), Ted Horowitz p150(5), Incamerastock p13(cl), jvphoto p52(9), itdarbs p169, Natallia Khlapushyna p69(8), Metta image p69(2), Minden Pictures p104(t), NakoPhotography p42(bret), Losevsky Pavel p150(1-band), Photo 12 p76(6), robertharding pp102(7), 150(7), Alexandre Rotenberg p12(r), Unknown p84(tr), Michiel Vaartjes p147(4), Alex Witt p101; **Anastassia Elias** p74(d); **Bananastock** p69 (background); **Banksy**, London, 2004 p75(d); **BrandX** p146(3); **Bridgeman Images** Little Dancer, Aged 14, viewed from the back (polychrome bronze, satin ribbon & wood) (see also 100777), Degas, Edgar (1834–1917)/Private Collection/Photo © Christie's Images p75(a), Guitar on a Chair (oil on canvas), Gris, Juan (1887–1927)/ Private Collection/Photo © BEBA/AISA p150(4), Mona Lisa, c.1503–6 (oil on panel), Vinci, Leonardo da (1452–1519) / Louvre, Paris, France p150(3); **Corbis** pp36(tl), 53(1),102(3); **Fancy** p56(1); **Getty Images** pp17(a), 28–29(background), 42(lena), 47, 48–49(background), 52(3), 52(5), 52(10), 70(a,b),146(2, 4,5,f,g,h), 147(1,2), 152(bmr), 151(1), p152(bmr), AFP/Timothy A Clary p51, AFP/John Macdougall p34(tl), AFP/ Justin Tallis p44, Age footstock pp13(bl), 16(clocks), Ajr images p42(helen), alexxl66 p166(bl), Daniel Allan p99(background), Altrendo p17(d), Jacob Ammentorp Lund p33, Sally Anscombe pp17(c), 61, Archive Photos p66(cr), ARB p66(tr), Raul Arboleda p66(cl), AYImages p163(cl), Baiterek Media pp36(b), 37(b), 148(l), Jonny Baker p18(b), Scott Barbour p56(b), Thomas Barwick p55(tl), jez_bennett p105(e), Bettmann p84(l), p150(6), Katarzyna Bialasiewicz p52(7), Blend Images pp14, 146(e), 152(br), Tyler Boley p111, bopav p89(scarf), Hervé Bois/EyeEm p81, Suphawinee Boonpeng p52(br), Caiaimage/Paul Bradbury p162(l), Adrienne Bresnahan p39(cr), Peter Cade p114(t), iStockphoto/caimacanul p89(jeans), Colin Carter Photography p105(b), Sandra Clegg p79(b), EyeEm/Pinghung Chen p69(c), Petar Chernaev p34(tr), China Photos p41, Chombosan p35, L Cohen/WireImage p152(t), The Print Collector/ Print Collector p150(1), Aurora Creative p148(8), Cultura pp56(5), 148(8), 152(bcr), Jim Cumming p105(d), Jake Curtis p32, DaveLongMedia p147(7), Caiaimage/Robert Daly p153(l), DeAgostini p102(5), Sofie Delauw p15, iStockphoto/demidoffaleks p89(jacket), domin_domin p163(bl), David Doubilet p102(6), DNY59 p58(br), Dorling Kindersley p28(br), Karin Dreyer p59(toothache), iStockphoto/Eshma p163(br), FatCamera p163(cr), filadendron p151(a), Antonio de Moraes Barros Filho P62(d), Fizkes p59(bad back), FotografiaBasica p58–59(background), Franckreporter pp19, 18–19(background), fstop123 p39(br), Mitchell Funk p148(7), www.galerie-ef.de p78(b), Katherine Gaines p151(4), Vladimir Godnik p59(headache), Vincent van Gogh p75(c), Bill Greenblatt/AFP p66(b), GretaMarie p48(b), grinvalds p112, Haag & Kropp p49(br), Izabela Habur pp36(tcr), 65, iStockphoto Thinkstock Images/halfbinz p151(7), istockphoto/StHelena p77, Hero Images pp2, 54(br), 72(background), Rolf Hicker p25(bl), Hindustan Times p55(bl), Blend Images/Ronnie Kaufman/ Larry Hirshowitz p151(e), Stephan Hoeck p154(r), Andrew Hounslea p52(bl), Andrew Howe p89(background), icreative Howe p89(shirt), The Image Bank pp42(t), 56(6), 148(6), Image Source pp52(8), 146(1), Emma Innocenti p114(b), Chase Jarvis p148(1), iStockphoto Thinkstock Images/johny007pan p118(background), Jokic p162(r), Mark Keelan p168(l), Dorling Kindersley p89(skirt), Thomas Koidhis p102(1), Kozorog p36(tcl), Nicole Kucera p102(4), Alexander Kuguchin p26(inset), Jason Langley p52(bcl), Liquidlibrary p86(t), simonlong p151(2), Loop Images p31, Lumina Images p89(bl), MariusFM77 p56(2), Dawid Markiewicz p62(f), Michael Marquand p59(br), Scott Masterton p168(m), Maurusone p98(b), Maximilian Stock Ltd p52(bcr), Ian McKinnell p113, Mervana p30(travel icons), Stuart Miller p146(g), Monkeybusinessimages p4(cr), Sabrina Bekeschus Monteiro/EyeEm p108(background), Dean Mouhtaropoulos p54(t), Naumoid p147(6), Steve De Neef p105(f), Nikada p13(cm), Michael Ochs Archives p62(b), OJO Images pp52(4), 59(stomache ache), iStockphoto/Thinkstock Images/Edu_Oliveros p69(4), Andrew Olney p16(inset), Omgimages p146(d), James O'Neil p168(r), PeopleImages p64, Prasit photo p93, oneinchpunch p83, Rudy Orozco P8(croissants), Pobytov p109(background), Perspectives p1, Getty/PhotoDisc pp98(bcr), 166(cml), Zoltan Polgar p56(3), Martin Poole p151(c), Prasit photo p167, Querbeet p147(3), Ranplett p38–39(background), Alex Raths p17(b), Jack Reynolds p105(a), RG–vc p166(cr), RICOWde p23, Nicholas Roberts/AFP p84(br), Paul Rojas p102(2), Kirill Rudenko p153(r), William R. Sallaz p148(2), iStockphoto/scanrail p166(cmr), Daniel Schoenen/ LOOK-foto pp62(b), 63(b), Science Photo Library p8–9(background), Davide Seddio p151(2), shayes17 p109(b), Jordan Siemens p21, Ariel Skelley p155(bl), skynesher p91, Slphotography p53(2), spooh p151(5), Daniel Smith p151(f), by sonmez p118(b), SolStock p92, James Steidl p147(5), kaisphoto p89(t-shirt), George Stroud p66(tr), studiocasper p166(cl), Santi Sukarnjanaprai p103, Superstock p150(2), Sundown100 p26–27(b), Svetikd p36(tr), Tarzhanova p89(dress), B. Tanaka p11, Tetra Images pp95, 151(b), Thinkstock Images/Jupiterimages p150(8), Tom And Steve p52(6), Shomos Uddin p8(bl), Lise Ulrich Fine Art Photography p105(c), Universal History Archive/UIG p75(b), Umbertoleporini p12(l), Universal Images Group pp59(sore toe), 62(a), Betsie Van der Meer pp7, 148(3), Vkuslandia p56(4), Wavebreakmedia p151(10.1–2), Fabian Wentzel p43, Westend61 pp46(b), p151(10.1–5), Barry Willis p155(br), iStockphoto/Thinkstock Images/Steven Wynn p66(tl), XiXinXing p146(h) Carol Yepes p151(d); **IMAGE 100** p40; **Image Source** pp52(tl,tcl), 146(c); **Mayer** McCann Erickson Slovakia p116(tr,cr,br); **Nature Picture Library** Ingo Arndt p104(b); **Mihaela Noroc** p4–5; **Photodisc** p146(b); **Rex/Shutterstock** p165, David Boily p86(b), Universal History Archive p76(2), Rob Latour/Variety p84(br), IMAS/JENNIFER LAVERS HANDOUT/EPA p106(t,b), Lucasfilm/Bad Robot/Walt Disney Studios/Kobal p76(1), Peter Schneider/Epa p157(tr); **Robertson Family Archive** pp24(bl,br), 25(br); **Robin Nilssen**, Boon Photography. Creative Agency: Animal p116(tl,cl,bl); **Shutterstock**/Cubolabo p69(1), Yulia Glam p62(e), Mark & Anna Wilson p152(bmr); **Solent News & Photo Agency** Stanislav Aristov p74(c); **STOCKBYTE** p151(3); **Stockphoto** Bulgac p155(b); **Thinkstock** pp52(tr),146(a),148(5); **Scott Wade** p74(b); **Max Zorn** p74(a); **123RF** Elnur Amikishiyev p62(c), Mile Atanasov p163(a,b), Tyler Olson p151(10.1–4), Baiba Opule p69(5), Andriy Popov p151(10.1–1), p154(l), Irina Roibu p69(6), Stockfotocz p151(10.1–3).

Commissioned photographs in the Café Hubs by Creative Listening.

The authors and publishers are grateful for permission to reprint the following copyright material:

p36 Helliwell, J., Layard, R., & Sachs, J. (2016). World Happiness Report 2016. New York: Sustainable Development Solutions Network; p42 Extract from 'One in five children just want to be rich when they grow up' by Keith Perry. Originally published in The Telegraph, 5 August 2014. © Telegraph Media Group Limited 2014. Reprinted with permission of The Telegraph; p106 Eriksen M, Lebreton LCM, Carson HS, Thiel M, Moore CJ, Borerro JC, et al. (2014) Plastic Pollution in the World's Oceans: More than 5 Trillion Plastic Pieces Weighing over 250,000 Tons Afloat at Sea. PLoS ONE 9(12): e111913. https://doi.org/10.1371/journal.pone.0111913; p106 Extract from '38 million pieces of plastic waste found on uninhabited South Pacific island' by Elle Hunt. Originally published in The Guardian, 15 May 2017. © Copyright Guardian News & Media Ltd 2018. Reprinted with permission of The Guardian; p107 Extract from 'Marine Conservation Society' © Marine Conservation Society (MCS) 2017. Reprinted with permission of Marine Conservation Society; p106 Significant anthropogenic debris on remote island, Jennifer L. Lavers, Alexander L. Bond. Proceedings of the National Academy of Sciences Jun 2017, 114 (23) 6052-6055; DOI: 10.1073/pnas.1619818114; p112 Extract from 'Here is Facebook's guide to fake news' by Aatif Sulleyman. Originally published in The Independent, 9 May 2017. © Independent Digital News and Media Ltd 2017. Reprinted with permission of The Independent; p114 Extract from 'How binge-watching has changed TV forever' by Sarah Rainey. Originally published in The Telegraph, 22 January 2015. © Telegraph Media Group Limited 2015. Reprinted with permission of The Telegraph; p164 Helliwell, J., Layard, R., & Sachs, J. (2017). World Happiness Report 2017, New York: Sustainable Development Solutions Network.

Printed and bound in Brazil

2024
28